Nabokov:

HIS LIFE IN PART

ANDREW FIELD

N

abokov:

HIS LIFE IN PART

HAMISH HAMILTON LONDON

First published in Great Britain 1977
by Hamish Hamilton Ltd
90 Great Russell Street London WC1B 3PT

Copyright © 1977 by Andrew Field

SBN 241 02479 X

Printed in the United States of America
Second Printing October 1977

The author wishes to thank the Myer Foundation of Australia and the Australian Academy of the Humanities for a
travel grant which aided in the research for this book.

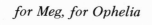
for Meg, for Ophelia

Hah! What Dr. Johnson would have thought about that book!

ILLUSTRATIONS

(Following page 208)

The Nabokov coat of arms
D. N. Nabokov
Nabokov's grandmother, Maria Nabokov
Maria Nabokov and her children
V. D. Nabokov at a masquerade ball, 1889
V. D. Nabokov, Berlin, 1919
Vladimir Nabokov, American passport photo
Nabokov with his mother, St. Petersburg, 1900
Nabokov with his brother Sergei, 1906
Nabokov at the Tenishev school
Nabokov at a family wedding
Nabokov on the streets of Berlin, 1934
Nabokov with his brother Sergei, 1916
Nabokov with Ivan Bunin, Berlin, 1934
Nabokov in the 1940s
Nabokov at Wellesley, 1943
At the Agassiz Museum, Cambridge, 1947
Nabokov with his brother Kirill and sister Elena
Nabokov with his wife and son, 1960
Nabokov, 1959

Nabokov:

HIS LIFE IN PART

CHAPTER

1

Yes, you wrote me the title of your book. What was it?
—You don't like it, do you?

A long silence of the sort that I associate with childhood visits to older or more distant relatives, when, seated on ungainly and almost desiccated upholstery, one is surprised by answers to questions which seem to have gone unheeded. Thirty seconds pass, time enough to think of other things. The choughs about which he invariably tells all visitors. They are, I think, flying behind my head now in the soft fog and radiator stillness of the late winter afternoon in Montreux. They fly, Nabokov (or his wife) has said, as though they were pieces of cut-out black paper moving across the sky. Aren't there choughs in *King Lear?* I often think of Lear   3 when I am with him. Edward. His face is loosely draped right now —very likely he looks like this when he sleeps—and the pads of his cheeks, which can be taut and quite prominent, especially in laughter, are, well, chuffy . . . His nose is handsome, though also slightly fleshy, in a Germanic way (the paternal grandmother's side of the family), and from certain angles it appears somewhat outsized. Frequently, as at this moment, he allows his head to go quite far back and looks not so much down as along or over it.

He shakes his head vigorously and very rapidly from side to side, and, when he has done, his face is again firm and full of features. The crow's feet at his eyes are exceptionally broad and long—they strain towards his large ears—and they are a natural, even a necessary setting to hold his eyes. Really, they are the eyes of an extremely alert and mischievous small boy.

Behind him the hotel-Grecian wallpaper, octangular, oval, and very small round blue-and-white cameos, pseudo-classical in subject. There are tiny, awkward double lamp brackets on the walls with cream-colored paper shades and dark edging. The sitting room is furnished on the understanding that it is vulgar for a hotel to pretend to be tasteful. It is quite possible that in at least a broad sense the room could have looked like this in 1845 when it was built.

—No, I don't.

That was said with some difficulty, and his entire body, which had curved into the chair, straightened, and it might have been noon again. In the late afternoon poor posture and excellent but loose tailoring often make him seem, especially when seated, a very much larger man than he is. Our conversation became more lively. The hotel's acceptable Swiss coffee with hot milk (he takes his demitasse a little tepid and with two pieces of sugar) was served up again by Véra Evseevna.

He held that the title is infeasible from a grammatical point of view. I have found that there are better subjects for conversation with Vladimir Nabokov than English grammar. Not infrequently his literary enemies have let it be understood that his mastery of the language is not quite good enough, but what is far worse, friends who have been given manuscripts to read have ventured to suggest minor points and nuances which might be corrected. He has admitted that there was a certain period shortly before and after he became an English writer when he lacked confidence in
4   his English—these were the years during which he sought advice

on the English translation of *Despair* and on his first English novel, *The Real Life of Sebastian Knight*—but he far more often stresses the fact that English is actually his first language. He cites with approval a proofreader who once discussed commas with him as though (—**which indeed they are**) they were points of honour. It is absurd but necessary to have to say that Vladimir Nabokov's English is superb and must have been so long ago when he published an article on butterflies in English as well as a few very competent English poems before he was twenty-one. Not only did he have English governesses, remember, but also his parents spoke English fluently. It is superb in an idiosyncratic way. His English does have faults, but his are all of a most obvious and hence inconsequential kind. In conversation he does confuse **who** with **whom** and sometimes even **I** and **me**. In fact, one of his first serious attempts to write in English was an essay lecture entitled *England and Me* or *My Past and Me* (there is a reference to a work called *It Is Me* in a letter of this period which could well be the piece in question) which he read on a short tour of literary readings in England in 1937, and he remembers having been embarrassed by so prominent a slip. There are brilliant riders who fumble a bit getting their foot into the stirrup. That is all there is to it.

Nabokov's words are his living souls, and the Lord of the Manner is himself the highest and final authority in even the most petty verbal disputes. That is one of his sources of artistic strength. He is very tetchy about his English. Once, reading *Ada* prior to its publication, I allowed myself to offer a minor suggestion, and I understood that this was a sensitive area, and it would have been better had I not. And on another occasion when suggestions were put by someone else, the conversation ended with a soft smile and a shrug —**Well, we'll just leave them.** That was very winning, and I think we all liked him for the way he said that. Everyone smiled.

On the occasion of this particular discussion we instructed each other, proceeding more gingerly than testily, in the proper usage and feel of adverbs in English. I elected to be vague but firm and avoid recourse to the *O.E.D.* or *Webster's Second* because the words in question were mine, and because I knew that this time (there were others, of course) I was correct.

The title is an admission and declaration of inconclusive evidence, of freedom from the fat of irrelevant fact, and that in itself could be disturbing to a subject such as mine, who has been known 5 to praise biographies only for their documentation. But of these things not a word was said that warm and dusky winter afternoon. No, the title was clearly not satisfactory.

—**You could call your book** *Nabokov—His Life and Parts.*

The remark just barely escaped from under a wave of rumbling laughter which shook him back and forth in his chair. His eyes were now gleaming with wetness, and he frantically slapped his chest, groping for his handkerchief.

—**Volodya, leave him alone. It's his book. Let him call it what he wants.** With this mild rebuke from Véra Evseevna and a clipped, perhaps slightly pouty **O.K.! O.K.!** the conversation shifted to other fields of interest.

I do not like biographies and in past years read very few of them, though by now I can pretend to some expert knowledge of the sorry genre. Nabokov does not like biographies either, and, when he taught, he used to refer to them as psychoplagiarisms. It still feels strange, after five years, that I should be writing a biography of this man whom—at what point precisely, I wonder?—I know how well? The reader, who it is understood is inquisitive, will likely want to know how it is that this biography came to be written.

I was preparing to quit America for Australia as my critical book on Nabokov was being published in the United States. This was in 1967. Nabokov and his wife, both of whom had read the book in manuscript very carefully and had refrained from any interference with the views I had expressed (which in many cases were not shared by them), wrote me urging me to arrange my itinerary so that I could stop by and visit them on my way to Australia.

Before that I had met and talked with Nabokov for only a few minutes in the lobby of the Commander Hotel in Cambridge, Massachusetts, in the early evening before he gave a reading in University Hall at Harvard. That was in 1964. I had in my library a book on criminal law by his father, published in 1904, which I had obtained in Russia, and I asked a mutual acquaintance to pass the book on to Nabokov but was urged to go and present it myself. I remember that he asked me where I had got my Russian, and I replied, which seemed the only possible answer to such a question from a man like Vladimir Nabokov (and the truth as well), that actually I never *had* really got my Russian, and that answer seemed to please him. He was clearly pleased, too, with the unexpected token of his father's past. He seemed radiant with the nervous energy and excess charm of an old professional about to go on. After a few minutes his wife came out of the elevator (—It's strange. I don't know why I persist in saying lift. Elevator is the older word), and then very shortly Professor Harry Levin, dapper and dressed in a dark suit which fitted almost too well, particularly in contrast with Nabokov's loose tailoring, and even more radiant though much less relaxed than Nabokov, arrived to take him to the lecture. I had forgotten where the reading was being held, which prompted Nabokov to recall how he had once lectured in that hall while outside his young son Dmitri had been ascending one of the building's ivied walls. The boy had explained to the grounds patrolman who accosted him: —It's all right. My father's lecturing inside.

I elected to go the other way around to Australia, but at the end of the year I had reason to go abroad for a few months, and, since one of the advantages of living in Australia is that from there anywhere in the world somehow seems on your way to anywhere else, I decided that I would pay a courtesy call to Montreux on my way through Europe to drink the champagne that, I was told, was being kept for my visit. It was a brief and most cordial visit. I recall that I was overdressed for the occasion—press accounts of the Montreux-Palace had tended to exaggerate its Edwardian rococo splendors rather much—but was made to feel quite at home. The biography began that evening, though it was far from my mind at the time.

—My only regret is that you won't be writing about me any more.

And three years later, when we were both wiser by far about what stresses a biography can bring to bear (in two directions), he shook his head sadly, sitting on the same side of the same small sofa, with a different drink in his hand. —Did I say that? . . . Yes, I suppose I did.

As it happened there was a continuing link with Nabokov through 1968 because it had been arranged with his new publisher, McGraw-Hill, to publish the complete bibliography of Nabokov's work, and he asked me if I would care to compose this bibliography. I had rather enjoyed the feeling of serene completion as regards my professional relationship to Nabokov, but I agreed to take it on. Because of the bibliography I was in regular correspondence with Mrs. Nabokov, and now Nabokov and his life 7 outside of art became an intermittent subject of household conversation. There were questions. Sometimes I had answers. It goes without saying that there were little bits and pieces of amusing biographical information that had fallen my way in the course of considering Nabokov's life's work, but I was aware of how little I knew with any certainty. Gradually I had a sense of a life portrait as a solid, discrete object, and I began to consider the unquestionable challenge of the genre and the subject. Something like scrubbing a quiescent but watchful rhinoceros with a large and unwieldy old-fashioned straw brush was the way in which it appeared to me. Of living authors known to me only W. H. Auden had spoken more vehemently against biography.

I wrote to Nabokov about the possibility of such a project in May 1968. —*So here I am, to my great surprise, answering an unplaced ad to be your Boswell.* The reply to my proposal (May 28) was warm approval and the hyberbolic though flattering assurance that he could not imagine anyone else whom he would want to accept as his biographer. The working relationship between us was almost entirely assumed, unspoken, very pre-1914. I assumed and relied upon the same calm, disinterested, aristocratic remove from the details of his own life that he had shown towards my treatment of his art. It will be surmised that I have had difficult moments as I worked on this book.

Quite late in the piece, after a short but sharp clash (all the cymbals were offstage) in 1971, we finally did discuss the biography. —**I told everything about myself in *Speak, Memory*, and it was not a very pleasant portrait. I appear as a precious person in that book. All that chess and those butterflies. Not very interesting. You remember what I said about myself:** *As far back as I remember myself (with interest, with amusement, and very seldom with disgust).* **Well, isn't that what everyone must say about himself?**

Before I had a chance to say anything, Véra Evseevna came in very quietly: —**No, I would say that is not an unflattering description of oneself.**

On my first biographical visit to Montreux in December 1968 we talked about the absence of specifics in *Speak, Memory*, the rich layers of detail accorded to very minor characters so that a governess has a whole chapter while his father and mother are scarcely present. Several pages about his father had been appended to the revised version of the autobiography in 1966, but

8   it still remains true that the specifics of Nabokov's *outer* life (we

have avoided the slippery word *real*) and a sense of the people who have been most involved in that outer life did not figure in the plans of the author of *Speak, Memory*. —**Yes, yes, of course. I planned it that way.** But with succeeding years that magic fairy tale—one of the works by which Nabokov's name will live—was represented by its author as not only a factual account, which it is, but also a wholly sufficient factual account of his life until 1940, which—how to put it?—is a notion I find contrary to my interest and belief.

—**Why did you want to have your biography written?**

—**Yes, I suppose I wanted to see the thing. The first biography, no matter what comes after, casts a certain shadow on the others.**

—**You wanted to see how you would look. You like good pictures of yourself.** Again, it was said so very quietly.

Our little difference occurred on January 23, 1971. Neither Nabokov nor I said a cross word to one another. It was a telephone call between hotels with his wife acting as plenipotentiary. It concerned how I was going about the business of compiling the material which would go into the biography. I was upset. There are, I must confess at the outset, ways (and I am not thinking now of his many virtues and attributes) in which I am too much like Vladimir Nabokov to judge him. I threw pieces of stale bread to the sea-gulls from the fourteenth-floor balcony of the teak-veneered interloper which now blocks so much of the view from the Montreux-Palace. The mountains across the lake did not move, and soon I was still, too. Puffs of choughs flew by below, and the last of the gulls, convinced now that the feed was over, slid sideways down the air to the lakeside. During the winter in Montreux all but a few of the larger hotels are closed for the season, and at certain hours every stroller and shopper can be idly followed from above. Some sentimental considerations made me, temporarily, a better person. I wrote a letter assuring Nabokov of my friendship. He liked the letter. I was expected for Sunday lunch as usual.

Sunday lunch is very often one of the more elaborate meals of the week for the Nabokovs. Since they have their own cook who comes in several days a week, they tend to eat the hotel's food mainly when they have visitors, which is quite often enough. Nabokov is a compulsive tipper. It is one of his most conscious and cultivated eccentricities. The Italian and Spanish and Yugoslav waiters swarm around the Nabokov party, opening doors, proffering menus and wine lists, smiling at his little French pleasantries. 9

A large cylindrical energetic susan is wheeled up to the table like a converted machine of war with several dozen different kinds of *hors d'oeuvre*. Many of the regulars are elderly women, most of whom eagerly acknowledge his greeting.

On this particular Sunday we were met in a sitting room off the bar for drinks before lunch. There had been no rift. Absolutely nothing was said. A Russian, one must understand, can quarrel and make up with nothing more than the spaces between words.

I had assumed that, even though it was Sunday, we would be eating in the rooms upstairs and had worn only a shirt and cravat. Véra Evseevna accompanied me upstairs to find something suitable from amongst her husband's jackets, and we selected a heavy wool sports jacket of variegated hue. Downstairs Nabokov complimented me on how well his jacket looked. As we walked to the glass doors of the dining room, Nabokov fell behind to ask me in a lowered stage voice not to let him forget to tell me about his daughter and his previous wife afterwards.

It was obviously discomfiting to Nabokov that his remark produced no reaction at all from me. —**Look, Véra. He does not even smile.** I could not explain that the joke was virtually an historical one for me, that it was one which he had been telling for over thirty years and which had fallen on most receptive soil. —**It is still spoken of at Wellesley,** I had been told *sotto voce* by an old staff member. I thought of Nabokov and his life and the business of understanding someone else's life. My mind cantered, I could not banter with the émigré gentleman at my side, and that was a fault in myself.

At the table he continued to stare at his coat. —**Now I can see for the first time how I look in that coat. I never realized that there was so much yellow in it.**

The ordering of the wine got under way, always a highly polished and amusing occasion for histrionics between the Nabokovs. They disagree about the wines, and then, when one finally is selected, they disagree about whether or not it should be sent back. Véra Evseevna thinks she detects sourness in the wine which Vladimir Vladimirovich has just elaborately sniffed, sipped, and approved. The always smiling young maître d'hôtel artlessly tries to agree with them both. —**You go through all the motions, rolling it about on your tongue, but that's all.** A new bottle is brought out, and I wonder if they are prepared to send it back again if need or whim be. —**Yes, yes, oh yes. We have sent the bottle back a second time.**

The table-talk somehow did not catch hold that day, and the conversation turned to easy shop talk, problems connected with the compilation of the bibliography.

Afterwards we retired to their rooms for coffee, and for the first time Nabokov gave me to understand—without words, of course —that he understood my position and was in concord with it. While we were waiting for the coffee to be brought from downstairs, he took me on a brief tour of their quarters, which stretch the length of the sixth floor of the old wing—this, I knew, is rarely done—and showed me a very old photograph of his wife, a charming and pacific girl of about six or seven with wavy light hair hanging down—this, perhaps, had never been done.

The conversation wended its way swiftly through another leisurely afternoon—St. Petersburg, the Nabokov summer estate Vyra, Berlin, Paris, New York, California, Cornell, the American Midwest, Harvard, Switzerland—the same skittish itinerary we had been travelling almost daily for three weeks. The Nabokovs are professionals, and there is little doubt that one of the attractions of the game we played was watching how everyone else played his part.

On occasion I used a recording machine, most often not. Nabokov affects—readers who know his work well will recall this theme at various points in his prose—a fear of electricity, which he insists we still do not really know anything about, and the dictating machine had to sit rather close to him, which caused some discomfiture. But whenever the thing was on and I offered, usually when the flow of conversation seemed in danger of stopping, to switch it off, he would gallantly wave me off.

—Perhaps the machine makes you nervous. Shall I turn it off?

—No, no, why? Darling, this *machine* is on. I'm not sure that I'm doing the right thing in speaking into it.

—You are very wrong.

—No, no, I am so careful. I am so careful that once or twice I was on the point of saying something really interesting and Nabokovian, and I stopped.

That was in 1969, the first year that we tried using the machine. In subsequent years he learned to be playful in its presence (—My sister always gives me all kinds of beautiful, interesting books. That was for the benefit of the machine) and sometimes even to forget about it: —Come on, come on, let's have another one! This is lots of fun. In 1971 we stumbled into an area of his youth about which he had not thought for a long time, and he was so enthusias- **11** tic about the electronic serf there at the ready to capture all that he remembered that he declared he would purchase one at the local stationers for his own use, but his ardour cooled, and he never could be induced actually to hold the microphone.

That Sunday, however, as on most days, I played it by ear and occasionally by notebook, little leatherette address books or pocket diaries which I would fill from flap to flap with snatches of conversation both for their own sake and to serve as memory pegs in reconstructing entire conversations later that evening. My method was to take down what I wanted with the utmost possible precision in improvised abbreviation, even to grunts and exceptional word stresses, but this method occasionally had its drawback, for as often as not, while I was still scribbling with my stubby little golf pencil, Nabokov would launch into some joke or recount some libellous rumour (or fact) about someone—some odd characters whom Nabokov encountered over the years evidently ended up as murderers, Nazi collaborators, and child molesters—and a look of great distress would spread across Véra Evseevna's face at seeing me apparently taking these things down. Once, when such an innocent overlap occurred, she could no longer restrain herself and put the matter to me directly: —**Andrew, I do not understand. Please tell me—how are you writing this book? What is your angle?** I replied that I needed to know everything . . . in order to be able to write a short book.

Nabokov himself tended in watching me watch him to pay more attention, as one would expect, to matters of form and composition than to content. One afternoon Véra Evseevna and I were sorting through bibliographical matters and he was napping. When he joined us, he was still slightly off balance as one sometimes is after a nap. He might have been sleeping in that cardigan and those baggy pants. As he came into the room, he was playing my part. —**I remember him shuffling in looking old and wretched, and a moment later he was bubbling with good spirits.**

I am reasonably adept at playing Russian when I want to, but that Sunday we had spent the entire afternoon chatting together, and it was scarcely an hour away from when it would be time to say good-night again. There had not been a single word about our difference of the day before. Though I knew that (like Véra Evseevna asking what my angle was) it was somewhat direct, I brought the matter up, and we all discussed it as though it had happened ten years ago.

He was defending his life. I was defending my task and my independence. Romance would be left out in particular—the names—but left in in general—a simple and depersonalized history (—**But all that, of course, was before my marriage**) of his love life. Véra Evseevna, for her part, allowed that as far as **she** was concerned I could write anything I pleased about his love life.

—**We'll make a deal, Andrew. I'll write your biography. We'll do each other. No holds barred.** I offered him the address of my first wife, and that stopped the conversation for a moment.

Nabokov was, in my opinion, much more ill at ease at the prospect of discussion of family matters than he was about treatment of his period of youthful romance. Two pages inserted in the new version of *Speak, Memory* about his brother Sergei seemed to him all that could be said on the subject of homosexuality. But even in these awkward pages he could not for some reason bring himself to say the word. He confesses there that a statement about his brother was something at which he had balked in the first version of his memoirs, and that Sergei was someone whom for various reasons he found it **inordinately** difficult to speak of. Yet I know well and with no possibility of error that Sergei's homosexuality was a subject about which his brother himself spoke with the greatest frankness and naturalness, even to his sisters and his mother. As for the rumour that Nabokov's father, the distinguished jurist V. D. Nabokov, might have been the illegitimate son of Tsar Alexander II, he was equivocal. At first he dismissed the topic out of hand, but then he said with a straight face: —**Yes, sometimes I feel the blood of Peter the Great in me.**

Over the years it had been my habit, naturally enough, to bring anecdotes and information back to Nabokov for verification and amplification. I could not but notice that my subject grew progressively more alarmed at what he chose to regard as the wildly unreliable memories of my informants, who also of course happened to be his relatives and friends. His sister Elena, who lives nearby in Geneva, adores her brother, and possesses a good measure of Nabokov toughness, was scolded by her brother because of something she had told me. —**Did you say that to him?** he asked her imperiously, to which she returned indignation and mock-injury: —**Well, if you think I'm that much of a fool, I won't ever say anything about you again!** Nabokov's best friend, George Hessen (he died in 1972), had related a tale Nabokov had told him years before. Hessen's anecdote sent Nabokov into a frenzy. He **13** slapped his forehead with his open palm and spoke directly to the ceiling above his head. —**To think that George Hessen could say such a thing! He's got it all wrong, absolutely wrong!** Previously, George Hessen's name had been held out as the example above and against other friends and relatives (especially the Nabokov cousins by the dozens) who seemed so often to stray from his truth.

On this particular afternoon of conciliation I decided to cease interviewing people beyond those few I had already established firm appointments with for this trip which it would be awkward to break. There were several people whom I was to meet after I left Switzerland, but one of the most important of these, an elderly and obviously very lively lady, had telephoned Nabokov in a state of jovial trepidation upon receipt of my letter: —**Vladimir Vladimirovich, why does he want to speak with me? I assure you I have never been your lover!** There had been some sort of quarrel with another old friend, so that meeting could very well prove awkward in another way. On one ground or another most of the many people whom I had not yet visited seemed artistically dispensable at this point. It was clear to me that Nabokov himself was growing more and more nervous at the thought of all these passers-by being gathered to give testimony to his life. In return for calling an end to the collection of personal impressions and anecdotes, I had but one request: I wanted my subject to try very hard to imagine a biography which was not written by himself.

—**That's a tall order, but I will try. I will try. Yes, yes. But just let it be in my lifetime!**

That assurance was given, and now that all the areas of sensitivity had been touched (or, more accurately, named) they seemed to have lost their previous power and importance. They had not.

—**I think that we have understood each other,** and to that I replied: —**At last.** We had not.

We had come back from a certain brink or precipice, which, by the way, we were to visit together several times more. I had seriously been considering abandoning the book (in my note I had in fact referred to the project in the pluperfect tense), while he very carefully and with a show of concern used a conditional present, unsure of my further intentions.

We parted warmly some days later, all in varying degrees enormously relieved that the seemingly endless days of conversation were now finished. —**We shall miss you**—that said with whimsy 14 —and—**Oh, you'll recover**—which is probably the spirit in which sensible strangers take leave of one another after an enforced comradeship on a liferaft. There was a going-away present, an elegant leather-covered Swiss travel clock.

—A good present for someone who almost never came or left on time.

—Yes, I wanted to say that.

—But I said you mustn't make such a joke.

The present wasn't really necessary or even usual by the standards of ordinary etiquette, but the Nabokovs keep their own account of such things, and I had brought some bottles of Australian wine and presented them with a portrait of the young Nabokov and his brother in a small turn-of-the-century frame. In a past visit to Montreux, when I saw how impossible it was to pick up the bill in the normal manner, I had bribed a waiter to have the parting meal at least credited to my account, but Nabokov was playing the grand host that evening—for dessert we had one of the hotel's lesser-known specialities, flaming **crêpes Nabokov**—and my joke had embarrassed him.

Before I left Switzerland, Nabokov wrote a letter to George Hessen, whom I was to see in New York in a few weeks, and he told me that he had a funny feeling while he was writing it because I was mentioned in the letter, and he suddenly realized that as his biographer I might someday read that letter. Neither of us realized that that time was but a few days off. The letter said that he should not tell Andrew Field very much as he knows too much already.

I had met George Hessen before and talked with him about Nabokov, but then it was all Berlin anecdotage. This year, however, he seemed to me to have things which he had decided to tell me. We sat and drank scotch and munched cashews in his West Eighties apartment and spoke of many things. The biography had reached the end of an important stage, and many stale rumours were being shucked and discarded.

Hessen was the son of one of Nabokov's father's closest political associates, Joseph Hessen. George Hessen had been with Nabokov regularly over the years, first in Berlin and then whenever Nabokov came down to New York. They referred to each other as best friends, and yet my impression was that they were really best pals. There were the ties of the two families—Nabokov heard the mysterious name Hessen from early childhood, mostly from between the clenched teeth of reactionary female members of the family **15** who were convinced that Joseph Hessen was personally responsible for having drawn V. D. Nabokov to the cause of political liberalism (they were wrong, but of that later). There was George Hessen's unqualified admiration for Nabokov as a writer. There was, perhaps most of all, Hessen's bright, squirrel-like sense of humour, his gift for **kidding around** in a particularly oblique Russian way which is also Nabokov's. George Hessen worked as a simultaneous translator at the United Nations. He was a small man, and—though I had been given to understand in Montreux that life had not been entirely kind to him—he always smiled as he talked, and it seemed as if he were even attempting to contain his smile, as though he thought it a social impropriety. He quizzed me about certain anecdotes he had told me the year before and expressed surprise that someone who was as absent-minded as I should apply himself to the craft of biography. I liked George Hessen and can well understand why Nabokov did.

Many years before, Nabokov was asked what his greatest desires in life were, and one of his replies was that someday he wanted to settle in a hotel de luxe. The Nabokovs left Cornell and the United States in 1959 following the success of *Lolita* when their financial independence was assured. They had no idea of the general region in which they wished to reside. They did want to be in England in case *Lolita* was seized upon publication there. The advance for *Lolita* had been very small, only six thousand dollars. There were in addition some foreign-rights payments, all in all a comfortable income by most standards, though scarcely too much for permanent residence in a first-class European hotel. The royalties and the motion-picture money came later.

Montreux and the Montreux-Palace were suggested to Nabokov by the conductor Igor Markevitch. A mutual friend, the actor-writer Peter Ustinov, was at that time living there in the old wing with his family. The Nabokovs moved in on the third floor below the Ustinovs—sound effect of joyful children's feet on the ceiling —liked it well enough, and have remained at the hotel, though in a state of permanent transiency. They moved up to the sixth floor, where they still live. They investigated buying a suite of rooms in the Eurotel when it was being built, but didn't; have poked about with an eye to purchasing various houses and flats in the region of Montreux, but without success; and they even almost bought an elegant villa in France, but, as Nabokov explained it to me, it had

16 a drawbridge and drawbacks. The Ustinovs moved on to Les Dia-

blerets, half an hour from Montreux, and the Nabokovs followed them to the extent of purchasing a thousand square meters high in the hills. The Ustinovs eventually built a châlet, but the Nabokovs remained at the Montreux-Palace in the slightly *démodé* wing of the hotel.

For a considerable portion of the year the Montreux-Palace is a vast, quiet, nearly empty hive of a place with close to four hundred rooms. The only noise is the night traffic on the Grand-Rue which runs hard by the hotel and actually separates it from its summer grounds, and that noise has perhaps been exaggerated in *Transparent Things.* There are many advantages of a private residence in such a situation. In an age when servants are hard to get and harder to manage there is nothing at all eccentric about people of a certain background and age residing in such a hotel. Rather, it is more difficult to imagine an alternative mode of existence half as suitable. When summer and the other American tourists arrive, the Nabokovs go into voluntary exile, sometimes by long-distance taxi, to one of the less peopled ends of Switzerland such as Lugano or by train to France or Italy or even Portugal. Butterflies have much to say about where they live and go nowadays, and there are, I am told, excellent butterflies to be had in the Swiss Alps reached by means of the prim little ski trains which several times a day winch their way confidently to near the top of the steep mountains which overlook the lake. Iran and Morocco and Chile would be good places to collect, but his wife holds him back from such vagaries in much the same way he holds her back from ever acquiring a permanent abode, and with every year it seems less and less likely or necessary, but there are always plans and irresolutions. The Israeli ambassador has asked him to visit Israel, and he agrees to go in the spring but then puts the trip off for a while. There had been more or less firm plans to return briefly to the United States—it would have been only the third visit in twelve years—but then Lerner's *Lolita, My Love* folded out of town, and there were health problems.

In the beginning Switzerland had seemed a particularly good place to be because their son was studying singing in Milan and his sister Elena, and later one of Véra Evseevna's sisters, came to live in Geneva. Montreux is on the way for American publishers travelling to and from other places in Europe, and it is of course an extremely convenient location to meet one's English, German, and Italian publishers from time to time. Now, however, Dmitri's **17** singing career often keeps him in New York for months and travelling around Europe much of the rest of the time. And Elena Vladimirovna has gone with her son and daughter-in-law to live in a modern condominium development on the far outskirts of Geneva, and whether for reasons of health or location they now see one another less often. So, in a sense, the original aims of the Swiss residence are no longer so well served. Moreover, the excellent manager of the Montreux-Palace, with whom they had become quite friendly, is now directing a new hotel. They lunched with him once, but still they have stayed put.

His sister feels that her brother's social horizon is too narrow and artificial in Montreux—publishers, journalists, academics, film people—and that he should move about more. Nabokov says that his sister does not know any of his many friends in Switzerland and has only the vaguest idea about "academics, etc." One must remember their many years in Germany, even past the point when Hitler's danger had become quite clear, or their unbroken stay in America, a large portion of it spent in the culturally raw region of northern New York State. The place for them is Russia, and that place no longer exists, at least in the way in which it did. A tourist brought him back a piece of brick from the site of the old Vyra house, and it is one of Nabokov's few not quite immaterial treasures. He still dreams about his return—too long and too intensely for it to have any point, he wrote in his Russian memoirs—and in his youth he wrote many poems on this theme, more even than were published (I have read them in manuscript), but he has not been really tempted to go back.

His sister claims that he intensely wishes to visit the family estate but will not admit it, and she sparkles with pleasure as she says it: —I don't think he would ever do it. But we discuss very often this problem. First of all I cannot imagine him walking the streets of Leningrad or Moscow. It would be impossible. He would attract attention, you know. The way he walks and the way he's dressed and everything. What would happen? . . . Véra. Véra says that he would be taken immediately. . . . I told her, but, Véra, listen, this would be a scandal for the whole world. He is an American citizen, and what profit would they have from this? No profit at all. But I can't imagine him there, you know. Seeing him in the Hotel Astoria . . . And then he would have to be silent. . . . People would come to hear him, and they would ask his opinion about things, and he would start talking about things as he does, and rightly, then I think they would ask him to leave. That would be all. I don't think that he would be afraid himself to go, but Véra would certainly be afraid. She would never ever go. The persistence of this theme in Nabokov's imaginary life is amply witnessed in *Look at the Harlequins!* And one must understand the intellectual tradition to which Nabokov, through his father, belongs to understand how obdurate and correct (from his own principles) Nabokov is on this point. Picasso, who had nothing whatever in common politically with Nabokov, could have understood this immediately, but I fear there are many who cannot.

So Montreux, or Berlin, or Ithaca is neither here nor there. One merely notes that there is a certain self-acknowledged indolence in Nabokov's attitude towards places, not really a form of Oblomovism, mind you, but the very softest shadow of laziness in a man who seems otherwise devoid of this common characteristic. This domiciliary indolence has caused him to remain for surprisingly protracted periods in those places into which he happens to fall, and one gathers that after only sixteen years Montreux is perhaps not used up yet.

The town of Montreux has had its Russians before, and in the local cemetery there is a marble figure of Christ spreading his hands standing between two cedars—it is the grave of Praskoviya Alexandrovna Nabokoff, née Tolstoy (the noble but not the titled line), who was the widow of a first cousin of Nabokov's grandfather. But there are richer associations than that. Nikolai Gogol once strolled by this lakeside as he prepared to write *Dead Souls*, and Tolstoy came here, too. Dostoevsky, who was in Herzen's eloquent phrase that *gentilhomme russe et citoyen du monde* (a description which, however, applies to Nabokov more than it does to Dostoevsky), prudently stayed at a slight distance from Montreux, in a lowly boarding house. The great nineteenth-century poet Fyodor Tiutchev wrote poetry about the mountains at Montreux. In years past one could have quickly formed an alternative government for Russia with the Social-Democrats and Social-Revolutionaries living by the side of this Swiss lake. The town is one of the wayside stations in the chain of an old tradition in Russian culture and literature: exile.

It is surprising how many of the reputed masterpieces of Russian literature were not written on Russian soil. In *The Idiot* Dostoevsky has one of his characters proclaim: —*All this life abroad and this Europe of yours, it is all a fantasy, and all of us abroad are* **19** *only a fantasy, too.* All the same, from the time of Turgenev it has been comfy (more than that, *uyutno*) for a Russian writer to be in Europe. The artist Aleksandr Benois, who was one of the editors of the pre-revolutionary journal *The World of Art,* described Europe's attraction for the Russian artist or intellectual in his memoirs:

—I don't know how they look upon "abroad" now in Russia, but in my childhood, in St. Petersburg and in our circle, abroad appeared as the most alluring earthly paradise. Old and young dreamt about this abroad, and the young did this scarcely more strongly than their elders. Everyone went abroad, even those with very modest means and those who out of patriotism were ready to denigrate everything foreign.

Benois was of the generation preceding Nabokov's, but nonetheless the time, place, and milieu from which this statement is made are right. Of course the Nabokov family was too sophisticated to permit one to speak of a passion for Europe. Simply, there have been Nabokovs in Europe constantly for over a century, and one expects to find them there. When Nabokov and his wife and child emigrated to America with the Nazis at their heels in 1939 it was, he wrote in his Russian memoirs, with a feeling of *boredom and disgust* for Europe. But they came back. Certainly Vladimir Nabokov, because of his international background, suffered less deracination than many because of the 1917 Revolution, but the young poet's intensity of feeling about his loss did much to dispel the advantage.

Other cultures have also paused at Montreux. Byron set *The Prisoner of Chillon* in a castle at the lake's edge in Montreux, and this castle is today the principal tourist attraction of the region. The Montreux end of Lake Geneva was painted by Kokoschka. Scott Fitzgerald bicycles in the environs in one of his novels, and one of Hemingway's characters wonders comically what the place is like while his passport is being examined and he is being advised to go elsewhere. The only previous resident *doyen* of the region was Romain Rolland, who lived very near Montreux. Nabokov, oddly enough, translated one of Rolland's novels, *Colas Breugnon,* into Russian when he was a young man, because of the challenge of rendering a novel in verse into Russian. But when he too was famous half a century later, Nabokov included Rolland among celebrated mediocrities in need of critical reduction. A Montreux photographer who has done portraits of Nabokov remembers how as a young lad he assisted his father in taking flash-powder pictures of Rolland when the news of his Nobel Prize came in 1916. But there is scarcely any remembrance of Rolland in Montreux—certainly there has been no effort on the part of the town to possess or commemorate his presence there—and Nabokov, too, despite the occasional television crews and the feature stories about him in the slicks, lives there more or less anonymously.

One of the invaluable functions which the hotel staff perform for him very well is to shield him from tourists who would like to include him among their sights. A man who has asked at the desk is requested to write a note rather than telephone, and, as he stands hunched over his little piece of paper, a dignified gentleman walks through the lobby. A bellboy discreetly approaches him, says something, and motions with his head towards the man who is writing. The European gentleman in camel-hair overcoat smiles, shakes his head from side to side, and continues out for his walk. Once some young ladies even made immodest proposals by means of hotel note, but, inasmuch as Nabokov was not aware of their sex, at first he thought he was being pointlessly abused rather than pointedly propositioned. There is a certain amount of this sort of thing in the mails, some of it amusing, but most of it merely a bother. They have learned that they need not return unsolicited books which have been sent to them to be autographed, but still this ethical annoyance is debated every time one comes. They did send one back signed because of a touching letter from a father who thought it might be some comfort to his son, who was dying. But in a year the miraculously recovered son wrote requesting an autographed edition for his dying father. When a *Time* cover story appeared in 1969 a deluge of covers for autographing (all unreturned) strained the homely butterfly-shaped mail catch hanging between the double doors through which one enters their quarters.

These annoyances of fame which are so carefully held at a slight distance obviously please Nabokov, though he would scarcely admit it. I was with the Nabokovs one afternoon when a young man, who had, he said, travelled across the ocean to see him, somehow made it through on the phone. Mrs. Nabokov set about to discover who he was and what precisely he wanted with **21** her husband, and while this bit of testing was going on Nabokov paced up and down the little rectangular room with his hands behind his back. Finally he took the phone from her and questioned the would-be intruder himself. His face was half aglow, and it seemed to me that at least some portion of him—the daredevil, the challenger, the impudent little boy—would have liked the stranger to be clever enough to fake his way in, but he couldn't, and Nabokov explained that he was terribly busy.

—**My life, I wouldn't call it boring . . . but it has been so . . . it has been centred so much on literature, on writing. . . .**

Nabokov writes and works in his seventies as he did in his thirties—intensely, relentlessly. Anyone who has written to the point of weariness and has sustained this writing over a long period of time to the exclusion of many other things may understand this. The publication remains as beautifully fossilized evidence of a vast plain of Vladimir Nabokov's soul. Smaller in scale perhaps though equally intricate and important to what and who he is as a man there is his relationship with his wife—for more than half a century—but this is something which is largely unknowable, for neither of them will ever speak of it. There are several allusions to but no direct mentions of his wife in *Speak, Memory.* Let it be clearly understood that almost everything beyond belongs more to the sphere of mere busyness. —**A serious biography is not adorned by good stories!,** my subject has proclaimed.

There are enough menials and casual acquaintances in Montreux to provide a pleasant and sometimes interesting colonial-style life. It is not in certain respects dissimilar in tone and incident to the life they led in Ithaca and Berlin, though it is very different in terms of circumstances. He sends his shirts out to a laundry which lies on his way to the railroad station where he buys a cluster of international papers every day, and he finds himself involved in the private life of the laundryman, who has a difficult young child—the boy draws on the shirt cardboards, and the drawings frequently soil the fresh shirts, but Nabokov cannot bring himself to complain. There is always a bit of jovial nonversation at the newsstand. Nabokov is probably their best regular customer. He takes the *International Herald Tribune, The Times, The Observer, The Telegraph, The New Statesman, Time, Playboy,* and *Lui,* a European imitation of *Playboy.* From time to time a French paper is thrown in, and he receives *The National Review* with the compliments of William Buckley, a sometime skiing partner of his son's; it is the journal closest to him politically. He also visits the town's other major newsstand because he feels that he must be democratic with his patronage. Whether cunningly or not, it is my impression that he cultivates ineptitude in the simple mechanics of living, and when from time to time he makes a foray to, say, the local bakeshop, the indigestible bounty with which he returns may be counted on to furnish some domestic amusement at his expense. An unlucky impulse purchase of a piece of jewelry has become a running joke —**I am going out. Can I bring you back something? Some bread? Milk? Pearls?**—but it is all in good humour, and they both enjoy it immensely. —**Such lovely pearls!** Because Nabokov does not drive (or rather, has driven twice, once into a ditch with a family car left idling on their summer estate in 1916 and the second time across a vast and empty California parking lot whereon he nearly collided with the only other vehicle then present) they live more or less confined to lake's edge. Véra Evseevna does drive a Lancia, and there are the taxis at the railway station, one of which is even driven by a Russian woman, but out of butterfly season they tend to stay within walking distance of the hotel unless there is some pressing chore or goal.

Nabokov has a part-time secretary now, a Swiss lady who knows English and does his typing and maintains a whole roomful of correspondence file boxes. They have a private cook who comes in to do simple meals for them, and they garnish her plain cooking with their jokes. A typical main course is critically examined and proclaimed to be a cross between a chicken and a turkey. There was an elderly relative of the Nabokovs in Montreux for many years, a woman with whom they had lived for a time in the early years and who had shown them great kindness. Véra Evseevna made a special trip to fly her to Switzerland from New York some years ago when she became ill, and they looked after her from a slight distance, with Véra Evseevna visiting her every other day until she died in 1973.

One does not notice it at first, but there are many strange people about on the streets of Montreux, and Nabokov confessed to me —**I should not do it, but I cannot help it** —that he sometimes follows and observes them.

There is a small English library at the other end of town where Nabokov has made some interesting purchases in the one- and two-franc used-book bin. At one of the local shops he buys, one or two hundred at a time, the index cards—*fiches Bristol* they are called—on which he has done all his writing in recent years. He keeps some under his pillow at night. He has a mechanical pencil which was given to him which he likes to use to correct proofs, but he is very fond of ordinary pencils and buys a goodly number of these, too. His boast is that he uses up the eraser when there is still long service left in the lead, and he cannot endure a pencil without an eraser. There is a kind of ballpoint pen he likes because it has an eraser and its ink can be rubbed away like graphite. That is about all, unless—which is hardly necessary—one wishes to add something about regular medical treatment of the sort that is common for wealthy people of advanced years in Europe, or the coin-sized packaged florentinas from the local chocolate shop of which they are especially fond.

Vladimir Nabokov ordinarily begins his day between eight and eight-thirty in the morning, but he may also start much earlier on occasion. Some years ago he would regularly start at seven-thirty. His insomnia, from which he has suffered all his life, may cause him to sleep in later but not too much. One day, I recall, he told me that he was fully awake until six A.M. that morning but had then fallen asleep until nine and felt fine. He takes a bath in the morning, every morning, always, and this practice is one of the small but essential continuums in his life. The bath is a long steeping affair during which with any luck a few creative gems, a sentence, perhaps two, emerge from the steam. If there are proofs to correct, which happens more and more frequently now that Nabokov has entered that stage of fame which necessarily acquires some of the functions of a light industry, he may turn to these first. When he has been seriously overworked it is more often than not due to things such as his pained and painstaking corrections of translations or the preparation of new editions. He should not be devoting the energy he does to such matters, but it seems he must. Worse, he has been threatening of late to compile a personal anthology of his favourite Russian poems in his own neo-Spartan translations, but this project, because of all that it will involve and take from him, is patiently but firmly opposed by wise Véra Evseevna every time it is mentioned. How serious and immediate his intention is no one can tell. It may be like his announcement one day in my presence that henceforth he was going to write only in Russian once again, a statement which was made, I judge, primarily in order to surprise or tease his closest confidant, who reacted to this sudden public pronouncement with amused lack of interest. One never can tell though.

Nabokov plays his game quite well. He should—he invented it. But I wonder sometimes that he does not tire of it, for he seems too good an actor to be satisfied with a lifelong character part. The person he usually imitates at the Montreux-Palace is the way he puts it. His dramatic ability is displayed at its best when he is playing someone other than himself, which usually happens when he is staging an anecdote: Edmund Wilson speaking Russian, or a Russian émigré secretly gesticulating and squirming on a sofa in an effort to indicate to Vladimir Vladimirovich that he, *too,* is a Mason. *Nabokov says* that it should be made clear that he is not. Much of the public face of Nabokov consists of well-practiced bits of vignettes—when he spoke of Edmund Wilson, for example, he would weigh their friendship and then slowly decide that, in spite of all that has happened in recent years, he was a very old friend —**in certain ways my closest,** and having said that he tilts his head and looks at his wife in an owlish and arch manner. I myself witnessed this particular scene, and as his biographer of course I have on record another instance when he enacted essentially the same scene for someone else.

When Nabokov has finished his morning of writing, he will potter about a bit rearranging his desk, which can be disorderly, but this does not interfere with his work since he writes standing up at an old lectern which was discovered in the hotel's basement. This, he says, has been the best part of his day because in the morning he feels young, there is the pleasure of creativity, the bath, and the very soothing view of the mountains across the lake as he writes. The lunch and dinner arrangements depend upon whether a visitor is due that day. If the day is free there may be a stroll in the afternoon, and then a nap if there has not been much sleep during the night. The Nabokovs retire very early, usually at eight-thirty. Sometimes, however, the pattern is broken, and Nabokov gets up from the dinner table full of creative energy. And the pattern does not apply at all during the summer when butterfly collecting all but eclipses writing. These are the fallow months, and what little work is done takes place deep in deck chairs.

The index cards accumulate in moderately large varnished wooden boxes. He brought *Ada* out to show one evening when the cards had nearly filled the two boxes and—perhaps it was a conscious parody—bounced them joyfully on his knees as though the boxes were a baby. It gave a fine sense of a book as a living thing.

Nabokov has pleasures of many kinds when he writes. It is a   **25** good feeling for him to see his images formed into words—it is Nabokov's claim that he does not think in words—and given some semblance of solidity on the cards. There is the first thrill of diabolical pleasure in cheating creation by having created something himself. There is the pleasure of reading what he has written to his wife, who is together with himself his best audience. —**I am going to read this to you, but I don't want any criticism now.** For the rest Nabokov is fond of repeating Pushkin's dictum that he writes for pleasure and publishes for money.

Pushkin is important to Nabokov, not only for his work but more subtly for the example of his life. In the lives of both men is found a fantastically fierce feeling of *amour propre*. In his youth Nabokov wrote much Pushkinian verse—his indiscreet 1928 long poem *Lilith* describing the itch of intercourse and the hell of historical desire is nothing if not a parallel to Pushkin's *Gavriliada* —and he played the dandy, certainly before the revolution but even afterwards in Berlin in strained circumstances though with a fine tuxedo and Pushkinian sideburns. His final tailor bill from England (for three pairs of pyjamas) was unpaid, which is what dandies do of course, but to his credit he enjoyed telling the tale against himself, especially how his English tailor traced him to Berlin when he wrote a letter to the editor in regard to an article on *audition colorée* in an English paper. The Pushkin sideburns were categorically denied until I produced a photograph blown up from a detail of a large group photograph of those years, and then the recollection returned. Later, however, it faded again, and Nabokov now inclines to the view that this amusing little discovery is a mere shadow blotching his cheek. Nabokov's first fiancée, almond-eyed and with what would in later decades be called a starlet's figure, had at least some of the attributes which biographers and scholars ascribe to Pushkin's wife, Natalya Goncharova, a famous beauty of her time. Nabokov has never to my knowledge fought a duel, but he has come close to it on several occasions. His father, it will be recalled from *Speak, Memory,* issued a challenge to a duel, but it was not fought when his adversary, Suvorin, whose father is well known in literary history as Anton Chekhov's editor, withdrew at the last minute.

The difficulty, of course, is that Pushkin with his early death is a hard paradigm for a protracted life, but one should note that Nabokov's imagination has surveyed these possibilities—in one of his poems he describes what Pushkin would have been like in exile, and in his prose he has imagined a dignified, elderly Pushkin glimpsed at the theatre by a boy, himself a future poet. Pushkin was the one great Russian writer who never went abroad, but at the same time he was far and away the most European of Russia's poets. This is important. The objection of many readers in the emigration to Nabokov's work was precisely that he was too Western, not Russian enough, but in vocabulary, syntax, and form this stricture would have to apply to a surprisingly large extent to Pushkin as well. The main thrust of Nabokov's scholarly commentary on *Eugene Onegin* was precisely to show how much the great poet drew from the French tradition, something which before him Pushkin scholars had stated but never demonstrated. And if you wish to find an antecedent to Nabokov's literary opinions—witty, rude, lightly acerbic—it is to Pushkin's letters you must turn.

Nabokov has even drawn up a Don Juan's list of all his romances for posterity. It was, he agrees, a Pushkinian affectation. It is none of my business, nor yours either, though Nabokov did once assure me in a letter that his romantic life has been more extensive than any of his biographers have assumed. Who, one wonders, are all these other biographers? . . .

He is a man with an enormous talent at once cool and febrile. He is, and confesses to being, a somewhat nervous person, but for some reason I did not ask him why he was nervous. Later, Nabokov strongly objected to the epithet nervous because of its common American meaning of "apprehensive" and explained that he had employed the word in the sense of "easily irritated, excitable," which he is most certainly. He has had a greater share of happiness than most men, enough at any rate to overshadow misfortunes which would loom much larger in other lives. All the same, he is by his own account a rather lonely man. He is, I reckon, a good man, oh, in a peculiar way perhaps, and with certain lapses, but a good man nonetheless. He is also a Russian, and though he intensely dislikes being made to fall in with any group, this fact is the one which cannot be left out, for as he himself once remarked to me: —**One Russian will know another Russian from I do not know what distance. A hundred miles perhaps.** These (perhaps) are the first and main things about this man, but still not the very man.

The book you hold does not come with the recommendation of Vladimir Nabokov. Another very difficult émigré whom I also like, Witold Gombrowicz, the Polish Argentine, has written in *A*   27

Kind of Testament (1968) about the "aseptic-aristocratic" artist, the one who feels an especial need to be inaccessible to others. It is this need which I did not see clearly enough in the early years of my work on this book and which lies at the base of all the difficulties and differences of opinion between Nabokov and his first biographer. I think. Nabokov sees his first biography as, among other things, an unsuccessful assault upon the *radiant, glacial, and final truth* of *Speak, Memory*. It is not, though it must be clear that the Nabokov of *Speak, Memory* and the Nabokov of *Nabokov—His Life in Part* may make each other ill at ease at times. Vladimir Nabokov insists that he exists **only** as a writer, in his written words. I gently but firmly disagree and hope that some part of posterity will thank me for my view:

> *Ah, would there power ga'e us*
> *To pierce some eyes tha' see us!*

Vladimir Nabokov has himself been much concerned with biography in his art. Much concerned. He has written several novels mainly devoted to the theme of biography, a novel in which the hero is a poet-biographer, and still another in which the narrator's sly following of his subject is a significant minor theme. He has also written a critical biography of Nikolai Gogol (I was curious and decided to take the trouble to count, finding that seventy pages of the 172-page-book may be reasonably called biographical), and there are at least half again as many as that devoted to Pushkin's biography in Nabokov's two-volume commentary to *Eugene Onegin* (given the rambling discursive character of the commentaries it is impossible to be more precise). As an appendix to the *Onegin* commentaries Nabokov wrote a long biographical investigation of Abram Gannibal, Pushkin's Abyssinian great-grandfather, which is perhaps his most serious attempt at the genre. There are, of course, numerous fleeting biographies within the context of *Speak, Memory*.

Nabokov's first attempt at biography caused a quiet scandal in émigré literature. His novel *The Gift* first appeared in instalments in *Contemporary Annals,* the most important and long-lived of the émigré journals and also the principle bastion of the Social-Revolutionaries and Social-Democrats in the emigration. For both of these groups Chernyshevsky was a figure of veneration, and the hero of *The Gift* has written a little biography which was to have appeared as the fourth instalment, but it had to wait thirteen years before it finally was printed in an American series of Russian-language books financed by the Ford Foundation. Fyodor Godu-nov-Cherdyntsev's rude biography of Chernyshevsky in *The Gift* —I have written of this elsewhere—utilizes intimate and embar-rassing material from his diaries, which had been published for the first time only a few years before, and Chernyshevsky is ridiculed with incredibly deft skill, not without a certain sympathy at times, to be sure, but also not within a horizon's sight of what people call propriety. The editors objected. A sonnet figures importantly within the biographical chapter of *The Gift*, and its substance is that the truth of the past is never accessible to the historian, and it is also hinted within the chapter that Godunov-Cherdyntsev's biography, drawn from the dry work of another (also invented) biographer may serve to redeem Chernyshevsky's life through the miraculous power of art.

I naturally was curious to discuss what we may term the bio-graphical licence in *The Gift* with Nabokov. Once I asked him whether there was anything he seriously regretted having done or not done in the course of his life. He did not think a minute and said that, yes, he regretted the overly sharp review he had written on the poetry of the talented émigré poet Boris Poplavsky, who was to die several years later. We spoke about the opinions which one may express about people who are alive (the dead whom he ridiculed—Nikolai Gogol, Chernyshevsky—did not come into it at all):

—I do think that when you criticize people, one should take into account the quantity and quality of happiness that has been allotted to them. Quite a number of people are unfortunate peo-ple, *neudachniki* in the Russian sense, and I would not criticize these people in the same way I would a very, very, very successful poet as Mr. (why should I) or Mr. (continue a fight?) who are really complete mediocrities. I had to remind my old friend of how well I knew his work, not merely the Poplavsky review but devastating things he had written about some truly minor contemporaries such as Rafalovich and Raissa Blokh.

—I shouldn't have. I was wrong. I think that I was just teaching myself to write. I was perhaps imbued with the spirit of cruel criticism of the sort that Gumilyov wrote. I may have been in-fluenced by that type of criticism. It was also current in English journals of the time when I was young. Rafalovich. Raissa Blokh. 29

I was horrid to her. She was saved by a misprint from a dreadful . . . She was a bad poet, O.K. But I should not have written what I did. Much later, in 1973, Nabokov preferred to say simply that she was a gentle young woman who happened to write mediocre verse. He also recalled that the misprint was corrected in a subsequent number. I mentioned Georgy Adamovich, one of the most important émigré critics, who had been very unfair and capricious about Nabokov's work, and who subsequently suffered some most unpleasant satirical jibes. Even here Nabokov relented: —**He's a difficult person. Still, I think I was wrong.** Later, in 1973, Nabokov had changed his mind about that and said: —**I would not go out of my way to attack him nowadays but I certainly do not regret the fun I had in exposing the frailty of his critical pronouncements thirty years ago.** Adamovich, as it happens, died in 1973, and in a bibliographic note to a Nabokov book being prepared for publication by McGraw-Hill (I read it in galleys) Nabokov used the occasion to note—an old joke of his—that the émigré critic had had two passions in life: Russian poetry and French sailors.

The biography within *The Gift* was written by a hero who was —**Sort of like me, but I myself wouldn't have written it that way.** There was a pause. —**The biography mustn't be written this way.**

When Vladimir Nabokov was young, he had an English governess who had three questions by which one's thoughts and words, she held, should be measured: —**Is it true? Is it kind? Is it worth while?** This litany was repeated to the young Volodya time and again, and more than half a century later his face still registered bemused incredulity as he recounted it.

The finest and most characteristic statement relevant to biography which Nabokov has made occurs in one of his obscure book reviews in which he refers to that narrow and elevated ridge where art and science may meet. But of course. The difficulty is that after several years of talking and corresponding with living and for the most part willing witnesses to a life, I find there is scarcely a shred or a shard, never mind the radiant truth which history coyly shields, which is not open to serious question or challenge. That's the truth.

Nabokov likes the game of trying to ferret and pluck out bits of unvarnished truth from the evidence given by chroniclers and artists. He likes to cite a Pushkin letter which strikes him as a pure snatch of a real voice heard across time. He told me —**Marvellous!** of a description by Louis XVI's valet of how Louis stood twisting the wedding ring on his finger before he was executed. He also likes an early French engraving of a tennis game in which all the moves, including a ballboy decorously removing a ball from under a skirt, —**seem right.** By that standard I possess only one fragment of pure Nabokov, half a sentence to be precise. Véra Evseevna and I had paused in the doorway as I was about to leave one day. Nabokov had said good-bye and gone to dress for dinner. While we were still standing at the door, Nabokov came back into the room turning his tie and saying in Russian—**Darling, can I really not write about him?** . . . Then he suddenly saw me. —**Oh, I'm terribly sorry, Andrew. I didn't realize you** *were* **still here.** The word stress was strangely out of place. An hour before Nabokov had been telling me about an extraordinary and pathetically tragic man he had known in California. I had asked—the man is now dead—if he intended to write about him in *Speak On, Memory,* but Véra Evseevna had interrupted and said that of course he could not. There was no essential gesture, truth, or information gained by me at that moment, but it is true that that half-sentence during the course of which I had been granted invisibility does live most resonantly within me, and when I summon up Vladimir Nabokov to myself he always begins with that Russian fragment spoken in a very particular tone and cadence.

Nabokov grieves over the past which has slipped away from him: —**I wish Véra had made me write down things when I was younger. You don't think you ever will, but you do forget** . . . but is positively appalled when he contemplates the prospect of pieces of his past which might somehow drag themselves into his present: —**It would be terrible. . . . Horrible!** Nabokov once pondered his own times and concluded: —**No one who hasn't lived through the émigré experience can possibly understand it. I myself don't know how to understand it looking back on it.** Later, he wanted the sense of that statement to be sharply qualified.

Vladimir Nabokov has never been satisfied with the mere possibility of truth, which is to his credit, but too often he has allowed himself to marshal his facts like an overconfident prosecutor, whether it be to prove his theory that Pushkin and his fellow poet Ryleev must have fought a duel near the Nabokov family estate (his case rests too heavily on supposition and personal information that cannot be either verified or disproved) or to prove that virtually nothing can be said with any certainty (he succeeds here) about Pushkin's supposedly Abyssinian great-grandfather. He 31 sometimes succeeds too well and might have done better to hang back a bit, but there is always that unrestrainable creative force which after a long struggle pushes the scientist over the ridge. Nabokov's account of how Pushkin used ciphers, in which he literally clambers into the poet's cranium, is brilliant fancy but fancy all the same. What, I wondered, would have been Nabokov's relations with Pushkin had they been contemporaries? **—Oh. He would have challenged me to a duel. There can be no doubt of that.** Yes.

In writing about his own life Nabokov is setting out to do something very special, and if he is in any tradition it may be that of Lord Herbert of Cherbury (1583–1648), who conceived that he should best declare himself in his autobiography by ignoring the outstanding facts and achievements of his life. Nabokov thinks of *Speak, Memory* as a lyrical book, and what troubles him about *Speak On, Memory* is that it is assuming the appearance of a mere epic peopled by anecdotes. Perhaps these anecdotes will yet fall away, but even though he is writing the book he professes no confidence that he will carry it through (in fact, he is proceeding briskly with it). **—There is an absence of that glow of affection I felt for *Speak, Memory*. It will not be violins but trombones.** For the time being he proceeds with neatly potted category chapters —the basic plan for the book has been in his diaries for two decades—such as university lecturing, or Edmund Wilson, but the only themes which really stimulate his interest and feeling, he claims, are the Museum of Comparative Zoology and his butterfly expeditions in the Rockies.

These are some of my competitor's problems, but his biographer had different ones of his own. Within the large Nabokov family, for one thing, there are those who are prone to exaggeration and to jest. Some of the Nabokovs speak of the various branches of the family by the first names of the grandfather's children, after the manner of medieval princely tribes, and in particular some of the Dmitrievichi (it seems agreed by all but the Dmitrievichi) have an inclination to find colourful things on the family tree. The best tale by far came from a member of the more rightist branches of the Nabokov family, who told me in all seriousness that Nabokov's father had been so liberal that all of the family's fifty servants had been Jews. When I questioned him about it, George Hessen laughed himself to the point where he had to lean against a wall for support over that story (**—Akh! Just think, where** would they have got all those Jewish servants from? You couldn't have found five in all of St. Petersburg. They would have had to have been specially imported from abroad!) and continued to laugh and wipe his eyes dry throughout that whole evening whenever it sprang back to mind. But his best friend, it seemed to me, heard this tale with far more serious glee. To be sure, it is a somewhat Gogolian picture—all those exotic Jewish butlers and footmen—but the thing of it is, there is no surety whatsoever that the story was originally (decades ago) transmitted in jest. Some other members of the family—and this goes back a long time prior to 1917—thought that V. D. Nabokov was *—practically a Red.* There were, in fact, more than a few right-wing Nabokovs who considered themselves the sole representatives of social propriety in the family.

Any given truth, I found, may stand very well by itself but be substantively modified upon being placed in proximity to another given truth, and even a statement which is patently false may more often than not involve capillary truths and histories which are interesting in their own right. The story of the Jewish servants, for example, is nonsense, but it may reveal something about relations and family politics within the various branches of the Nabokov family, the credulousness of some of them, and of course the presence of anti-Semitic feeling in the Russian aristocracy. Or again, there are the family tales such as the one that V.D. Nabokov was really the son of Tsar Alexander II. If for no other reason than that Alexander was deep in another affair at the time and nowhere near Nabokov's grandmother, V. D. Nabokov could not possibly have been his son, but the legendary romance was known to Nabokov and to my mind it ties in with certain narrative themes in his fiction. Another theme—the dream of the Russian exile returning to the deeply loved land, but not a land controlled by the Soviets —is one that might have come true for Nabokov: when the Germans pushed the Soviet army back and laid siege to Leningrad, the Vyra estate come very close to falling out of Soviet hands, and this at a time when the Nazis had a policy of returning estates to their pre-revolutionary owners in appropriate cases. But it is absolutely certain that no matter how fascinating the theme of return may have been to Nabokov, he would never have been tempted to resume the Vyra estate, not under German auspices.

A small truth may give the appearance of giving essential testimony but is usually not sufficient in itself. Thus Nabokov spoke to 33 me of his tremendous will power, a characteristic that he was anxious I should perceive, and as an instance of his will power he cited the way in which he abandoned his chain smoking in a single day. True. But it is also true that at just that time he is recorded as having developed a passionate attachment to molasses kisses, which he consumed at a steady rate, causing a great increase in his weight. Still, I know, without his having had to tell me, that Vladimir Nabokov is in fact a man of tremendous will power.

Once I asked Véra Evseevna what she thought her life would have been like had the revolution not occurred, and she was only midway through the second sentence of her speculation when Vladimir Vladimirovich lost patience and interrupted with forced gruff humour:

—**You would have met me in Petersburg, and we would have married and been living more or less as we are now!** He spoke very emphatically and rapidly, almost in an English imitation of that unique form of Russian rapid speech called *skorogovorka*. It was not a joke. It was a point of essential order in his very private universe. And if a man does not wish to allow anything to history, fate, chance determinants—call it what you will—who is to say that it is a conceit or a deceit? The point is that he cares very much indeed about such things, and as far as I can make out he has no lucky stars to thank or bad luck to curse in his own view of his life. There is much to be said for such a point of view.

Major outlines of the life that Véra and Vladimir Nabokov have lived together are described in perfect concord by them; but there was not such unanimity in the recall of particulars in my presence; they were not accustomed to being quizzed on the details of their personal lives reaching back for fifty years. Disputation about the particulars of the past seemed one of the vital nerves of their relationship:

—**A very charming and very intellectual young lady, and she boarded with the Hessens. And she was instrumental in suggesting I read *South Wind*, which I liked very much, and *Some People* by Nicolson. So that *Some People* and *South Wind*, though very different books, remained for a long time on the same shelf at the back of my brain.** But before the conversation can touch on Douglas, Nicolson, or any one of several interesting subjects it must first pass through an intellectual visa checkpoint:

—**Excuse me, but that's absolutely wrong because I know that**
34 **I read *Some People* in Landhausstrasse and translated it for my**

father. . . . Nabokov is no less certain than his wife:

—**No, no, no, no!! That is all wrong.** . . . The two versions of reality struggle with each other, until at last I ask the obvious question, knowing full well in advance what the answer will be. —**It is not important.**

While on one hand Nabokov clearly enjoys both the retrieval of bits of the past and a good fight, he has also on the other an ingrained conviction that all *facts,* especially the minor ones, but rather large ones as well, are basically extrinsic to his self if they do not come from himself. Here is a not atypical discussion of a not unimportant event, Nabokov's engagement and marriage:

—**Oh, we were engaged for a very short time. Perhaps a year.** —**Two years.** —**Two years. We were married in the Berlin Town Hall.**

—**I vot i vsyo. [And that's that.]** The conversation, as invariably happened when personal matters arose, was from this point waged on two fronts between Nabokov and his wife: factuality and reticence. It also slipped into Russian.

—**I vot i vsyo. I vot i vsyo. And my mother, I think, didn't know about our marriage.** —**She knew.** —**She didn't.** —**That's that.**

CHAPTER

2

You must use those German barons!

The barons—actually they are better described as Baltic barons —are the Germanic ancestors of Nabokov from his grandmother's family, the von Korffs. They figure neatly and stolidly in an elegant genealogy which was prepared for Nabokov as a gift by his German publisher Rowohlt Verlag, though there is every likelihood that these medieval souls were for the most part not stolid at all but members of the Teutonic Knights, a harsh military caste in what we would call Klanish costumes, which very effectively controlled large areas of Eastern Europe under special papal licence for several centuries. The medieval name Korff derives, I am told, from basket *(korb)*. That is straightforward enough, as is the name **39**

Rukavishnikov, the family of Nabokov's mother, which derives from *rukavitsa* in the sense of a warrior's gauntlet. It is a much more chancey feat to trace and parse some functional sense from the name Nabokov itself. I looked the von Korff family tree up and down, but I am sorry to say that there was little in it of interest apart from Nabokov's grandmother, who interests me very much indeed and who has already been mentioned, and his great-grandmother, whose morals Nabokov has called into question in *Speak, Memory* on the basis of information unknown to me. Heinrich Korff was a thirteenth-century knight who went on the first crusade led by King Louis IX (St. Louis), and the legend has it that he saved Louis' life and was awarded a *fleur de lys* for it. While Nabokov allots considerable space to the von Korffs in *Speak, Memory,* he gives no indication of any discernible von Korff traits in the Nabokov family life, apart from an obdurately transgenerational birthmark. But it is reliably hearsaid that there are many specific traits in the latter-day Nabokov family which may in all probability be traced directly back to the von Korffs. The intense fastidiousness which Nabokov has and his father before him had (especially those never missed daily baths in still-mysterious-to-me portable rubber tubs) may well, according to one family source, be a specifically Korffian characteristic. *Nabokov says* that in all probability the Korffs were bathless barons, and he reminds me that *Pushkin* used to take a bath every day, and that his own wealthy great-grandfather Rukavishnikov used to travel abroad with his carriage *and* his bathtub.

I learned from Nabokov's sister Elena of a costume ball when they were children to which her brother had worn the costume of a Spanish matador, a little fact which was duly noted but which seemed to have no more to offer than Heinrich Korff's *fleur de lys.* It leaped back to me, however, when I came upon a very old picture of V. D. Nabokov as a young man, at a costume ball, dressed as a Spanish matador. Nor was that the end of it, for a casual remark in the reminiscences of one of Nabokov's aunts about childhood games among ancestral trunks in the large box-room of their St. Petersburg house suggests that the use of a Spanish costume in the family (I have no idea whether the actual costume or pieces of it were actually one and the same) goes back at least to his grandfather D. N. Nabokov, who was four years Pushkin's senior, who is registered as possessing 390 souls shortly before the emancipation of the serfs, and who died in the same house and only three years after the birth of Nabokov's father. *Nabokov says* that *all* Russian families of their set loved masquerades and that toreador costumes were the most popular and banal at such balls, which may be, but it was not that which I had in mind. A masquerade costume is fairly conspicuous and hence easy to note and follow. Think of the countless gestures, habits, routines, and traditions which have likely trickled down through generations. They can never be known, and yet they are not without importance. Vladimir Nabokov would be infinitely less comprehensible as a person if considered apart from his rather unusual family, and in particular his father.

Why, then, is Nabokov himself as interested as he is in even the farthest tributaries of his family? Apart from a very few families descended from the Varangian first rulers of Russia, the lines of nobility in Russia are in comparison with other European countries carelessly recorded—coats of arms, for example, did not come into use until the very end of the eighteenth century—and it has been the custom among the modern Russian nobility to speak in a half-serious scoffing manner about their more distant forebears. Nabokov's father is recorded as having followed this fashion. There are several possible explanations for Nabokov's latter-day interest in genealogy. The natural scientist in him would of course want precise taxonomic knowledge. The ironist in him would, for example, take pleasure at the thought of so many bloodthirsty Huns in the family tree of a writer who has ridiculed the Germanic with such gay ferocity. The fact of emigration and the disregard and lack of interest with which Nabokov regarded family history as a youth and young man may have served, with time, to heighten the value and intrigue of family history so that these family trees eventually were given a modest place in the garden of his childhood and his Russia.

In *Speak, Memory* Nabokov refers to the founder of his family as Nabok Murza. Murza is the title of an ennobled military leader. His source of this information, a cousin of his father's, told Nabokov in the 1930s that this Nabok Murza was a russified Tartar prince living in the vicinity of Moscow in the late fourteenth century. My researches into Tartar nobility of the period were, however, fruitless; in a scholarly listing of the retinues of the first four Khans following Genghis Khan (translated from the Chinese by a monk in Saint Petersburg in 1829) there was no possible variant of the name Nabokov to be found. On the other hand, **41** though, one has only to examine a photograph of Nabokov's grandfather to see at once the undeniable presence of Tartar or Mongol blood in his face: the Minister of Justice under Alexander III used, in fact, to be called *Kitaets* (the Chinaman) behind his back. The answer may lie to the South, in the Tartar incursions and consequent intermarriages in Persia, Turkey, and Egypt. The Arabic *na'ib* means something like deputy or viceroy, and that word goes back to Genghis Khan. If that is the derivation of the name one cannot but notice that Nabokovs were still fulfilling this function in the nineteenth and even twentieth centuries. There is an Indian title, *navab*, deriving from the time when part of India and South-East Asia became Moslem, and, of course, the Bengal form of the title, *nabob,* is an accepted and well-known English word. At any rate, there are today Egyptians with the name Naboka. So we may imagine that the initial Slavic Nabok came into Rus from a southerly direction—perhaps he was a Turkman or a Circassian even—that he could have been a Mohammedan before he was a Christian, and that, judging by the probable meaning of his name, he would have been an ennobled colonial functionary of a Tartar prince rather than a full-fledged prince in his own right. The name Nabokov is not at all a common one, but I have found that there were Nabokovs of low estate but purportedly noble lineage living in the south of Russia prior to the revolution.

There is a difficulty presented by the fact that both parts of the name Nabok Murza might be titles, but the sense of one of them as a title could well have been lost by the fourteenth century. For some reason Nabokov and other relatives with a genealogical bent do not favour the possibility that the name Nabokov might have referred quite simply to a founder who had been afflicted with, say, polio and thus was twisted in body to the side (as the name in Russian could imply), though Nabokov the goalkeeper and contented loner has written that personally he would have preferred his name to derive from someone who stood *to the side* of the road *(na oboch'e),* which it could mean, too, and which would suit him very well. Russian names, and Tartar names as well, were originally surnames or nicknames (there were no family names at this time), and some of the most famous old Russian family names such as Dolgoruky (long-armed) were formed from prominent physical characteristics, quite like English names such as Longfellow. Though less likely in the case of the Nabokovs because the information was acquired by reliable members of the family, the possibility, I feel, should not be entirely dismissed inasmuch as we have no way of knowing how accurate this information was when it was recorded sometime in the eighteenth century. Nor should I pass away from the subject without mention of King Nebuchadnezzar, the illustrious ruler of Babylonia and destroyer of Egyptian armies in the sixth century BC, whose name has come down to us in much corrupted form, earlier discarded variants of it being Nabukudurushur and Nabokodnossor. In the hinterlands of mythology there is Nabu (or Nebu), the inventor of writing.

In order to understand the historical place of the Nabokovs in Russian society it is first of all necessary to clarify what the term prince signified in medieval Rus. I draw my information from a long essay by K. Karpovich entitled "Princely Titles in Russia" which appeared in the *Historical Messenger* (*Istoricheskij Vestnik*, Vol. XX) in 1885. The princely families of Rus were comparatively few in number, or, to put the matter in another way, it is estimated that the number of princely titles of Tartar, Mordovian, Georgian, and such-like origin exceeded the number of Russian princes at least tenfold. At a later date, beginning in the sixteenth century, a crafty stratagem was implemented by the Russian ruling class to lessen the importance of non-Russian nobility, in particular the Tartar nobility. It was decreed that *all* Tartar Murzas who accepted the Orthodox faith had to refer to themselves with the title of prince. In medieval Rus there had been certain buffer principalities in which Tartars were welcomed and their numbers used to bolster the strength of those states against their rival Russian principalities. It would in all likelihood have been in one of these buffer principalities such as Ryazan that Nabok Murza was russified. But the deflation of the value of Tartar nobility was so successful by the seventeenth century, and especially after the reign of Tsar Aleksei Mikhailovich, that whether or not Nabok Murza was a *real* Tartar prince or nobleman (the fact that Murza follows the name is another indication that he was), his descendants had to share the title of prince with literally thousands of old-clothing merchants, simple peasants, and soapmakers. The title prince meant nothing in Russia after this time unless it was in reference to one of the Russian princely families. In fact, according to the Ukase of 1675 it was an insult and slander to address someone simply as prince without the use of his Christian name or surname, since in common usage by that time this was tantamount to calling someone a Tartar and thus casting aspersions on his family background.

Of course the fate of the Tartar nobility in seventeenth-century

Russia did not in any way affect the Nabokovs, who were completely russified by the fifteenth century, but it is necessary to understand this bit of social history in order to understand what would have happened to the princely title of Nabok Murza which Vladimir Nabokov mentions in *Speak, Memory.* The title, anyway, appears to have been dropped by the fifteenth century. The Nabokovs were noble, to be sure, but the family did not stand as high as did some of the russified Tartar nobility.

For there had been a genuine Tartar nobility which was russified, enjoyed privileges of property and station (generally slightly below but in certain cases exceeding those of members of some Russian princely families who for one reason or another had gradually lost their material advantage in society), and this Tartar nobility was recognized by the Russian court as being (the exact distinction is an important one, though it is too fine for me to sort out here) noble but not aristocratic. Evidence points clearly to the fact that the Nabokovs were such a family, and there is no reliable evidence known to me which gainsays it.

The most distinguished and powerful of the Tartar princely families such as the Urusovs (descendants of one of Tamerlane's princely lieutenants) and the Yusupovs (one of the recent members of this family participated in the assassination of Rasputin) were included in the lists of the most distinguished boyars very shortly after their acceptance of the Orthodox faith. The Nabokovs were not among these ranking families, but on the other hand there is evidence which points to the fact that the Nabokovs are one of the families which are placed too low in Prince Dolgorukov's *Russian Genealogical Book* (1858), in which they are located only in the thirteenth table, which contains families having attained nobility by virtue of being in the first two classes of the state service in the table established by Peter the Great. Peter was hostile to much of the old Russian nobility, and his reign marks a drastic change in Russia's social structure, for not only did Peter create a class of clerks and civil servants, he also by this means created a very large upstart or parvenu nobility. As the Tartar nobility had been effectively debased, so, too, the importance of the Russian nobility falls markedly after the time of Peter.

The Nabokov family should in all likelihood be entered in about the seventh chapter (the succession of chapters in Prince Dolgorukov's book is also deceptive, and one can be led astray by attaching too much importance to the mere number of a chapter), that is, among nobility established prior to 1600. Pushkin's family, for comparison, is listed in the sixth chapter; Moussorgsky's, in the fifth. Nabokov, standing slightly lower, comes from the *moyenne noblesse,* which has historically furnished Russia with the great majority of her writers and poets, and the family origins of, say, Turgenev or the philosopher Chaadaev are essentially similar to his. *Nabokov says* that on the social ladder, as opposed to mere genealogical scales, his family stands incomparably higher than Moussorgsky's and considerably higher than Pushkin's or Turgenev's.

The more reliable indications which we have of the earlier nobility of the Nabokov family than is given in the seventeenth-century *Velvet Book* or the nineteenth-century *Russian Genealogical Book* are the family crest, which utilizes motifs traditionally present only in the older Russian coats of arms (and showing, incidentally, that the early Nabokovs were military men); the existence of records showing that Nabokovs owned land prior to the seventeenth century, before which time land ownership was with rare exception reserved entirely to nobility; and, finally, the fact that the earliest of these known registers (I have not seen it —it is cited in *Speak, Memory*) shows that the Nabokovs, landowners with no traces of their Tartar origins in their Christian names, were already using their surname in the fifteenth century, by no means a common practice at that time. When Konstantin Nabokov served in the Russian embassy in England just prior to 1917, he found in the records there that a Nabokov had been a junior officer in the deputation which Ivan the Terrible had sent to the Court of Elizabeth I.

A family history, particularly one of any length, is not likely to tell one much about an individual. All the people in it, if they were to be magically gathered together at one time, would likely be surprised at how little they held in common apart from their name. Features and dispositions shared through the generations would caricature themselves. And also, the mathematical progressions as one moves backwards in time are such that it would not be terribly difficult for any skilled genealogist to establish some link eventually, however tenuous, between virtually any Parisian taxi-driver of Central European ancestry and the Bourbon dynasty of kings. Besides that, families, whether or not they possess trees, do from time to time have a bend sinister, and then, well, what is the point of it all? Nabokov's youngest brother Kirill only regret- **45** ted that in his brother's memoirs there is too much of family matters which are of no interest to other people. I propose to be satisfied to use what we know of the Nabokov family tree simply to make us conscious of what the Nabokovs themselves perhaps have taken for granted when they have written about themselves: the particular heritage, half historical, half genetic, which has produced a certain Nabokov tone and sense of place and function in the world which is shared by Nabokovs who in more obvious respects could not possibly be more different. That is my view of the family tree, but various members of the Nabokov family see it somewhat differently, too.

The question which needs to be asked here is whether or not there ever was any social grouping in Russia which corresponds to the English notion of upper middle class. Not really. A family which might have been seen as being upper middle class such as the family of Nabokov's mother, the Rukavishnikovs, became ennobled as soon as its wealth reached a very high level, not automatically, but in practice. The Rukavishnikovs were ennobled quite late, in the 1890s. They were then very, very wealthy mineowners; in the eighteenth century they had been schismatics or *raskolniki.* One of the Rukavishnikovs was in Pugachov's rebellion. The Russian social order did not really provide a separate place for a *haute bourgeoisie,* unless one wishes to apply this term to the very small group of millionaire merchants such as the Tretyakovs who became famous for their support of Russian art. Class distinctions and privileges were sharply drawn so that wealthy and cultured individuals and families could exist, true, but without exerting themselves as a class as they naturally did in other European countries. And the few exceptional families such as the Rukavishnikovs, who *were* middle class in fact, were marginally ennobled. So we may put the matter this way: the Nabokov family belonged to the affluent portion of the lower nobility, the *grand monde* which consisted of high bureaucracy and court circles. They had a professional tradition, first as soldiers, then for the most part as statesmen and courtiers. From the eighteenth to the twentieth centuries the Nabokovs were distinguished and important with surprising frequency. They were snobs like the rest of the Russian nobility, but their snobbery was based for the most part upon intellectual ability and bureaucratic achievement rather than class. The Nabokovs were loyal to their country in a
46   way that the higher aristocracy in Russia too often was not, and yet

they were also able to be true Europeans in a way that Russia's aristocrats, again, often were not. These are generalizations drawn from and spread out over generations, but I have not come to them quickly.

We may now enumerate some of the traceable Nabokovs beginning with Nabokov's great-great-grandfather, General Aleksandr Ivanovich Nabokov (1749–1807), who commanded a military regiment in Novgorod and fought under Suvorov, and whom I mention only because of his nephew Nikolai Andreevich Nabokov, who served in that regiment after having been attached to the Preobrazhensky Guard Regiment. This nephew's wife, Olga, was related to several of the officers who had prominent parts in the Decembrist Revolt of 1825. Was there a Nabokov Decembrist? There is a tradition in the family that there was one Nabokov who was involved, though not in a prominent way. There are even rumours that there were two Nabokovs actually arrested at the time of the uprising. Nikolai Andreevich, though he would have been forty-seven at the time, would seem likely to have been one of them or the one. The involvement was supposedly serious enough at any rate to warrant Siberian exile, and it has been reported that in the secondary literature on Dostoevsky there exists mention of a conversation which Dostoevsky, serving his sentence in Siberia, had with the Decembrist Nabokov. I have not been able to find this reference myself, but neither can I bring myself to let it go unmentioned. What is a fact, though it is a meagre one in comparison with that possibility, is that one of the brothers of Nabokov's great-grandfather (who was married to the sister of Pushkin's closest friend) was the commandant of the Peter-and-Paul Fortress during the time Dostoevsky was imprisoned there. He is of no use to me. I am thinking, of course, about the possibility of finding the farthest origins of the fine but strong line of liberal commitment within the Nabokov family.

We have no information which would suggest such a social disposition in the next Nabokov, our Nabokov's great-grandfather, Nikolai Aleksandrovich (1795–1873), except, and it is a strong exception, that he married a Nazimova, a sister of one of the most prominent of the Decembrists. It was this Nabokov who went on the 1817 expedition to the Arctic island of Novaya Zemlya—our Nabokov, of course, prefers the English mumble or bumble, Nova Zembla—where a small river (he was a very young officer on that expedition) was named for him. It is not shown on most maps, but **47** it may be seen in the 1912 *Geographical Atlas* published in St. Petersburg.

In his memoirs Nabokov speaks of the next Nabokov, his grandfather, who, in his declining years, was closeted up in a single room which had been decorated to resemble a room in Nice, which is where the old gentleman strongly preferred to be resident. Nabokov dimly recalls showing his grandfather a pretty stone—this was when he was four and the family was actually in Nice, a very short while before the old man's death—which Grandfather Nabokov, who, as Nabokov was told by his mother, was then quite mad, placed slowly in his mouth. In the memoirs of one of Nabokov's older aunts, Véra Pihatcheff, she describes *her* grandfather—that is, Vladimir Nabokov's Nova Zemlyan great-grandfather—as an equally old man, also closeted up in St. Petersburg (in an earlier Nabokov house, however, on Glinka Street):

—I remember him as rather a haughty and imposing old gentleman with a beautiful white beard and snow-white hair. He never left his room, but received a great many visitors. We children were formally taken down every morning to pay our respects to him. He used to give us a look of benevolent indulgence and then opening a drawer—which was kept carefully locked—he would hand us each a few sweets, saying "There you are, you little mischiefs." Like well-bred children we accepted them with thanks, but experience had taught us to be careful about eating them, for they frequently were old and rancid.

What was the seventy-eight-year-old grandfather, D. N. Nabokov, thinking of when he placed that little stone given to him by his young grandson in his mouth? Vladimir Nabokov values most highly the discovery of such patterns of repetition in telling of a life. But I would hesitate—not that I could not do it—to write Nabokov's own life according to this speculative prescription. These are merely the question sparks of reality.

I shall skip now the several pages of von Korffs and Grauns as catalogued in *Speak, Memory* who seem important to the history of the Nabokov family mainly for the musical aptitude which they contributed to it. Nabokov's cousin Nicholas Nabokov is a well-known composer. Nabokov's father (like many of his brothers and sisters) was a passionate lover of music, and his son Dmitri is a professional *basso*. Nabokov himself, if he is not actually tone deaf, cares little for music.

N. A. Nabokov, Vladimir Nabokov's great-grandfather, had thirteen children, only two of whom died at an early age. D. N. Nabokov, who was N. A. Nabokov's second eldest son, had nine children. V. D. Nabokov, who was D. N. Nabokov's third son, had five children. V. V. Nabokov has one son. Through a combination of martial ability, state careers which were well-rewarded, and some fortunate marriages the Nabokov clan flourished throughout the nineteenth century. Of D. N. Nabokov's brothers one was a landowner in the province of Saratov, one was a provincial vice-governor, two had successful military careers, and the fifth furnishes me with another of those first-rate Nabokov legends. . . .

Vsevolod Nikolaevich Nabokov was born May 13, 1834. While his father was by Russian standards a modestly wealthy man—he owned the equivalent of about 14,500 acres on two estates—the number of his children naturally enough limited the degree to which he could provide for their careers and marriages. Vsevolod Nabokov was either the youngest or next youngest of the six sons (there are some dating errors, I have found, in the family records), and thus, according to nineteenth-century family custom, probably one of the last in line for most things. However that may be, he seems to have been the black sheep of the family, and one of Vladimir Nabokov's cousins can remember as a boy hearing him referred to in this way in family conversations on the Batovo estate. The Russian genealogist Rummel refers to him simply as a retired mining engineer and a bachelor. He dropped from view, and no one knows when or even in what country he died. Family accounts of him have it that he went to Siberia, which was something ordinarily done only under special circumstances in the last century, but the fact that he was a mining engineer long induced the assumption that Vsevolod Nikolaevich had not been exiled or sent there as a prisoner but had gone for simple career considerations. There is one tradition which has it that he eventually left Siberia and immigrated to Australia, which in the second half of the century attracted world-wide notice because of gold discoveries in Victoria.

The most colourful story about the black sheep Nabokov is that he followed a prostitute to Siberia, and that it was his story which inspired Leo Tolstoy with the plot of his third major novel, *Resurrection*. We know from Tolstoy's papers that he had the basic idea for the novel in 1889, nearly a decade before he actually wrote it. The hero of the novel, the repentant nobleman Nekhlyudov, it has been established, has many autobiographical features, and that particular name is used by Tolstoy elsewhere when he has a character who is especially close to his own thoughts and disposition. But the story line itself, needless to say, does not come from Tolstoy's life, however repentant he may have been about his numerous youthful dalliances with peasant girls. The story is recorded as having been told to Tolstoy after an actual occurrence by his friend A. F. Koni, a minor writer and in his time one of the most distinguished lawyers in Russia. The identity of the repentant nobleman has never been established. But we do know that Koni knew the Nabokov family very well indeed and wrote at some length about Vsevolod Nabokov's famous brother (Vladimir Nabokov's grandfather) in a book on the judicial reforms of Alexander II.

Tolstoy himself also had a slight acquaintance with the Nabokovs. Nabokov, in fact, recalls Tolstoy tousling his hair in 1909, when he was ten, while his father and Tolstoy, who had come to St. Petersburg for the opening of one of his plays, stood talking on the street together. It is a nice vignette, and I will take its absence from *Speak, Memory* as a pure sign of Nabokov's extraordinarily reserved character. Not many people, I daresay, would be able to count those fingers in their hair for so little when they came to tell about their lives.

Someday no doubt registries and municipal records from the nineteenth century will be able to be examined in key Siberian stopping places. After several inconclusive efforts among Australia's Russian community, I discovered with some excitement, by the simple expedient of combing telephone books at a post office, that there are Nabokovs in Australia. But my prize was swiftly taken from me when I wrote to them, for they were of the Crimean Nabokovs, simple folk who were among a large group of people forcibly transplanted from Southern Russia to Siberia at the end of the last century (that sort of thing has always happened from time to time in Russia) and who settled in Vladivostok. If Vsevolod Nabokov did go to Siberia and thence to Australia in search of gold, his name likely nestles somewhere among the endless pads of shipping registers, all preserved, of ships that called at the ports of Brisbane, Sydney, and Melbourne in the 1880s and 1890s.

Nabokov has written of how his family is connected by marriage with the family of Pushkin's best friend and also with the man who was Pushkin's second at the fatal duel. There are other interesting oblique connections as well. One of the relatives of the famous anarchist Mikhail Bakunin was married to a Nabokov —a Soviet source notes that there were *links* between Bakunin's family and the family of the commandant of the Peter-and-Paul Fortress when Bakunin was imprisoned there. And the novelist and publicist Saltykov-Shchedrin's sister-in-law was a Nabokov through her mother. All of these connections are mere curiosities, of course, but they serve to underscore the point which I made earlier about the position of the Nabokov family in precisely that level of Russian society from which most of her writers came.

Vladimir Nabokov's grandfather Dmitri Nikolaevich Nabokov (1826–1904) had far and away the most successful career of all his brothers. He completed a distinguished career of state service by becoming State Minister of Justice under Tsars Alexander II and Alexander III in the critical period from 1878 to 1885 when so many legal aspects of the great reform of serfdom in 1862 were under severe stress. More than that, D. N. Nabokov became a confidant and trusted friend of the Tsar-Liberator. When the tsar was felled and mutilated by a well-coordinated nihilist bomb attack on March 1, 1881, D. N. Nabokov was sent for in the country by special messenger and rode at full speed to the palace in time to be present at the tsar's bedside before he died. His son and the new Tsar Alexander III, who was to cancel much of the good that his father had done, presented D. N. Nabokov with the buttons he tore off the blood-stained shirt of his father after his death, and they became a valued family keepsake. It was in the summer of 1876 that the first special messenger from the Court had ridden up to Batovo as the Nabokovs relaxed and chatted on their broad outdoor terrace. He had a personal letter from the tsar inviting Nabokov's grandfather to come to the capital and join the Privy Council. Not long after, he was asked to choose either the portfolio of Justice or the Interior. The latter Ministry was the more important one, but Nabokov took the one which best suited his own training and interests. Thus it was he, after the murder of the tsar, who had to head the enquiry over the assassination and the activities of the five conspirators (two of them women and one of these pregnant at the time) and ultimately to pass the death sentence **51** on them. He had to interview the prisoners in their cells in that same Peter-and-Paul Fortress on numerous occasions, and it is recorded that this duty would upset him physically each time. One of the women in particular, Perovskaya, had a sinister other-worldly manner and gaze, and she had occupied herself in her cell by painting a life-size autoportrait on the wall with the aid of a mirror. It was a public execution; the other, pregnant woman, Gelfman, was executed separately later, after she had given birth. I note that in the thirteenth chapter of *The Russian Genealogical Book* one finds together with the Nabokovs the family of Perovskaya and also the family of Shabelsky, one of the two killers of D. N. Nabokov's son (Vladimir Nabokov's father) forty-one years later.

D. N. Nabokov was most closely identified in his public life not with Alexander II but with Alexander's brother the Grand Duke Konstantin Nikolaevich (1827–1892), who, as one Russian source writes, *. . . found in him a spirited and talented advocate of his ideas for reform.* If Alexander II was the best of the Romanov tsars (he was, little praise though that may be), much of the credit for the epochal Great Reforms which took place in his reign (and several years before Lincoln freed the slaves, incidentally) must belong to his dynamic and prodding brother Konstantin. The brilliant men who gathered around Konstantin included, besides Nabokov, Boris and Nikolai Mansurov (both served as Secretary of State), Prince Georgy Obolensky, the influential senators Saburov and Glebov, and N. A. Miliutin, a gifted jurist from a family even more distinguished for its state service than the Nabokovs. Many of these men and others like them in the government had attended the Imperial Juridical Faculty with the Grand Duke. They were all popularly linked together under the rubric Constantinists.

Nabokov's involvement with the Grand Duke's circle did not come about by chance. Because his parents' estate was far removed, in the region of Pskov, he had spent the greater part of his adolescence in St. Petersburg with the family of his Uncle Ivan (Peter-and-Paul Fortress again, I cannot keep it out), who had been very close to the Court. His son and D. N. Nabokov's cousin Pyotr Nabokov became a gentleman-in-waiting at the Court and the Grand Duke Konstantin's librarian and secretary to his wife, the Grand Duchess Aleksandra. In addition, there was one other, even more important connection between the Nabokov family and the Grand Duke. Konstantin's tutor had been Admiral Count Lütke, and this Admiral Lütke was a schoolmate and lifelong friend of D. N. Nabokov's father, who had accompanied him on that Zemblan expedition under Admiral Golovnin, whose son, by the way, became Education Minister under Alexander II when D. N. Nabokov was Minister of Justice. It's all reasonably complicated and intangible, but that's the way these things usually are.

A few years after his graduation from the Juridical Faculty in 1845, when he was not yet twenty-five, D. N. Nabokov was taken onto the staff of the Grand Duke at the Ministry of the Navy, which Konstantin (only a year older himself) then headed as Grand Admiral. In the Navy Ministry Nabokov's grandfather helped to effect many of the reforms that the Grand Duke wished to introduce, and in time he became his closest aide and one of his closest friends. The Grand Duke had quickly acquired the reputation of being a staunch liberal in his Ministry. A new naval manual was compiled under his direction which had a progressive tone and bettered the lot of Russian sailors in scores of small and large ways. Corporal punishment in the navy was abolished entirely.

Konstantin was deeply committed to the issue of freeing the serfs and on the most generous terms possible. His views were widely known, though neither he nor they had any real support in society apart from the small group of progressives he had gathered round himself. And, of course, there was his brother the tsar. The French *chargé d'affaires* in St. Petersburg at that time described the political balance in Russia on the eve of emancipation in the following way:

—*The Grand Duke Konstantin, who, for all his feverish activity could not evoke any support in any class in Russia, had at this moment a stronger influence than ever before on the excellent but disturbed and perplexed mind of his brother.*

Konstantin had taken over the educative function towards his brother of their old mutual tutor, the poet and friend of Pushkin, Zhukovsky. Konstantin succeeded to the detriment of his own career, for the Constantinists around him, including D. N. Nabokov, passed naturally over to Alexander, and the Grand Duke ended a rather sad and isolated figure.

After he left the Ministry of the Navy, the Grand Duke together with Nabokov went to Poland, where he assumed the Re- **53** gency of Congress-Poland, then as now a dependency of Russia with certain show-window pretences of independence. There had been a very serious rebellion in 1863 which was put down by force. The Grand Duke made the serious mistake of assuming that he could ameliorate the Polish situation by dynamic persuasion brought to bear upon certain influential Poles. He failed badly, and his reputation suffered a severe blow. Commentaries on the personality of the Grand Duke tend to speak of his extraordinary intelligence, his energy, and his naïveté. He could be arrogant to the point of insolence, and he could also be familiar to an excessive and offensive degree. One of the many things Konstantin did in Poland was to set D. N. Nabokov to work reforming Polish law. The Grand Duke evidently did not see the inherent contradiction in reforming laws in a state which was being held by main force. It was not long before he had to request further military support.

D. N. Nabokov probably derived a large portion of his liberalism from his friend the Grand Duke Konstantin, but it was held within bounds by his sense of measure and his methodological way of looking at things. His talents and his personality were better suited to the needs of those difficult times than his royal friend's. When he became Minister of Justice he was able, under Alexander II, to institute changes in the jury system necessary to support the reforms. While many of these changes—the right of indigent jurors to refuse the obligation of jury duty, the limitation of the number of jurors that each side could refuse—seem small enough, they were the fruit of highly intricate planning, and much of the social order in those confusing years rested on them.

Of the twelve years Nabokov served as Minister of Justice, four were under Alexander II and eight were under the young Alexander III. These last eight years were perhaps the most important in D. N. Nabokov's career, for it was left to him almost single-handedly to defend and preserve as best he could the essentials of the reforms in the period of dark reaction which followed the assassination. There were vicious attacks made on Nabokov from the right in these years. Many compromises had to be made, and this is the context of the Brokhaus-Efron encyclopedia article which Nabokov quotes in *Speak, Memory*, comparing D. N. Nabokov with a ship's captain who must jettison much during a storm in order to save his ship. But there were compromises he would not make. Russia was ruled in those years by Konstantin Pobedonostsev, the harsh arch-reactionary who had been young Alexander's mentor. In his memoirs Miliutin recalls how Nabokov refused on principle to shake hands with the powerful Pobedonostsev.

A. F. Koni, the author, legal expert, and friend of Nabokov's grandfather, wrote of D. N. Nabokov after his death (in his 1914 book on the judicial reforms in Russia) that he had felt a true calling for his life's work:

—Always courteous and plainspoken, Nabokov brought out a gratifying consciousness of mutual solidarity in their work in all those who had occasion to deal with him regularly in regard to juridical matters. He was able to understand properly the great difficulties involved in much Court work, to express deep joy when it was successful, and to bring to bear a delicate understanding of the complicating moral and material factors with which his subordinates and co-workers had to cope in their work. People naturally grew to depend upon him, and thus they were able to see how from behind the official façade of a Minister there looked out a cordial human being who was aware how often the burden of life could be a heavy one and who understood, therefore, that **stricte justice n'est pas justice—justice c'est équité,** *as Nikolai Turgenev informs us Catherine the Great said. He was inclined to give a sympathetic hearing to "mitigating circumstances" and even, when it was absolutely necessary in several instances, to exercise his power with resolution. D. N. Nabokov would not hesitate before the possibility of personal unpleasantries or distasteful explanations in connection with the initiation of measures which he knew by his experience and his sincere conviction were necessary for the good of the judicial process.*

In 1884 Nabokov made a prolonged tour through Russia to observe the provincial courts at work. He had been personally responsible for the enormous amount of bureaucratic work which had to be done when the government assumed ownership of all private railways, and as a sign of gratitude the tsar had placed an elegant private railway car at the disposal of Nabokov whenever it was needed. It was in this period that the courts and Nabokov himself were under heavy fire from reactionaries such as Mikhail Katkov (himself a former radical), who wrote scornfully that the Russian state could not endure a challenge to its authority by its own judiciary and that one scarcely needed to travel around **55**

Russia to grasp this. Nabokov successfully withstood all the attacks upon him, and most of the measures he fought for were enacted, though some had to wait several years and came to pass only after his retirement. There have even been those who hold the view that, when one considers the dark and trying period in which he worked, D. N. Nabokov, who is not ordinarily spoken of as a liberal at all, may deserve as great a place in the history of Russian liberalism as his more famous son, V. D. Nabokov, Nabokov's father. Like his son, D. N. Nabokov did much to defend the rights of Jews in Russia.

Nabokov's grandfather was evidently not a happy man in his private life. One of his daughters describes him as *an overworked and very busy man, often tired, ill, and irritable;* and the other memoirist-daughter writes:

—We saw very little of our father, whose official duties took up so much of his time that he lived a life apart from us in our childhood and adolescence. Occasionally, however, he would snatch a moment to come in and talk to us and then there were great rejoicings in the children's quarters. But it was another story when one of us had been guilty of some grave fault. Then recourse was made to his supreme authority and he would arrive in our apartments looking very severe, though his face was drawn with fatigue and worry; but the contrite air of the culprit quickly mollified him and the punishments he inflicted were always light.

Though Vladimir Nabokov does not rate his aunts' autobiographies highly (—**So you have even found those books!** my subject said to me with a soft grim sigh when I first spoke of them), and admittedly they are maudlin and have many inaccuracies, the reliability of the two women, provided only incident and not insight is required of them, is vouchsafed for me by the remarkable number of events in the upbringing of the children of Nabokov's grandfather which repeat themselves for Nabokov's own childhood as recorded in *Speak, Memory.* The stern reprimands and lectures on social conscience for being rude to servants, lessons given by famous tutors (just as Vladimir was taught to draw by the fashionable *World of Art* artist Dobuzhinsky, one of his aunts was given piano lessons by Anton Rubinstein), contests of will between governesses and cunning little Nabokovs, such things and many others like them span at least a full generation in the Nabokov family.

Nabokov's grandfather did not marry for love, which was not unusual in the nineteenth century, but, which is unusual, the marriage lasted forty-five years, until D. N. Nabokov's death, with no certainty that there were any bonds of even friendship between them. If one knew how the marriage had been arranged, many things might be explained. It is enough to say that it was in all probability arranged either by or in consideration of the Court. The bride, the Baroness Maria von Korff, was from a more noble family than Nabokov's grandfather, but, as I have already explained, D. N. Nabokov by this time in his life—we are talking of 1859—had already been in a particularly favoured position in the Russian Court for a full decade. His fiancée had barely turned seventeen but was acknowledged to be one of the beauties of her day, as her mother had been before her. Her granddaughter (that is, Vladimir Nabokov's aunt) makes the claim that her grandmother had refused forty offers of marriage (a little bit short of those fifty Jewish servants, one fears!) in the winter before she accepted the hand of Baron Ferdinand von Korff. The von Korff beauty continued in time, for the most beautiful of Maria's daughters, Nadezhda, was also a Court favourite and lady-in-waiting to Empress Aleksandra Fyodorovna. It was from the start an unequal marriage. D. N. Nabokov was sixteen years Maria's senior and taken up with affairs of state. The marriage took place very much against her will.

Nabokov men used to have a reputation for being not so much rakes as easily inclined to fall in love. After the turn of the century a most unkind saying was current in Russian high society that —*all the Nabokov women remained loyal, all the men betrayed.* There were Nabokovs to whom such a statement might apply, but the inclusive way in which the proposition is phrased is patent nonsense—in the particular line of the Nabokov family with which we are concerned the men have, in fact, tended to have relatively or absolutely uncomplicated personal lives. Maria Nabokov, on the other hand, has been called a tragic and passionate woman by many members of the family. Was she the mistress of the Tsar Alexander II? One of Vladimir Nabokov's cousins once told a reporter who questioned him about this:

—*With my formidable grandmother one can never be sure. She certainly had many lovers, and it is not unlikely that one of them was Alexander. . . . Personally I don't trust the story, though, for when I look at the photos of Vladimir's father and my grandfa-* 57 *ther I see considerable family resemblance. But as Count Tolstoy was supposed to have said, beyond one's own father and mother one never knows.*

Some evidence for the theory of a dalliance between Maria Ferdinandovna and Alexander II comes from the manner in which she herself over the years spoke of him always as My Tsar and hinted that they had once nearly been lovers. Speaking of the woman who became the tsar's lover she boasted to one of her grandchildren: —**He wavered for a long time between me and Katya Dolgoruky.** But the case is closed, the truth of it is now unknowable; all the rest is gossip, the biographer's Tenth Muse.

At the end of his life Nabokov's grandfather could look back on: a special medal presented to him by the tsar for fifty years of distinguished service to the Empire; memories of a world which had died and the beginnings of a new world which he had done much to make a better one; a life spent in luxury though not at ease; a very large and energetic family; and what else? The picture in *Speak, Memory* which Nabokov gives of his grandfather denouncing his children to grinning strangers, Lear-like, in Italy (but *why* did he denounce them?), if it is true, is chilling even if we ascribe the incident to mere senility.

Nabokov's grandmother lived later and longer and her mind remained lucid in her last years. Nabokov's Aunt Vera recalls her reunion with her aged mother in Germany after many years of separation:

—*I saw an old lady walking up and down with slow and unsteady step, and leaning on a stick. It was she, my mother, and yet not she. Where were her majestic carriage, her quick movements, her vivacity, her fresh and brilliant complexion, her beautiful, clear, expressive and laughing eyes? Alas, it was not only age that had transformed her, but deep, inexpressible suffering. Greatly moved, I watched her for a long time before she was aware of my presence, for she was blind.*

The old woman kept a box of relics, and among them was a new addition, a wax death mask of her recently murdered son Vladimir.

I stare at clusters of old photographs and strive to set in motion a puppet show of memories which are not even mine. The tall and slender Minister of Justice. He is supposed to have been a witty man, but I have no example of his wit. The very German beauty Maria von Korff, who is supposed to have had laughing eyes, but I cannot see these eyes in any of the pictures I have, only her hard mouth. Their son Vladimir. Alexander II and his brother Konstantin, who was godfather to one of the other Nabokov children.

Vladimir Nabokov does think about this past, and there are incidental motifs in his fiction which take on a special meaning when you know the history of the Nabokovs. One such, for example, is the amusing jibe at Freudianism in *Solus Rex* in which we are presented with an Italian psychiatrist who has evolved the theory that all psychological disturbances are the result of a subconscious memory of the misfortunes suffered not by one's parents but by one's ancestors. *Ada* is the Nabokov novel which parodies a family chronicle, and Nabokov was widely complimented by many reviewers for having invented a whole new world in that novel. But the exotic customs and characters of *Ada* do have vague counterparts in the flamboyant old Nabokov family life. There is no—repeat—no direct or indirect usage of real people and stories in *Ada*, but **that sort of people** (even a few kissing cousins) were in and around the family, and Nabokov, when I spoke with him about it, did cautiously and reluctantly allow that there are more bits of real Nabokoviana in that novel than in any other. The catherine's wheel of languages in *Ada* is the way the Nabokovs, not just Vladimir, really do speak—in the households of Nabokov's father and grandfather it was French at the table, English in the nursery, and Russian elsewhere, with complete freedom to use macaronic combinations as the mood or need was felt—and so in this respect, too, *Ada* is an historically accurate voice of a family. *Ada* simply could not exist in the form that it does were it not for the rather special Nabokov family history.

The importance of cultural training had been established in the Nabokov pattern of life certainly no later than the beginning of the nineteenth century, due probably in large degree to the inclinations of Nabokov's great-grandmother. As one of Nabokov's aunts described it, perhaps a shade awkwardly: —**Generally speaking, Aphrodite and the Graces were the household gods and my grandmother was at great pains to cultivate in her children all the beauties and graces of mind and body.** Dress rehearsals of parlour and dinner-table conversation on political and intellectual subjects were held for the benefit of the children. The children had **59**

French, English, German, and Russian governesses and tutors, and, of course, there were drawing and music teachers, and they were given systematic and top-rate training in swimming, riding, fencing, and dancing. The only part of this regimen which had been dropped by Vladimir's generation was the German tutor. One portion of the Nabokov family, largely through marriage, turned back towards Germany, and Nabokov's paternal grandmother was said to be **water-tight** against all things Russian, but Nabokov's father was one of the children who became thoroughly and unquestionably Russian in outlook.

Even in entirely different social and financial circumstances more than forty years later Vladimir Nabokov used recognizably the same curriculum for his son Dmitri: he himself gave language lessons in order to make Russian their son's "first language" despite his early English schooling, Véra Evseevna supplied the first (and very fruitful as it turned out) music lessons, and, when outside help was required, only the best people and institutions were considered. Dmitri's grammar school was the Dexter School (its most famous alumnus is John F. Kennedy), he prepped at two exclusive New England schools, St. Mark's and Holderness, and he finally went to Harvard. He was taught to box by one of the finest instructors in New England, and his singing teacher was also the best one available in the Boston area. The schools were very often attended without benefit of scholarship, and these were not years of plenty for the Nabokovs in a material sense; Dmitri's education was the Nabokovs' first and virtually only luxury in this period of their life.

On the paternal side of Nabokov's family I note a regrettable (to his biographer) decline in certain quaint eccentricities and incidents of absent-mindedness over the generations. Four generations back Nabokov's great-grandmother, who believed in the power of fresh warm milk to impart a smooth and clear complexion, arranged that a cow should live in one of the wings of her house in the country where the children's rooms were so that none of the milk's magic power should be lost in transport from the barn. And it lived there peacefully, all its wants being attended to by servants and loving children, for many years. In the following generation there is a lovely story about Nabokov's grandmother, who lived above her means and drove her husband into many successive mortgages (from which he was rescued in the end by his son V. D. Nabokov) but who had a real and generous concern for the predicaments and desires of people who presented themselves to her. And thus it happened that on one occasion she mixed up two petitions so that she successfully arranged for a local priest to have a post at the Imperial Opera in Moscow, while a musician who had come to her was given a very good diocesan appointment. V. D. Nabokov, however, was the very model of not only a generous, but also a sensible modern *barin*—true, he was swindled on all sides by certain servants, as the Minister of Justice had been swindled before him, but given the conditions by which society successfully malfunctioned in old Russia there was nothing extraordinary or even distressing about this—and his son, my subject, has not a single colourful eccentricity that I can think of, except if it be the simple fact that he is an old-world gentleman from Russia, which has, I guess, been tantamount to eccentricity for certain people who have written about him.

It was the maternal side of Nabokov's family which, though it figures in only a small way in the life at Vyra, furnished some of the traditional Russian excess at the end and beginning of these centuries. I am thinking particularly of Nabokov's Uncle Ruka, who is given special privilege of place in *Speak, Memory*. The Rukavishnikovs had become (precisely the clichéd word will do here) fabulously wealthy through their Siberian mines. Nabokov's maternal grandfather on this side of the family was the morose old Russian landowner one tends to image up out of classical Russian literature. Nabokov tells us that his grandfather Rukavishnikov had a violent temper and apparently a strong dislike for his son. In those early years the family lived at Vyra, which passed to the Nabokov family as a gift when Elena Rukavishnikov married. The brother of Nabokov's mother, Vasily Ivanovich (Uncle Ruka of *Speak, Memory*), lived close at hand on the other estate of Rozhestveno, perhaps the most magnificent of all, which the Rukavishnikovs had purchased in mid-century. In its time it had been owned and used by the Romanovs for assignations, and there was a secret staircase in the house. V. D. Nabokov's mother and various younger Nabokov children and cousins continued to live at Batovo, though the house, never attractive, was now rather badly run down as well. Eventually Nabokov's grandmother had a small separate residence built for herself on the Batovo estate and moved there together with the family portraits. Two other estates a short distance away also had connections with this central family compound. It should be mentioned, too, that for many years the **61** royal family summered in the environs of Vyra, Batovo, and Rozhestveno. About twenty miles away was the estate of Zarechie, on which for decades an old retired officer-turned-naturalist had encouraged and preserved all forms of wildlife to be found around the Oredezh River. It had a large lake in the waters of which literally layers of indolent fish could be observed. Although the manor house at Zarechie was in rather rough and simple taste, the royal family purchased the estate after the old man died because of the unequalled fishing and hunting which it provided, and Alexander and the Grand Dukes spent much time there.

Uncle Ruka was looked upon most affectionately by the whole Nabokov family, though V. D. Nabokov did have a tendency to be cross with his brother-in-law. One can surmise why. Vasily Ivanovich was a consummate dilettante in life, a person whose only answer (albeit in five languages) to the first question of modern cocktail parties would have had to be: —**Nothing.** He had a diplomatic career, but only of the vaguest sort, and even it had been given rather than sought in recognition of Vasily Ivanovich's substantial contributions to charity. (The Rukavishnikovs had come to be noble in more or less the same fashion.) He had villas abroad, wrote music and poetry in French, and was somewhat out of place in Russia and in Russian, and yet he could only have been a Russian by virtue of the simple fact of subtraction: he could never have been a Frenchman or a German or an Italian. There is to my eye something about Vasily Ivanovich, with his cape and his airplane and his codes, which might almost qualify him to be a character out of Vladimir Nabokov.

Like Nabokov's younger brother Sergei, Vasily Ivanovich stuttered badly and was a homosexual. Uncle Ruka was Italianate in appearance, though not in manner, and had extremely dark eye concavities, almost as dark as a pantomime artist. He had an exaggerated mincing walk (he was quite open about all of this, particularly for the times and the country), a swooping moustache, and carried a silver knobbed cane. He was very fond of his handsome nephew, whom he embarrassed and made terribly awkward.

V. D. Nabokov was an expert, among other things, in certain of the legal and social ramifications of homosexuality, and he was for this reason doubly distressed when the tendency became apparent at a very early age in his own son Sergei. Vladimir Nabokov shares his father's view of homosexuality as an illness—a view which is not universally accepted—transmitted exclusively by heredity—a view which has been almost overshadowed by the vast network of psychoanalytic theory of this century, until, that is, in very recent times when purely biochemical factors such as the level of testosterone in the blood (*New England Journal of Medicine*, November 1971) have come under investigation. It would appear now that V. D. Nabokov's attitude has much to be said for it, though in my own mind I myself cannot disregard entirely the hothouse atmosphere in which the Nabokovs lived at the turn of the century and which seems to have allowed so many propensities of all manner and kind to grow and flourish exceptionally well. I hasten now (too slowly, thinks Nabokov) to leave this subject. The discomfiture which it caused decades ago in the Nabokov family has, at least in part, inspired an artistic interest in the subject which has provided a remarkable gallery of homosexual characters in Nabokov's writing.

The most important things I know and wish to convey about the Nabokov family are the very things which are impossible to prove or even state with any precision. In spite of their great wealth and their many possessions, they were not a materialistic family. It may derive from a certain not-quite-mystical disposition which is to be found in one degree or another in virtually every member of the family. It may be that the pre-revolutionary life which the Nabokovs lived could not really be expected to last forever, particularly in a country like Russia. In exile in countries all over Europe the Nabokovs ran tea rooms and restaurants, served as petty officials, sold cars, took in sewing, gave lessons, but to my knowledge not one of them was bitter. They remained Nabokovs without benefit of their wealth.

The Nabokovs were a close and distant family through the two generations about which we know enough to make such a judgment. It is true that life was organized in such a way that husbands and wives and brothers and sisters and parents and children resided in the same house but often without seeing too much of one another in any given day. But it may have been that the sense of family was actually heightened by this limited contact. It was a natural way for a family such as the Nabokovs to live then, and one did not think about it, just as one did not think of playing with the children of the servants. Such considerations arose only many years later. There were unhappy Nabokovs, even unfortunate Nabokovs, but never without some compensating passion or grace or talent. Most of the Nabokovs did not get their share of unhappiness until much later in life. Tolstoy has taught us, of course, that there is no such thing as a happy family. (All happy families are alike; but no two individuals, much less families, can be alike; therefore, there are no happy families.) The issue is debatable. But there are happy childhoods, especially in Russia where there is a tradition of providing compensation for what life may offer later, and this was particularly so in the Nabokov family. Nabokovs who differ in almost every other respect share this one thing. It is no small matter. This undemonstrable factor seems to me to be the most formative and significant pattern that I have been able to trace to the present from the furthest known reaches of Nabokov family history.

CHAPTER

3

My first animated picture of V. D. Nabokov—it is quite out of character with subsequent records of him and so all the more valued for that—is of a young lad holding a jar of apricot preserves on high and leading his brothers Indian file in a mock-solemn procession while they all sing in a discordant choir. They are teasing their younger sister, who especially covets that particular jar of homemade jam (stolen from under the less-than-watchful eye of the pantry servant, nicknamed "I'm hungry") and who is at that moment practising the piano. There are a very few still photos between that time and adulthood. In the first known photograph of him he is an exceptionally composed and thoughtful boy of about ten. I have a picture of Vladimir Nabokov, taken at a **67**

much younger age, which looks astonishingly like this picture of his father in every way, but for the rest there is a constant difference to be observed in all the childhood pictures of father and son. The eyes of the father show a serenity and balance, of a sort usually associated with paintings of the Renaissance, which is succeeded in his son by a look of precosity and mischievousness. Nabokov tells us in *Speak, Memory* that his father maintained the aura of lightness of spirit and good humour about which V. D. Nabokov's sisters testify within the family all through his life. One does not see it, however, in his brilliant but rather judicial public personality or his terribly heavy and latinate prose style.

When V. D. Nabokov died in 1922, Joseph Hessen, who was his political and editorial colleague and a close friend for a period of exactly twenty-five years, delivered a speech in honour of his memory in which he said:

—Whoever says anything about V. D. Nabokov always makes mention first of all of the extraordinary harmony and integrity in this man's nature. Nabokov was a great man. Great people, powerful forces usually coincide with great wants and great gaps. Nabokov possessed great strength without this expected drawback or blank in his character. He was strength in harmony, organic harmony, he was a man of many sides without any dissipation of his powers, he was abundance without excess.

Even allowing for the friendship, the occasion, and the rhetorical style which is obligatory at such times, Hessen's words are repeated in a full score of estimates of the man, and not all of them are written by those who were close friends or in political sympathy with him. Ivan Bunin wrote an article entitled "A Great Loss" about the assassination by mistake of V. D. Nabokov, whom he knew only slightly. Nabokov's death was seen by Bunin as another almost unbearable loss in the seemingly endless chain of chance tragedies falling upon Russia in those years, and he took Nabokov and the Nabokovs (the unspoken reference here was undoubtedly to the Minister of Justice, D. N. Nabokov) as representative of what was finest in old Russia:

—God grant all good things to the future, "new" Russia. But when will she again have her Nabokovs? In the former, old Russia there were such people. She can be proud of them. For now, alas, Russia
must be in mourning.

Like Hessen, Bunin takes for granted the virtual unanimity of opinion about the character and merits of the man: —*There are no two opinions about the deceased,* he writes, —*and is this not in itself a stunning commentary in our time especially?*

At the other end of V. D. Nabokov's life we find much the same opinion about his promise and his place in the family. Both his sisters report that from a very early age Vladimir Dmitrievich was looked upon as the pride of the family. And that generation of the Nabokov family was a particularly distinguished one. One of V. D. Nabokov's brothers became a senator like his father (this son upon his majority was given an estate in Poland which Alexander II presented to his Minister of Justice to be presented to the eldest Nabokov son); another attained the highest academic distinction, the Gold Medal, awarded at the Imperial School of Law and Political Economy and subsequently became a provincial governor; and yet another entered the diplomatic service, in which he was one of the representatives of Russia at the peace treaty presided over by Theodore Roosevelt between Russia and Japan, served in Brussels and then Washington and as Minister at New Delhi, and, finally, was the *chargé d'affaires* at the English Embassy, of which he became *de facto* ambassador for a short time after the revolution. (This brother, Konstantin Dmitrievich, wrote books about India and his experience in the diplomatic corps at the time of the revolution.)

The young V. D. Nabokov, a prodigy among prodigies, was for several years a promising social lion at the highest level of St. Petersburg society. St. Petersburg Court society was a league in which the prettier of the Nabokov girls fared very well indeed, but the young V. D. Nabokov was probably (I am guessing) neither aristocratic nor wealthy enough to be truly successful in such society, where mere intelligence and giftedness did not (I am not guessing) count for much.

Why did V. D. Nabokov leave his natural class milieu and ally himself with Jews and classless intellectuals—all from other classes —who had banded together to fight against great odds for the cause of constitutional democracy in Russia? No one really knows. One version within the Nabokov family had it that he had been won over to radicalism—as liberalism was familiarly referred to by most of the Nabokovs—by one of his tutors. But that view comes from a reactionary side of the Nabokov family, as does another silly theory which ascribes primary importance to the mild Anglomania which had been introduced into the Nabokov family in the preceding generation and to a St. Petersburg shop, described not only in *Speak, Memory* but also in one of the aunts' memoirs, which specialized in imported English luxury goods. It is less than likely, in my opinion, that V. D. Nabokov received his liberalism together with Pears Transparent Soap, though it is true that his public speaking manner was a very conscious imitation of the English fashion, so strange in the Russian context that no historical commentary of the period fails to mention his *calm, even, unemotional* way of speaking. No, V. D. Nabokov's liberalism derives quite simply and logically from the views and activities before him of his father and other Constantinists, attitudes which were eclipsed but not extinguished in Russian intellectual life when V. D. Nabokov was a boy. It should be mentioned that there was only a handful of other noblemen in V. D. Nabokov's generation who figured more than peripherally in the Constitutional Democratic or Kadet movement.

The political convictions of Nabokov's father were deep and constant. When he was still a student at St. Petersburg University he was active in student strikes against repressive measures taken by the government. He stood at the barricades noticed but untouched by the police because he was the son of the recent Minister of Justice. At least once, however, he was briefly arrested by mistake, and this incident foreshadows his more real term in prison in 1908 for his part in protesting against the tsar's dissolution of the First Duma, or Parliament, of which he had been a member.

The formal break with the tsarist regime came in 1903 in connection with the anti-Jewish pogroms. The article which Nabokov wrote created a sensation, and it is not too much to say that the liberal movement in Russia grew greatly in scope and maturity as a result of that article. It also marked the emergence of V. D. Nabokov as a political leader.

When one speaks of the career that Nabokov forfeited by his resolute liberalism one is embarking upon impure speculation. Nonetheless, Nabokov was made a junior gentleman of the chamber at twenty-five, and he is supposed six years later to have been about to become (the stories vary) a minister without portfolio or leading prospect for a portfolio. Given his father's excellent and faithful service to two tsars and his own intellectual qualifications, there is no reason to suppose that V. D. Nabokov would not in the logical course of things have occupied a minister's chair.

Vladimir Nabokov is fond of saying that, although there were later many retroactive liberals, his father was actually the only liberal in the entire Nabokov family. Because of his father's advanced age and illness and the informal separation of his father and mother, V. D. Nabokov became, if no longer the pride, then at least the effective head of the large family. The rest of the family learned to live with his liberalism, but that is all. After his three-month prison term in 1908 for having been a signatory to the Vyborg manifesto, expressions of solidarity and support were organized in various places to greet the returning prisoners, and there was to have been such a welcome in the villages surrounding the Nabokov estates, both because of actual support for the movement among the peasantry and because V. D. Nabokov was popular among the peasants. But his mother staged a successful counter-manoeuvre by threatening the peasants with economic reprisals if they demonstrated in support of her son.

After his graduation from St. Petersburg University in 1891, Nabokov's father served his term of military service. His hair was cut in close Prussian fashion as it had been since his late teens, and it is about then, I believe, that he begins to wear a moustache and slight beard, though I have no photograph to fix the beginning of this change in his appearance. He went on a tour abroad, where he continued to study jurisprudence, and on his return to St. Petersburg he became a prominent consultant on legal questions (**not,** his son took pains to inform me, a lawyer) and a lecturer in criminology at the St. Petersburg Imperial School of Jurisprudence. The memoirs of his sister, Nadezhda Wenlar-Larsky, make an interesting addition to his *curriculum vitae* here, but one which is unfortunately not confirmed by any other published or family source:

—*In politics, a liberal, and by profession professor of criminology and of literature; two strangely assorted subjects. He had the reputation of being a conspicuously clever young man.*

The most one can say at the moment is that V. D. Nabokov did years later publish articles of an old-fashioned appreciative sort on the poet Fet and Charles Dickens, and it could well be that he did indeed lecture on literature as well as law.

In 1897 V. D. Nabokov married and received, in addition to the country estate of Vyra, a most substantial *dot* (the Russian dowry). The two things were, in fact, not at all related to each other in the event. The deep love and devotion between man and wife are not open to any question, and V. D. Nabokov had the means to be modestly rich without the dowry. But there were two natural results of his additional acquired wealth, one pleasant and the other to be expected. Nabokov and his young wife began to live *na bol'shuyu nogu,* in high style. This life style of total luxury without (no easy feat) any affectation is beautifully and delicately rendered in *Speak, Memory.* But V. D. Nabokov's rise to political prominence was also accompanied by snide remarks from the petty and the jealous about the manner in which he had acquired his wealth, and these remarks sometimes wiggled their way into print. It was said that he felt himself so much above things Russian that he sent his shirts to London to be laundered. In a cartoon in the journal *City and Country Manor* (much the same genre as *Harper's & Queen* or *Vogue*) Nabokov was caricatured as a merchant's wife, a clear (and, by the way, absolutely inaccurate) allusion to the sources of the Rukavishnikov wealth. The Rukavishnikov family into which V. D. Nabokov married had no connection with that famous family of wealthy merchants. The 1911 challenge to a duel about which the young Vladimir learned while at school and which is recounted in *Speak, Memory* arose from an article in the reactionary *New Times* in which the insinuation was made that V. D. Nabokov had married for money.

In the years following his marriage V. D. Nabokov grew somewhat portly (a problem with which his son also would eventually have to contend), and a new *Kammerjunker* uniform for Court functions had to be ordered for him a month before he was deprived of his Court title in January 1905. It did not see much use, that new uniform, nor should too much importance be ascribed to the fact of its being ordered, though it is tempting to see it as a sign of how suddenly and sharply V. D. Nabokov's attitude turned against the government in revulsion at its anti-Semitic policies. As for the story that Nabokov coolly advertised the uniform for sale in the classified columns of a newspaper, I find that wholly in keeping with his character, though enemies of the family in the emigration claimed that the story was made up long afterwards, the insinuation here being, I suppose, that V. D. Nabokov had unsuccessfully tried to get himself reinstated at Court.

Vladimir Dmitrievich suffered from a sour stomach, which was perhaps a nervous condition arising from the enormous working obligations which he undertook—he was an editor of the daily liberal newspaper *Speech (Rech')* and the legal paper *Law (Pravo)*, was president of two associations and served on several more, actively engaged in legal research and writing, played an important role in Kadet Party formulations, and of course there were many family interests to be looked after. But perhaps the sour stomach was simply the natural consequence of the gourmet tastes which he inherited from his father. He habitually consumed almonds to aid his indigestion. Ordinarily he carried them in his breast pocket, and he kept a large quantity in an ornate inlaid black Japanese box in his St. Petersburg study. Once most of these almonds were eaten by Vladimir and his cousin, who had been playing in the study, and at dinner that night his father merely remarked: —**It's funny. Something is happening to my almonds** while looking fixedly at his son. I have no record of his ever resorting to more direct authority than that in his family life, but his tongue could be sufficiently biting in the old-school manner so that nothing more was required. The strongest words that ever passed between father and son came after a gauche adolescent joke that Vladimir Vladimirovich played on his father. They were in the country together, skiing, one sunny morning, and Vladimir Vladimirovich for reasons unknown to himself placed a large purple grape upon his father's chair seat just as he sat down in his white or pale grey skiing togs. —**That was a cretinous prank,** he said, and that was all.

In the First Duma, which came into being in 1906 as a result of pressures after the abortive 1905 revolution, Nabokov's father did not at first so much attack the government as speak of the obligations of future governments in Russia in a way which was, however, transparently condemnatory of the situation at that time. But the political situation was so execrable that direct criticism could not be withheld for long. His speeches were admirable for both their content and the manner in which they were presented, and yet some of the very features of mind and manner which made V. D. Nabokov so attractive in the first political forum also served to place limits on his possible effectiveness, quite apart from the pressures of the reactionary tsarist government, in political life.

In her memoirs of the period V. D. Nabokov's political colleague Ariadna Tyrkova-Williams, one of the first and most important women to be active in Russian democratic politics, presents a portrait which highlights Nabokov from the particular perspective of his class origins:

—He had grown up in proximity to the Court, and in his tastes and customs he was a man of the world. He glided along the floor of the Tavrichesky Palace with the small dancing walk he had used at balls in the past in which he had on more than one occasion artfully led a cotillion. But he had early outgrown all these gleaming inconsequential things in the extraordinary life that he led. He had too energetic a mind to be satisfied for long with success at balls. A political conscience burned in him as it did in many enlightened Russian people of the time. He became an outstanding jurist, a professor, and one of the most prominent activists in the Liberation Movement. Nabokov read lectures in the Institute of Jurisprudence, wrote legal articles, and was one of the editors of the St. Petersburg weekly **Law,** *where a group of Liberationalists like himself cleverly skirted the censor and advocated the same extreme liberal ideas as put forward by Struve in his émigré* **Liberation.** *After the 9th of January Nabokov read a speech in the St. Petersburg Duma, of which he was an elected member, an indignant speech against the firing upon workers. For this speech he was deprived of his status as a* **Kammerjunker.** *[A variant explanation which is not confirmed in any other source, but many are the tales that Clio, the goddess of history, has to tell.—A.F.] His removal in disgrace from the Court was not very pleasant for him, though he would speak about this only in passing and in an extremely careless way. In the ironic grin which often flashed across the regular features of his sleek and healthy face [some of his colleagues] saw the condescension of a nobleman. But in fact, if there was a degree of condescension in his smile it was purely of an intellectual nature and not at all rooted in class. Even the representatives of the working class could not but agree with the political thoughts of this talented deputy, but all the same Nabokov's person gave rise to class hostility among certain of them, a feeling of unfriendliness which he did not at all experience towards them. . . . Several of Nabokov's utterances were remembered and repeated. A great success was enjoyed by his long speech delivered as an address in which he developed in detail the idea, much valued by the Kadets but completely unacceptable to the government, of the responsibility of the Ministers to the State Duma. Nabokov ended this speech with the words which even now*

are sometimes repeated by people who have not forgotten the Duma period of Russian history: —Let the executive power be subordinate to the legislative power! *And having thrown forward this call, Nabokov ran lightfootedly, in spite of a certain premature tendency to corpulence, down the steps of the Duma rostrum to the accompaniment of stormy applause . . .*

But V. D. Nabokov's political career was short-lived, for, after his protest at the dissolution of the First Duma by the tsar and his three months' imprisonment, he was barred from taking part in subsequent Dumas, and thereafter he turned primarily to journalism. As it happened, V. D. Nabokov was fated to spend the rest of his career as a more or less detached observer, a part which bore excellent fruit in the dispassionate memoirs he wrote of the Provisional Government as observed from his post as its procedural Executive Secretary.

It is sad that V. D. Nabokov never had the opportunity fully to utilize his talents in a Russian government, but he belonged to a too small class of highly educated and principled men, the Russian liberals, who were perhaps not by disposition capable of wielding power. The opportunity came very close indeed, though, since in July 1906, shortly before the First Duma was dissolved, the tsar's government had been seriously considering asking the Kadets to form a ministry. The decision to dissolve the Duma, according to some historians, was not motivated by the government's fear of the strength of the Duma, but, on the contrary, by fears that the liberals who dominated the Duma were incapable of holding power and that the power to govern would immediately be snatched from their hands by extremist elements, which after all is more or less what did happen eleven years later. When the Duma was dissolved there was a very real possibility and expectation that there might be another revolutionary uprising in 1906, but the liberals missed or chose to miss their chance to call upon the country. A more ineffectual political move (assembling in Finland to sign a protest letter which called upon the Russian people to protest by such means as non-payment of their taxes) could scarcely be imagined; the only real effect, of course, was that the government was presented with a splendid and safe opportunity to disenfranchise some of the liberals and so further weaken the movement. At about this time a keen and trustworthy witness, Maurice Baring, who was then stationed as a correspondent in

Russia, knew many of the Kadets personally and was sympathetic to their aims, made the harsh judgment: —*The Liberals were journalists, men of letters, professors, and able lawyers, but there was not one man of action in their ranks.* Perhaps V. D. Nabokov was the right man but at not quite the right time in Russian history. Had there been a democratic revolution or evolution, he had the talents of an Alexander Hamilton or Benjamin Disraeli to bring to the service of his state.

V. D. Nabokov's family thought of itself as a little nation and even had its own national anthem, a popular song of the time called *We Went into the Garden,* which was played with sentimental regularity on a brass-horned gramophone. Reverberations of it, Nabokov once acknowledged to me, can be heard clearly in *Ada,* though he feels the song is a painful and insignificant lyric. There were many philanthropic good works in evidence to provide schooling and hospital care for the peasants within the cluster of the Nabokov estates—V. D. Nabokov did not initiate this custom, nor was he alone in practising it among the Nabokovs: —*No èto—tol'ko pokazukha!* says the Soviet guide showing weekend excursionists around the estate of Rozhestveno: —**But that was just for show!** No, the problems of the staff and the peasants were attended to with real concern and intelligence, and, if the social order depended upon great differences in means and station, V. D. Nabokov did as much as anyone could to deserve his privileged place. After his death one of his contemporaries wrote: —*With the tactfulness which was peculiar to him he knew how to deal with those who were in need, bringing to bear all his lightness of touch and refinement of character.*

In *Speak, Memory* Nabokov's son touches only for a moment on this question, and he notes, quite rightly, that Soviet women streetcleaners are hardly better off than were the women who weeded the park avenues at Vyra. But that is not an answer. The problem is as old as the history of political liberalism in any country. When V. D. Nabokov became the leader of the moderate faction of the Kadet Party in emigration, he was one of those attacked by the leader of the left faction of the Kadet Party, Pavel Miliukov (the man whom he died defending and whom Vladimir Nabokov years later described as the "world's most ungifted man"), because he was unwilling to renounce all previous privilege such as large land holdings in the event—which was deemed more than possible at that time—that the Bolshevik regime should fall. One may

postulate that V. D. Nabokov evidently believed in the defensibil-
ity (or inevitability) of social inequality so long as it does not trans-
gress social justice and basic social rights. Miliukov, however, believed that this question was the essential one to make any
democratic or socialist order viable in the future in Russia. I have
raised the question, but it is not my purpose here to look for an
answer, though one cannot help but note that Pavel Miliukov did
not have a large estate to renounce. There is one more thing to
be said. The occurrence of repentant noblemen such as Tolstoy
described and almost was himself went back at least a generation
in Russian society. The phenomenon was already a little trite and
vulgar by the time V. D. Nabokov came into his estate, and anyway it is my conviction that psychic self-flagellation was and is
quite foreign to the natures of these Nabokovs, grandfather, father, and son.

Vladimir Nabokov once told me that there was something of
Tolstoy's Pierre Bezukhov in the character of his father. While on
the surface he seems too polished a *peterburzhets* (and of the
elegant old St. Petersburg of Pushkin), certain reported incidents
do lend themselves to an image of a good and charmed nobleman
bobbing perilously but safely in the torrents of history. At an evening in commemoration of the anniversary of V. D. Nabokov's
death, Joseph Hessen related how he had been walking along the
Nevsky Prospect with Nabokov's father during the days of the
revolution when shooting commenced along the street. To Hessen's reasonable enough suggestion that they take refuge in the
close-at-hand public library Nabokov replied, prophetically, that
the bullet destined for him had still not been cast and continued
calmly on his way. There were several other incidents of this
nature before Nabokov escaped from Russia in 1919.

He was a fatalist, I gather, or at least there exist published
recollections of him which assert that he was. He had a strong
character which showed itself clearly in his public deeds and writings. He was certainly one of the very few men in Russia who
naturally spoke with the rolling r's of a St. Petersburg aristocrat (an
accent which his son also has, by the way) in defense of the rule
of law and democracy. It is useful to bear in mind that, when he
defended the rights of the Jews in the Duma, there were twenty
Jewish members among the several hundred deputies, but they
themselves evidently felt constrained to keep their silence on this
matter which was so charged—until Nabokov spoke to the ques- **77**

tion—with the awkward and unbearable tension of silence in even the most advanced quarters of intellectual society. V. D. Nabokov even had difficulties on this score at home since many members of the family who frequented the town house on Morskaya, including V. D. Nabokov's own mother, were at least genteelly anti-Semitic, and the young Vladimir keenly recalls how concerned he was whenever he invited Jewish schoolmates to his house lest something might be said. —It never was, but the fear and the possibility were always there. Later, in emigration, when he married, Nabokov recalls that his old grandmother, using an archaic form of speech, asked: —Of what religions is she? Like so many other stands on public issues which V. D. Nabokov took, his position on the Jewish question was good and right in itself, and in this particular instance it may have served to save the life of Vladimir Nabokov's wife and child. For they received their berth on one of the last ships to leave France before it fell to the Nazis through a Jewish relief organization, yes, because Véra Evseevna was Jewish and, yes again, because Vladimir Nabokov was one of the best-known writers and poets of the emigration, but in no small part because the name Nabokov, V. D. Nabokov, had a magical effect upon grateful Russian Jewry.

His role as Executive Secretary of the Provisional Government was filled with torment for V. D. Nabokov. The Provisional Government of Kerensky was constantly in peril due to juvenile fights, empty bravado, threats of resignation, and, above all, a very weak sense of the reality all around it. Nabokov's father saw all of this very well. His published account of those months contains many harsh personal judgments—one member of the government, for example, is described as *imbued with the most simple-minded Philistinism, the grossest provincialism,* and Nabokov does not even fail to note that the speeches of Miliukov, one of the most cultured members of the government, *masterful though they are, lack any imagery and structural beauty.* But in spite of this severity his memoir attains an extraordinary level of calm objectivity and depth of perception in regard to the broader and more essential questions such as the importance of the Kerensky-Miliukov relationship for the Provisional Government, the influence of Germany on events in Russia, and the legitimacy of the various contending forces. V. D. Nabokov would probably not have wanted that memoir of national failure and despair to be considered one of his foremost achievements in public life, but it may well be.

78

In November, having narrowly avoided arrest on several other occasions, V. D. Nabokov was finally imprisoned by the Bolsheviks under an order calling for the arrest of all members of the Kadet Electoral Commission. He and a dozen or more of the Kadets were placed in Smolny Prison in a cramped, low-ceilinged room. The furniture was minimal, and the prisoners were offered no food at all the first day, though fortunately one of the men's wives, who had heard of the arrest, managed to bring a basket of food. Nabokov slept on one of the narrow benches. The next day the prisoners were fed in the prison's common room. They received mattresses and linen, and relatives were allowed to bring provisions. Vladimir Dmitrievich records that the company was in good spirits and even gay, though there were fears that they might be shifted to the much more dreaded and permanent prison, Kresty. As it happened, however, they were all unexpectedly released, for no apparent reason, on the fifth day, and then Nabokov, who had been forewarned not to return home, where a new arrest would almost certainly await him, began the long hegira southwards which many months later reunited him with his family in the Crimea. Before they left Smolny, the men did a very Kadet-like thing. They sat down for a parting tea and resolved to draw up a document about their imprisonment and interrogation.

Nabokov's arrest in 1908 for having signed the protest at the dissolution of the Duma was out of an operetta in comparison with the dangers and discomforts of this Smolny episode, even though the term at Smolny was but five days while the earlier sentence had been for three months in Kresty. The Vyborg sentence was not served until a year and a half after the event. We have an excellent record of that term through some letters which were smuggled out to his wife. They were written on toilet paper; he asks his wife to think of it as exotic Oriental stationery. It is evident that Vladimir Dmitrievich is concerned to set his wife, who was evidently distraught about the sentence, at ease. He describes his daily routine in minute detail. He arises at five, bathes, and reads the Bible. Breakfast is eaten between six and six-thirty, then he gets dressed, and in the remaining time until nine-thirty he studies Italian and is allowed his first walk of the day in the prison court-yard. Before lunch he studies problems having to do with capital punishment for two and a half hours; in the early afternoon he rests and then has a second walk, and between four and seven he does serious reading, while standing (as his son writes, come to 79 think of it), and gymnastics. His reading includes Anatole France and d'Annunzio and Dostoevsky. In the evening he reads Italian for nearly two hours, followed by some light reading before going to sleep at ten or ten-thirty. The cell is large and airy with a beautiful view. He has tipped one of the warders, who in consequence is now virtually waiting upon him. The *parashka,* or steam bucket (a good Russian word—Solzhenitsyn's Ivan Denisovich uses it, but things have changed in the course of fifty years), is evidently brand-new and does not smell in the least. Cleaning it once a day is a most unpleasant operation, but it lasts only ten minutes, and there are lavender salts to help reduce the smell. He has his portable rubber tub with him, of course, and so has a full bath every day.

V. D. Nabokov lived in interesting times. But his life was conducted on two distinct and wholly separate levels so that fierce political opposition, journalism, work towards legal reforms, and World War I military service alternated and shared seasons and years with a splendid and luxurious Russian version of Edwardian timelessness. Fate seems to have been saving him as it was saving Russia, just for a time.

The murder of Nabokov's father was an absurd mistake, really essentially not at all unlike the murder of John Shade in *Pale Fire.* Moreover, he died with a literary work caught precisely at a moment of assured pause, just as John Shade's poem ends. When V. D. Nabokov died he had shortly before handed in a new chapter in his memoirs of a lifetime's passionate observance of opera and theatre in St. Petersburg, and the concluding sentence of the instalment which appeared posthumously a few days later in the émigré journal *Theatre and Life* was: —*But about this—and how Wagner took our opera scene by storm—another time.*

Pavel Miliukov was delivering a speech at the Berlin Philharmonic Hall. He was to be introduced by Nabokov, his opponent within the Party of the People's Freedom (as the Kadet Party had by then been renamed). The evening, it was anticipated, might be of importance in determining the course of post-Bolshevik rule (it was 1922) in Russia. It was hardly likely though that there could have been a significant rapprochement between the left (or young) and moderate (or old) Kadet wings. The renunciation of personal property was the least of it. Miliukov was flirting with the Bolsheviks, or, rather, with the idea, evidently counting on a Bolshevism which would mellow to a degree that the emigration's more radical left could eventually join forces with it. This was his New Tactic, which he initiated in 1921. Whether it was his lifelong antipathy to totalitarian politics or simply his realistic awareness that Miliukov's hopes were quite chimerical, Vladimir Dmitrievich privately expressed simple boredom with the intellectual antics of Miliukov. He complained to his family that he didn't even want to go to the talk but had to in his capacity as editor of *The Rudder,* which was the largest circulation émigré daily newspaper in Berlin and one of the principal organs of émigré Kadet thought. *The Rudder* on the previous day editorially called Miliukov one of the finest statesmen of modern times, a gesture of fine courtesy on the part of Nabokov to his former political and editorial colleague now turned opponent. The hall was filled to overflowing. But the Nabokov family stayed at home. One of his daughters sewed a button on for him just before he left. —**Such a waste of time. Just think of sewing a button on for such a short time.** She sighed softly, as if that button was somehow attached to the incomprehensible tragedy-by-accident.

The talk was on the theme *Russia and America,* and Miliukov, who suffered from prolixity, had reached the conclusion of the first part and was being applauded when a young man got up from his seat in the second row and ran towards the dais, gun in hand. There was consternation in the hall. Shots rang out. Five, perhaps six. A second man also ran forward. V. D. Nabokov had leaped up at the first of the assailants. It might have been an attempt to disarm him. It might have been an attempt to shield Miliukov, at whom the assailant was firing. It was the instinctive action of a brave man. He had succeeded in deflecting the hand of the one man. They both fell to the ground. When they pulled V. D. Nabokov off the assailant, it was found that Nabokov had been shot twice, once slightly below the heart. He probably died instantly.

The second assassin remained free for some minutes. He leaped onto the stage and began to shout melodramatically and wave his pistol about in unintentional parody of John Wilkes Booth. —**We have avenged the murder of the tsar!** He managed to fire a third shot into the prostrate body of Nabokov before he was tackled, and it was never satisfactorily determined which of the bullets had killed Nabokov. Both of the gunmen were now set upon and badly beaten and bloodied before they were tied up on chairs. The police and ambulances arrived to take away the assassins and the wounded. Several other people had received flesh wounds.

The killers were named P. N. Shabelsky (or Bork-Shabelsky or

Shabelsky-Bork) and S. V. Taboritsky. The subsequent investigation and trial revealed that the two men had been roommates in a shabby Munich rooming house. Both had a history of mental disturbance, and both were connected with extreme reactionary groups. Another man, F. Vinberg, who edited a sporadic and most scurrilous journal in which Shabelsky's articles had appeared, was also arrested and charged with heading the conspiracy to kill Pavel Miliukov in which V. D. Nabokov had been murdered. He very likely did, but there was insufficient evidence against him, and he had to be released after four days.

The cause of the attack had been yet another of Miliukov's rhetorical flourishes for what he considered sound tactical reasons. Miliukov had declared publicly that in his opinion a democratic Russia could function very well without a monarchy. There were those, especially among the rabid monarchists, who held Miliukov indirectly responsible for the murder of the royal family. The accusation had no justice, and the assassination, had it succeeded, would have been an empty foul gesture serving no conceivable purpose. The killing of the wrong man merely carried the absurdity one step further.

The Nabokovs, understandably enough, do not like to talk of the murder, which is still a very immediate and painful topic even after half a century. I attempted once or twice to talk with Vladimir Vladimirovich about his own feelings at the time, the funeral, the two poems he wrote about his father's death, but each time the conversation was abruptly curtailed: —**I am not interested in funerals,** or —**Those poems are my *worst* clichés.** What I know then comes mostly from others, but it is not hearsay. The event so shook the twenty-three-year-old Vladimir that he was not entirely in possession of himself for some time. Although outwardly calm, he was obsessed with and spoke openly of challenging the killers to a duel, in spite of the fact that they were both, in the terms which Nabokov outlines in discussing his father's challenge in *Speak, Memory,* unduellable, and it is just as well quite apart from simple justice that both remained in jail for several years.

In his memoirs Nabokov mentions how one of the assassins was eventually released and attained a position of some importance under Hitler. That was Taboritsky, who became the head of Hitler's department of émigré affairs during the war. Its main functions were ferreting out Russian Jews and maintaining a corps of Russian fascist translators and intelligence agents to interrogate prisoners of war. I do not know what the fate of Taboritsky was, but Shabelsky lived a long and apparently untroubled life in Brazil, where he published a book—a digression which I will be forgiven for avoiding—and died only in 1950. As for Vinberg, I have found only some of his quite incredible hate-cramped publications in the years after the murder, including an issue of *Ray of Light* in which the event itself is discussed. The manner in which the spectators dived under their seats is recounted with gleeful relish. There is some uneasiness at the fact of V. D. Nabokov's heroism— the only human instance in the entire screed—which is finally merely doubted, but particular vilification is saved for Miliukov, who, it is claimed, hid himself in a cowardly manner and subsequently returned directly to Paris rather than attend Nabokov's funeral. That last at least is true, but it is also true that there was a convention of reactionaries in Berlin at this time, and there were grounds to fear that further attempts on the life of the Kadet leader might be made. Miliukov was followed by such accusations throughout his political life, for it had long been rumoured that he was the author of the 1906 Vyborg Manifesto for which V. D. Nabokov and its other signatories had served their prison sentences, but that he had deftly avoided signing it himself. Vladimir Nabokov, however, subscribes to the view of those who knew Miliukov that, whatever his other failings, he was an absolutely fearless man.

The office for the dead *(panikhida)* was held at the Russian Embassy Church on the Unter den Linden. In 1922 it had not yet passed over to Soviet control. One man, the well-known satirical poet Sasha Chyorny, who had been a particularly close friend of Nabokov's, could not restrain himself and fell into a fit of hysterics. Nabokov's friend and colleague on *The Rudder,* Avgust Kaminka, organized things for the family, and it was he who managed the family's affairs for Elena Ivanovna in the months afterwards. V. D. Nabokov was buried in a sylvan Greek Orthodox cemetery in Tegel, a suburb of Berlin. Today Nabokov pays a small yearly sum to have the grave well tended. It was arranged for Elena Ivanovna and her three youngest children to go to Prague, where she was eligible to receive a small widow's pension from the Czech government. Prague was, after Berlin and Paris, the third major center for Russian émigrés, and Czechoslovakia had shown itself to be more sympathetic to the problems and needs of the Russian émigrés than any other country in the world. One of Nabokov's sisters, Olga, remained in Prague. The young Vladimir, who had only by chance happened to be in Berlin at the time of the murder on vacation from university, returned to Cambridge, where he was in his last year.

How important was his father to Vladimir Nabokov? I can only say this: There are rather many facts and features in Vladimir Nabokov's life which have some precedent in the life of his father.

V. D. Nabokov believed in a state of patrician democracy which allows for the existence of an intellectual, monied élite. His son's belief in democracy as I understand it—and I am well aware that he himself would state the matter, already has in fact, in far more attractive and less blunt fashion—is the same. V. D. Nabokov had a professional interest in abnormal psychology and criminology. His son's novels are peopled with the subjects of such studies. V. D. Nabokov was a passionate lepidopterist, having acquired the interest as a young lad from a tutor; his son has studied lepidoptera from the time he was a boy. V. D. Nabokov was a dandy as a young man; V. D. Nabokov was, by his own description, a fop, which is admittedly not exactly the same but generically close enough. V. D. Nabokov possessed an extraordinary capacity for sustained work. There is a good illustrative anecdote from a German source relating how V. D. Nabokov stayed behind to complete the transcription work after the executive committee of the Kadet Party had worked itself to the point of exhaustion on the drafting of its party statutes. He worked through the night, and the next morning he had a neat and meticulously ordered codicil to be signed by the committee returning from their night's sleep. Similarly, his son for years strained even the generous legacy of insomnia to earn a minimal income, produce an *oeuvre* on the old-fashioned scale, in terms of its size, engage in literary research, and, during one protracted period of his life, also pursue research in lepidoptery with equal zeal. V. D. Nabokov counted Jews among his closest friends; Vladimir Nabokov's wife is Jewish—there is no direct connection between the two things, of course, but they are not entirely devoid of connections either. Both father and son show the unusual combination of great reserve and great gaiety in their personalities. And finally this: when Nabokov briefly grew a moustache in the 1940s, it was precisely his father's brush moustache. There are many differences between Nabokov and his father, too, but the signs of emulation are not to be passed over.

84   There is one other way in which V. D. Nabokov played an

important part in the early life of his son. It was an oblique influence and probably not noticed by the young Vladimir himself though others did speak of it in later years. Vladimir Nabokov was the epitome of the precocious child. He was handsome. He was nurtured and attended to with all the means and wisdom that his very wealthy and very well-educated parents had at their command. There was, in short, no opening for the despised Dr. Freud in that family situation. Young Vladimir literally revered his father, even as the elderly Vladimir Vladimirovich still reveres his memory. These things do happen . . . though not as often as one would wish to future writers. For, all signs to the contrary, the young Vladimir Nabokov was not a spoiled child, and, whether through imitation or necessity, he inherited not only his father's superlative self-assurance, but also a sufficient measure of some of his other virtues, too. Favoured though he was, the boy must have known that he was not the centre of the family universe, a useful lesson in every perfect upbringing.

His mother, Elena Ivanovna, was called Lyolya in the family. While Nabokov's mother was relatively untouched by the revolution *per se*—she had, from completely different premises, perhaps even a keener sense than her husband of Russia's fragility—she never recovered from the shock of Vladimir Dmitrievich's murder, and the last seventeen years of her life were difficult ones with three children to support and educate on a small pension. Vladimir Vladimirovich, who was not living in the hackneyed style but nonetheless on the same financial level as the traditional impoverished artist, could not help much.

Nabokov was able to visit Prague on odd occasions when he had been invited to give literary readings. (It will be remembered that he gave Prague to one of his novels, *Despair*.) In *Speak, Memory* he pictures his mother as living in pitiful surroundings but wholly immersed in thoughts of the past as she played solitaire. She received some comfort, too, from Christian Science, to which she had been converted by an American lady, but she did not like to talk about this with her son because she objected to a certain almost imperceptible smile which would appear on his face whenever the subject came up. It had always been her custom to copy out poems which she particularly liked in albums, and she did this not only with all his poems which appeared in *The Rudder* and other émigré publications, but also with most of his early short stories, thereby eventually preserving for her son's bibliography 85 several items which otherwise might have been lost. These she read to her daughters and to her companion Evgenia Khofeld, who had been her daughters' governess in Russia since 1914, and in one instance that I know the albums were even taken with her on a social visit. Once, in *Glory*, Nabokov gave a small habitual hand gesture of his mother's to Martin Edelweiss's mother, and she was greatly upset by this.

In addition to keeping a voluminous scrapbook of poetry which appealed to her, Elena Ivanovna was herself an industrious albeit unpublished poetess. The poetry wasn't of very high quality. She used to tell the story on herself of how one morning she wrote a rapturous poem about a young bird at daybreak, but it turned out later in the day that the young bird was a young donkey, and the poem had to be destroyed. All the branches of Nabokov's family had amateur poets for at least a generation, and one of Nabokov's cousins, Dmitri Pihatcheff, was a published poet (not without talent, as they say). Given the intensity of feeling which Nabokov's mother brought to all things, whether important or trivial, it is not unreasonable to credit her for some portion of the young boy's very early poetic vocation. It should be mentioned, too, that Nabokov's youngest brother Kirill occasionally also published verse, of a very high standard, in the emigration. Like her husband, Elena Ivanovna was also a music lover, and when she entertained in St. Petersburg, it was often with private concerts, some of which were given by Koussevitsky.

Nabokov's mother died in Prague in 1939. Nabokov himself was by that time in Paris. He came into a room in which George Hessen and Mikhail Kaminka (another old friend, who was the son of Avgust Kaminka) were preparing to play a practical joke on him. —**My mother died this morning** was all that he said in a simple uninflected voice, and he rubbed his forehead with his fingertips for just a moment.

Lyolya—we are back for the moment on the other side of the revolution—almost always dressed in light colours. She was not an outstanding beauty when measured against the Korff women and the prettiest of her husband's sisters, but she was a beautiful woman by standards which perhaps eluded them. In all the pictures of her that I have seen one observes an ever-so-slight pendulous tension in the outlines of her features, a languorous demi-embellishment which was very well suited to the *World of Art* St.
Petersburg of her time. She had a very high forehead which she

accented with a steeply rising arrangement of her hair, curled back over an artificial cylindrical bun at the front. Her wardrobe was not inferior to Vladimir Dmitrievich's much-talked-about closets; it was merely more noticed in him because he was a man. Many years later she would tell her daughters in Prague how relieved she felt to be poor. In St. Petersburg she would awaken and lie awake worrying which of fifty hats to put on that day, whereas now, in Prague, there were no such worries and only one hat to put on if she felt like it.

Nabokov has confessed that he is subject to what he calls the embarrassing qualms of superstition and that he can even be affected obsessively by a dream or a coincidence. His mother, though far from alone in the Nabokov family in this respect, had these experiences, and it is not too much to say that her belief in manifestations of the supernatural was one of the dominant, though not dominating, characteristics of her personality. She frequently would experience the true pre-visionary glimpse of a future event or feeling that one has been in a certain place before, the *déjà vu,* that phenomenon and term which Nabokov complains is so badly misunderstood and misused by journalists. One scarcely knows whether to consider such a gift or propensity as genetic or cultivated; like *audition colorée,* it was recognized and shared between mother and son. Nabokov experienced the *déjà vu* sensation in regard to the death of one brother and a prophetic coincidence in regard to the death of the other. Shortly before news of Sergei Vladimirovich's death in a Nazi concentration camp reached him, Nabokov had a dream about a concentration camp. A few hours before he received the cable informing him of Kirill Vladimirovich's death, Nabokov purchased a black scarf. All of his novels, Nabokov told me once, have an air—**not quite of this world, don't you think?** I didn't, or hadn't, though I granted there were very many such works in his canon. He promised—this was in 1971—that this sense would become even more pronounced in his future works, and it did. When I discussed the seventeenth-century writer Archpriest Avvakum with Nabokov on another occasion, Nabokov pointed out that it is in the work of Avvakum that occult phenomena first appear in Russian literature, and then he spoke in general: —**Electricity. Time. Space. We know** *nothing* **about these things.** These, of course, are major themes in many of his English works. Mother and son seem to have (or want to have) an innate ability to perceive things which science and reason **87** cannot explain (—**I try to keep an open mind on these things,** says Nabokov the unnatural scientist). Both Elena Ivanovna and Vladimir Vladimirovich have explored other avenues and shores in the manner of Nabokov's invented poet Shade. Nabokov's sister Elena Vladimirovna told me that a medium had predicted her father's death shortly before the murder.

Both Vladimir Dmitrievich and Elena Ivanovna were religious. In *Speak, Memory* Nabokov says that his mother was not fond of institutionalized religion. Nonetheless, the Nabokov children were taken to church fairly regularly. Nabokov did not like the confessional, where, he felt, you could not speak of your real sins and so had to make some up especially for the occasion. When he was slightly older, he complained to his father that church was boring, and his father said: —**Well, if you feel that way, all right. You don't have to go.** The place of religion in Nabokov's childhood and youth is relevant primarily because of the large number of Biblical and religious poems, published and unpublished, which he wrote at the beginning of his literary career. It was another slightly awkward subject.

—**What do you mean, those angels?**

—**Not only that, dear, but the tone of a number of my poems. . . . They accept the religious view of the world. That's what he means. I still say that it was a stylistic pose, a stylistic posey—a slight pun if I may—I don't know why I tell this kind of pun—there is no more to it. They have as much reality as the Dark Lady of the Sonnets.**

It is a hard disclaimer to accept (especially after Dr. Rowse's plausible identification of the Dark Lady), though I recognize the sense in which the statement is true. These poems constitute the one area of his life's work which, I feel, may constitute something of an embarrassment to Nabokov not simply because they are weak—the poems are not technically juvenilia because they were for the most part written between the ages of twenty and twenty-four, but they nonetheless play the part from the perspective of several decades of an art which is essentially very very different from all his later writing—but rather they are a potential embarrassment because their calm acceptance of an old-fashioned deity serves to contradict and even belittle the playful metaphoric questing and implied sophic wisdom of the later Nabokov. The poems are stylistic exercises. The style is drawn from the framework of Christian belief within which both his parents lived. The

88

images were, I believe, family objects with which a young man furnished his first art and which were in the natural course of things outgrown and discarded. Religious imagery at any rate ceased to obtrude in Nabokov's poetry after 1925, though there are of course occasional instances in which it plays an important part. *Nabokov feels* that religion has no significance whatsoever in his early Russian poetry and that the religious metaphors are simply borrowed from his favourite poets (Pushkin, Blok, Gumilyov, and Soforth).

—Well, it happens, shall we say, it happens with many Russians. It happens in Tolstoy's *Childhood and Youth*. The little Tolstoy crying in the nursery: it was the same Tolstoy who walked to that desolate railway station. Thus Nabokov explained to me the specific gravity of childhood in fixing, forever, the character of a Russian to a much greater degree than happens with other people. **—Well, look at your books. They've changed,** I said. **—Not so much,** he said. **—Of course he grew,** she said. The importance which Nabokov attaches to his own youth can be amply demonstrated by the way in which, although his memoirs are ostensibly supposed to cover his life through the year 1939, in fact *Speak, Memory* is three-quarters devoted to the writer's childhood.

Nabokov was born in the large townhouse on 47 Morskaya Street, now Herzen Street, which his grandfather had built, more an embassy than a private home (and it in fact became the Danish legation for a brief period after the revolution), on April 23, 1899. It was a coincidence full of promise—the birthdate of Shakespeare, the centenary of Pushkin's birth. Nabokov was born in one of the finest sections of St. Petersburg, the Admiralteiskaya region, comparable to the best portions of South Kensington in London or the East Sixties in New York. Morskaya Street (we are, of course, using the designations of that time) ends facing the Moika Canal for a stretch of several city blocks before both the street and the canal come to a right-angled juncture with another canal, the Kriukov. The Nabokov house lies on the other side of Morskaya, that is, facing the canal side and scarcely a block from it. The whole of Morskaya runs in the most undulating sort of parallel to the Neva, separated from it by four blocks and several very wide streets. The street begins on the side of the Palace Square opposite the Winter Palace, then it crosses the famous Nevsky Prospect, runs apace for a short while with Gogol Street until the Isaakievsky square and bronze-domed cathedral which extend into yet another large open area, the Mariinsky Square, through both of which another important Prospect runs at an angle, and on the other side of all these begins the portion of Morskaya on which the Nabokov house is situated. The house was not far from the Admiralty Building with its famous gardens and golden dome and also close to the State Council and the Senate buildings. Numerous concert halls and theatres were not far off, too. It was a posh quarter of that silver city.

Nabokov has listed the occupants of the neighbouring buildings to the left of his house in *Speak, Memory.* My source, the massive two-thousand-page telephone and telephoneless directory *All Petrograd for 1916,* would indicate that by that twilight year of the Russian Empire Prince Oginsky had sold No. 45, the house next to the Nabokovs, to another princely family, the Gagarins. (A previous Prince Gagarin had been one of the main leaders in the half-successful attempt to push Alexander II farther to the right, an effort which was vigorously opposed by the Grand Duke Konstantin and D. N. Nabokov, after the first attempt that was made on the tsar's life.) And, while the Italian Embassy remains as No. 43, the German Embassy, evidently as a consequence of the war, has been vacated. But nothing has happened to the neighbourhood: to the immediate right of the Nabokov house live members of one of Russia's oldest princely families, the Meshcherskys, and skip a door farther there is a baron. On the other side of the street there is an imposing string of millions of rubles in the form of the managing offices of some of Russia's main insurance companies and land agencies.

St. Petersburg is one of Europe's cities which has a life and style uniquely its own, even to a certain extent today in the Soviet Union. St. Petersburg has its poets and writers in a way that Moscow does not; poets and writers, by contrast, seem for the most part merely to happen to come from Moscow. The St. Petersburg tradition among poets starts with Pushkin, who exemplified the Europeanized Russian and several of whose long poems introduced the note of the cruel and grotesque spirit residing within the coldly beautiful city, a theme which was elaborated by Gogol, Dostoevsky, Blok, Bely, and Mandelstam, to name only the giants among the Petersburg poets and writers. The air of unreality of this city, forced upon a swamp and a nation, has been another particularly frequent St. Petersburg theme: Dostoevsky saw the city as a mirage in the waters of one of its own canals; Andrei Bely put forward the claim in his novel *St. Petersburg* that the city simply did not exist and was a fiction. A little man walks fearfully or proudly or angrily through this city as it appears in Russian literature, and more often than not the city mocks him. Nabokov's relation to his city, figuring as a major theme in his early poetry and an especially rich motif in his memoirs, is radically different. Quite simply, Vladimir Nabokov's St. Petersburg and his youthful years in the city *were* different, happier, lived in perhaps better emotional and material circumstances than any other major St. Petersburg writer before him.

I hold an old French Baedeker of the period for St. Petersburg and Russia—in V. D. Nabokov's library there were no less than twelve Baedekers covering all of Europe!—and approach the city through its eyes and advice. It is a beautiful city, but it is not a healthy city, the pre-revolutionary Venice of the North. In the summer there is a slight stench which at times is discernible on the Neva, and nets are set on the river to filter out effluent believed capable of producing dysentery and diptheria, for much of the city's drinking water is taken directly from the river. During this period of the year, of course, the Nabokovs are in the country. Serious illness and death through contagion do occur throughout the year, though the Baedeker is exaggerating a bit when it declares: —*C'est alors l'époque de la grande mortalité a St-Pétersbourg.* And in addition, of course, there are the normal climatic hazards of the region to be considered; pneumonia and severe fever are nothing out of the ordinary at this time. Nabokov himself contracted pneumonia twice in his youth. But for all the dangers the residents of the city are an amiable people even though—the Baedeker adds quickly—they do have some most peculiar habits such as the way in which men, women, and youths smoke furiously and even passionately without cease, in public and in private and even between courses while eating. At the beginning of the century this was evidently a uniquely Russian habit. As a young man, Nabokov told me, he smoked up to a hundred hollow-barrelled Russian cigarettes a day, a habit which he very likely acquired from his mother, who also smoked too much.

Nabokov was a sickly baby and the second child Vladimir Dmitrievich and Elena Ivanovna had attempted to have. The first was stillborn. The baby was pampered and adored by the parents, at **91** least that is the impression which is unequivocably stressed in the unpublished memoirs of V. D. Nabokov's friend Joseph Hessen:

—I knew V. V. Sirin, the adored first-born son of my deceased friend V. D. Nabokov, when he was still a child, but even though I am very fond of children, I did not take much notice of the slender, well-proportioned boy with the expressive, lively face and intelligent probing eyes which glittered with sparks of mockery. True, one rarely had occasion to see the children when one visited V. D. Nabokov at home: they were "in their own quarters" (more precisely, they were on their own floor, which had been con-structed especially for them) with their own tutors and gover-nesses and servant, and I would meet them only when I happened to dine at the Nabokovs. And even at the dinner table the conver-sation did not take the presence of the children into account, for the two girls turned to the instructress sitting between them and the two boys, to the tutor between them. I was well aware that the family circle of my friend was disposed against me, and it seemed that such an inclination had even communicated itself to the children. For his part V. D. Nabokov loved to speak about his children, particularly his oldest son whom, I repeat, he literally idolized, and his wife and her parents did this even more so than he. . . .

In retrospect the amount and intensity of parental love which he received has perhaps the very slightest strange aftertaste only because of its marked contrast—then, of course, it meant nothing —with the affection which fell to his four brothers and sisters. Nabokov mentions the difference between the affection shown him and that which his brother Sergei received in *Speak, Memory,* but he does not like to expatiate on it.

Nabokov's sister Elena, who has a very matter-of-fact view of the particular place that each of the children had in the emotional spectrum of their parents, notes that her eldest brother was raised differently in at least one significant respect. Speaking of their mother she told me:

—My mother adored him. Of all the five children. This was really an adoration. . . . Later in emigration if she didn't get a letter from him she was practically ill for a week. But with the other children, it was a little different because we were brought up that way—which perhaps is wrong—by governesses, you see. And so

we were much closer to our governesses than to our own mother. I never remember playing with my mother, you see, or sitting on my mother's lap. I got close to my father when I was about fifteen, and then I think he loved me as much as he loved Vladimir. This was when I was fourteen, fifteen years old, but before that, no. . . .

It is, of course, not an inevitable pattern but a very common one, the favoured position in childhood and very often throughout subsequent life of the eldest child. In Switzerland brother and sister often discuss the matter, and he tells her: —Well, you exaggerate. But she is firm: —I am not exaggerating, I am sure I am not exaggerating because I felt this so much in my childhood. We knew this. I knew that I was not loved as Vladimir was loved, but it didn't matter.

The conditions of social life of such upper gentry or lower aristocrats as the Nabokov family tended to underscore and develop not loneliness but certainly separateness. Though he may have had advantages in parental attention over his brothers and sisters, the young Vladimir was himself first given to a wet nurse and then to a nurse before graduating to a governess. One must imagine an enormous house in which a number of people, a rather large number of people even, can live their day on different floors and in various wings and rooms without ever seeing each other at all except at the appointed dinner hour. The children were dressed up for dinner. When the children were still young they were allowed twenty to thirty minutes after dinner during which time they sat and talked with their parents before bedtime at eight. Under such circumstances it is not surprising that the Nabokov children were not terribly close to one another, since they often did not see each other too much.

In the mornings it was Elena Ivanovna's habit to sleep quite late. The governesses took care of getting the younger children up. During the course of his childhood Vladimir Vladimirovich had three valets: two Ivans, and a Christopher who played the balalaika. Once V. D. Nabokov caught his son—he was thirteen then—leaning back in a chair so that his valet could remove his shoe for him, and afterwards he was sternly told that that must never happen again. The training in regard to the deference one must show to servants is still very evident in the way Nabokov acts towards the hotel staff in Switzerland. Nabokov's father himself behaved in an exemplary though surely somewhat awkwardly **93** equalitarian manner towards his own man. Democracy in the Nabokov household never reached extremes, but the children, with the exception of Vladimir, were taught to be just a little bit ashamed of their wealth and privilege. Whereas Nabokov tells us in *Speak, Memory*—the smart can still be felt decades later (—*The grin can still be seen*, says Nabokov)—how one of his teachers once asked him to at least have the chauffeur drop him off a block away from the school, his sisters, by a curious coincidence, on their own initiative did beg the chaffeur *not* to stop the car in front of the school.

The regimen of lessons in languages, subjects, and sports was a hard one, and it was in general not an idle Russian household. The house breathed activity: political meetings, literary meetings (V. D. Nabokov virtually single-handedly had brought to life the previously moribund Literary Fund which aided indigent writers), editorial conferences with his legal colleagues, and occasionally important visitors such as H. G. Wells, whose stories the children already knew in the original. In England Nabokov would attend Cambridge with one of Wells's sons, and later he became friendly with Wells himself. The house library was substantial enough to require its own printed catalogue and full-time librarian. The catalogue was done in 1909 and then subsequently a supplement was issued, but it is reasonable to estimate from these sources that by the time Nabokov was a teen-ager the library probably contained something under ten thousand entries, more if separate volumes are counted because many of the entries are collected editions. Foreign books seem to have been supplied by a library ordering service in Leipzig. The girls were not supposed to go to the library—the books were chosen for them—but Vladimir and Sergei did. In the Nabokov family even hobbies tended to bring technical literature and equipment with them, and so the scientific direction which the young Vladimir's butterfly collecting soon took also has a natural explanation within the life of the family. The contents of V. D. Nabokov's library represent a clear personal taste. (Wealthy Russians had always had libraries, but frequently they were ordered collectively from Paris like furniture, for the decorative effect of their leather bindings.) V. D. Nabokov's library is, as regards literature, decidedly old-fashioned. The books, predominantly in Russian, French, and English, could be found in any well-equiped school library. Pushkin,

94 Gogol, Aksakov, and Herzen are particularly well-represented,

and together with the expected standard Russian poets of the nineteenth century one finds a good representation of the middle-rank parlour poet Apukhtin, for whom Nabokov has confessed a certain foible when he was young. There is in my view a very high correlation between the Nabokov library and the style and contents of many of the poems in *The Cluster* and *The Empyrean Path,* Nabokov's first two collections of verse in 1923, which were in fact criticized for their imitativeness of nineteenth-century models at the time of their appearance. Among English books we find Conan Doyle (whom V. D. Nabokov also knew personally and whose works were well known to his son), Dickens of course, Ruskin, and Mayne Reid *(The Scalp Hunters, The White Chief).*

Nabokov shares the spirit of his time—it was the Silver Age of Russian literature, the Symbolist and Acmeist periods—only in the general sense that he possesses the flair and style and propensity towards extremes in all things about which memoirists speak, but there is absolutely no influence upon Nabokov by the artists of the Silver Age except perhaps for Aleksandr Blok, and who in St. Petersburg during those years did not know Blok? Apart from an occasional best-seller such as Fyodor Sologub's novel *The Petty Demon* and some odd Solovyov and Rozanov the library contains very few of the Sirin books, the publishing house which printed most of the modernists of the time. Characteristically, the two primary Russian literary and art journals, *The World of Art* and *The Scales,* are present in the library's catalogue only for their first years: the subscriptions were evidently not renewed. There is a four-volume set of another contemporary writer, however: Maksim Gorky. Though he has denied the influence of the Russian Symbolists upon him in an interview, Nabokov says that he had digested "the entire population" of the "so-called" Silver Age in the soft-cover ivory Sirin volumes which he purchased at a certain table in Volf's, a large St. Petersburg bookstore. He had, he says, several hundred volumes (mainly poetry and lepidoptera) in his own library upstairs. At any rate, Nabokov's taste for post-Symbolist poets such as Mandelstam and Annensky came later, in the emigration, and he did not experience the influence of Andrei Bely, particularly important to him for his theories of metrics and his analysis of Gogol's style, until after 1917 when he was in the Crimea shortly before the family went into emigration.

The situation is very similar in regard to French literature in V. D. Nabokov's library—there is as much Hugo as you could wish, **95** but a very scanty representation of the French Symbolist and Decadent poets who were at the height of their activity in the 1890s.

The substantial portion of V. D. Nabokov's library which is devoted to his professional interests is considerably more interesting. There one may find titles such as *The Sexual Instinct and Its Morbid Manifestations* and a good collection of Havelock Ellis, the psychologist whose work Nabokov knows best and holds up against Freud. In whatever time he took from his lepidopteral studies, the young Nabokov certainly did acquire a taste for this sort of reading, for when he was confined to bed for a time years later in Berlin, he sent a friend to the library to take out psychological case studies for him. It is a very simple and unexciting but sufficient explanation of the origins of Nabokovian neurotics and psychotics such as Smurov in *The Eye,* Herman Karlovich in *Despair,* and Humbert Humbert. One also finds in the library Przhevalsky's 1883 work *Third Journey to Central Asia, From Zaisan through Khami to Tibet,* which furnishes a portion of the expedition described in *The Gift.* That fictional trip is a kind of artistic compensation, inasmuch as it had been arranged for Nabokov to go on an Asian expedition with another naturalist, Grum-Grzimailo (also in *The Gift*), in 1918, a trip which was unavoidably cancelled by history.

Nabokov had his own pocket money at a very early age, a substantial enough amount that when he was fifteen he was able to have one of his early juvenile poems privately printed between lilac paper covers in an edition of two hundred copies. Nabokov recalls that there was a rhododendron in the poem wearing its stress on the wrong syllable. At the rear of 47 Morskaya there was another house which was also owned by V. D. Nabokov and let out to rent, and the green lamp of a printing establishment could be seen from a rear window. A survey of the classified section of *All Petrograd* shows that the neighbourhood of the Nabokov townhouse was prophetically endowed with printeries, with many to choose from within a few blocks. The young lad's great confidence in himself was soon to be outstretched by the wealth which came into his possession, together with the estate of Rozhestveno, upon the death of his godfather, Uncle Ruka. But, as recorded in *Speak, Memory,* this wealth—something in excess of a million rubles—never had the opportunity to make its presence felt. He enjoyed the feel of shiny five-ruble coins in his pocket, and in the winter, when he was being unfaithful to his first love (as he has said he considered a young *littérateur* should, to gain experience for his poetry) he was able to take young ladies to the finest and most expensive restaurants in St. Petersburg—there were several of first-rate European standard—with no financial hesitation or even need to consult with his parents.

The one lasting use to which his inheritance was put in the short time that Nabokov had it was the private publication of a book of his best youthful love-sad poems. It was a smallish book and in soft cover but on the best paper and with a very elegant and tasteful typeface. There were five hundred numbered copies. V. D. Nabokov, like his wife, took a great deal of pride in his precocious son's poetic efforts. Joseph Hessen recalls that his friend told him about his son's poetry, adding that the poems themselves were: —*Not at all bad (—Ochen' nedurnye).* When Hessen, who was rather firmly of the opinion at that time that the young Vladimir had far too much of too many good things to come to a good end, protested vigorously that the book of poems was an untoward display on the part of a seventeen-year-old boy, Vladimir Dmitrievich became awkward and defensive: —*But after all he has his own means. How can I stand in his way?* It is evident that, for all his love and confidence in his son, V. D. Nabokov shared at least a portion of Joseph Hessen's doubts about his future. He had not wanted him to inherit his uncle's estate. Not only was it perhaps not the best state of affairs to have a still immature boy so totally independent, but there was the further complication that the Rozhestveno estate was managed by a man who was an out-and-out scoundrel even by the undemanding standards of that particular profession in Russia. Uncle Ruka had known this very well, but he had never dared say a word to the man.

Neither his parents nor his tutors ever punished the boy physically, though Mlle. Miauton—the famed Mademoiselle O of *Speak, Memory*—was from time to time known to set *une bonne dictée* as punishment for some transgression. But there were not overly many even of these. Decanters of claret and port wine were always on the dining-room table, and, although it was forbidden, the furtive young Nabokov would usually manage to cadge a sip of one or the other. His father frowned on his drinking as he did on his smoking—although he was a great lover of good wine, V. D. Nabokov was far from what would be called a drinker, and he did not smoke at all—but nothing was done about it, and his mother in any case was more lenient. As has already been noted, Nabokov's parents were also inclined to be slightly permissive when he began to be interested in girls at seventeen, though he was brusquely lectured on the duty of a young man not to get girls into trouble, and his father occasionally showed harsh displeasure at his antics.

The young and the mature Nabokov has always been called Volodya—the standard Russian affectionate form of the name Vladimir—by members of his family and a handful of friends, but the simple informality has not extended to all that many people in his lifetime. When he was a child he was called Volodyushka (very Russian), Loddy (one of those oddly anglicized Russian names reminiscent of "Roddy" Raskolnikov in a bad old translation of Dostoevsky's novel), and Poops. He had rusty or reddish-brown hair when he was a boy which subsequently became mat brown. When Nabokov grew his moustache it was jet black, but his son Dmitri's brief experiment with a beard many years later yielded red.

Nabokovs know how to cry. One of Nabokov's earliest memories is of his mother crying with him in tender commiseration at the foot of the staircase of their country house when he was three. There were many tears, too, related to his lepidopteral passion and the bitterness of close misses of some prize specimens. This passion has subsided only a little after many decades: —**Not tears, but you remember how unpleasant I would get. And after that I was so pleasant, so charming. After catching it.** Tears figure importantly in Nabokov's childhood and youth and in his poetry and prose. But they seem to be tears of intense feeling and unspeakable loss (—**Russia. That was the most terrible stress in my life**), and Nabokov had, has—from his father, I daresay—an almost morbid fear of showing any fear or common emotional pain. It was in part that same quality, plus the slight added advantage or attraction of the fact that his cousin was eighteen months older, which lay behind his close friendship with Baron Yury Rausch von Traubenberg.

Yury, or Yurik, was the son of Nabokov's Aunt Nina by her first marriage. Nabokov says in *Speak, Memory* that his cousin's family was not as cultured as his own, which is not altogether a fair judgment inasmuch as a cousin of Yurik's father was a talented sculptor and porcellanist, illustrations of whose interesting pieces (mostly military figures) can be found in the journal *Apollon* for 1913. It is probably more accurate to say that the culture of that particular family, whatever it was, seems to have been swept along in the tempo of a military march and guided by courtly considerations such as honour and dalliance. Yury's most beautiful sister was married to the youngest general in the Russian Army. Yury was a baron, and Nabokov himself might have been a count had his grandfather accepted the tsar's offer of a title instead of an estate (though, in an American letter to his friend George Hessen many decades later, Nabokov jokingly refers to the bypassed title and signs himself Count Nabokov—it would have been a pleasing touch: *Lolita* by Count Vladimir Nabokov), but in other respects, principally the means of their respective families and their education, Vladimir was in much the favoured position. It was the custom for Yury to be invited to spend the summer at Batovo, and they also spent some time together in St. Petersburg. Wherever they were together, they soon gravitated to playing at and later actually performing deeds of bravado. On the occasion when his father's almonds were eaten, Nabokov and his cousin were searching his father's elegant study—dominated by an enormous desk made of black stone—for his Browning, which they fondled. Then one day not too long thereafter Nabokov's father, suspecting that the pistol had been tampered with, examined it, and it discharged by accident. The shot pierced a painting which is now part of the collection at the Hermitage in Leningrad. In addition to their games with spring-gun darts and the brief episode with Yury's pearl-handled revolver, both of which are described in *Speak, Memory,* the two boys met frequently on the wooden bridge over the Oredezh River connecting the Batovo and Vyra estates and shot it out with air-gun pellets. In retrospect it strikes Nabokov as a miracle that they did not kill one another.

A few years later the two friends were together again in the Crimea. They were helping to shift some furniture on the estate of Countess Panina, where the Nabokov family was staying, and, as the two of them hefted out a sofa, Nabokov's father remarked casually: —**This is the way you will carry my coffin someday.** It was only a few years before that did happen, but Yury von Traubenberg was to die in a few months. He was an active participant in the futile last-ditch White resistance in the Crimea. Seen from afar it does seem that Yury von Traubenberg is one of those for whom death—there is one theory, usually identified with Henry James, which says that this is what happens—smoothed out and simplified a short lifetime. In a chronicle such as this there are more than a few secondary personages who tempt the biographer and threaten to distract him from the main thing. It is perhaps just as well then that I do not know poor Yurik better. I see a very young face with very old eyes, Clark Gable matinee eyes, set in shadow (Nabokov calls them luminous, and he has seen them, I have not), with Lermontov's trim, close moustache and, come to think of it, very much Lermontov's expression, too. He was, beyond doubt, in the peculiarly strong Russian tradition of the poet-hussar as one sees it in the lives of nineteenth-century soldier poets such as Lermontov, Marlinsky, and Davydov. Chekhov parodies the latter-day imitators of this type rather harshly in *Three Sisters*, but there was clearly an intensity of purpose in the character of the young Baron von Traubenberg which stills any such caricature and which was and is the cause of Vladimir Nabokov's admiration then and now. Otherwise, the young soldier who is given more prominent pride of place in *Speak, Memory* than any of Nabokov's boyhood friends had very little in common with him. That one thing was enough.

It is my impression that the summer months at Vyra claim particular primacy in the young Vladimir's affection and memory, though much more of his boyhood, of course, was spent in St. Petersburg, and in spite of the fact that Vyra had to compete with the fairy-tale appeal of opulent trains and resorts in Southern France. Winter at 47 Morskaya was long, slogging-hard lessons and homework. Winter was parents who were tremendously busy, so that one was left much more to the guidance of governess and tutors and the servants. Winter was serious colds and fevers with *kompressiki,* compresses of cotton wool and American cloth administered by the family pediatrician, Dr. Sokolov, and lessons such as drawing and dancing, which were on the whole less interesting than, say, the boxing lessons in the summer given by a crack instructor whose own son trained a French champion. There were some particularly vivid and memorable adventures and experiences associated with Biarritz—being caught by a narrowing strip of beach between a clayey cliffside and the surf with his brother on bicycles in 1909 as the bikes slipped and foundered and the swift tide rushed in—or St. Petersburg—where about a year later in a grandstand box with his father, who chatted with the poet Blok in an adjoining box, he watched the Wright brothers perform a short flight in their highly unpredictable machine—but the summers at Vyra possessed a quieter and richer charm, a fuller sense of family and festivity.

An extant photograph of Vyra has yet to come to light, and so it remains rather more a ghost house for me than 47 Morskaya, Batovo, or Rozhestveno. It was, I gather, an unpretentious mansion, light green, wooden, managing to be at one and the same time both extremely luxurious and yet a simple country estate in a sense. The house no longer exists, the very subject as it happens of a jocular little prefatory paragraph to *Conclusive Evidence* which Nabokov for some reason did not use. After the revolution it is said that a veterinary clinic operated from the house, and later that it was an agricultural college of some sort. Some say that the house was burned by the Nazis in 1944; others, that it simply became ramshackled and was dismantled for its materials. There are traces of the foundation remaining, but with a snow on the ground the scene might be any tranquil wood, more New England than Russian somehow, containing a gnarled and a forked and a perfectly straight tree with the tops of bushes showing through the snow like cast-iron reeds. Off in the distance one can see the hill where Nabokov used to sled when the family came down to the estate by train in the winter. If a photograph were found, then, someday, when Russia is rather like America (—**Our country.** —**Which country, Vladimir Vladimirovich?**), a perfect Williamsburg-type replica of Vyra might be constructed in that woods, and twenty-first-century tourists may see an ecstatic and slightly plump young lady dance through the house on twice-daily tours as she does at Tolstoy's Yasnaya Polyana. Unless sketches and plans are drawn quickly the interior decoration of Vyra will also be not without difficulties. From Nabokov himself I have the impression of a country house which was elegant but tended towards the old-fashioned. There was no electricity, Nabokov said, because his mother wanted to keep the house as it was. But cousins who used to visit Vyra from Batovo remember a house which was very richly appointed and rather modern in some respects. At homely Batovo, to which the young Vladimir and Sergei would be taken to see their grandmother and their aunts in an elegantly polished two-pony carriage, everything was shabby by comparison. Batovo was full of chintz, a fashion among the St. Petersburg smart set of the time (largely due to the fact that the Empress Alexandra was a chintz empress) and the saving grace in the homes of many comparatively poor Russian noble families. There was nothing chintzy about Vyra. Vladimir and Sergei would descend from their carriage always very elegantly dressed, usually in the English style, sailor suits were very popular too, and Vladimir would charm his **101** waiting aunts with a few moments of his self-assured gaiety and then go spinning off to play, leaving behind his timid, tense, and stuttering brother to bear the burden of conversation.

Nabokov is very partial to landscape in his or other people's writing, and on occasion—for example, the stepping-stone path of parks across Europe which marks his son Dmitri's earliest years in *Speak, Memory*—landscape can be most important in the Nabokovian perspective. Joseph Hessen claimed to see details of the Nabokov city and country life in many of Nabokov's novels, and he termed these casual autobiographical markings one of the most characteristic features of his art, which may or may not be —there are now few people who were not merely children then who can recall what life at 47 Morskaya and on the estates at Siverskaya was like. I am inclined to accept Hessen's view.

The grounds and paths of Vyra were kept as meticulously clean as the house itself. The grounds were kept to an English standard. There was an apple tree with a circle of pansies. Beds of poppies and violet flowers, hawthorne. Close to the pond vegetables were grown. Carrots, cabbages. There were extensive strawberry beds. A greenhouse. There were few leaves on the ground because the groundkeeping staff was rather large.

As he has noted in his memoirs, the young Vladimir did not have a great deal to do with the servants. His cousin Yury was much more at ease with subordinates. Nabokov told me about how once Yury made a sortie to the servants' quarters to investigate whether the prospects for the seduction of a certain young serv-ant-girl were worth while. He returned sadly shaking his head. On the occasions when he himself was in the servant's quarters Nabo-kov was most struck and even a little puzzled by the **odd smell.**

But the paths and gardens, the patios and drives, the ponds and marshes, the grounds and the fields, the roads, the river, the bridge, in a word, all (except the villages, the servants' quarters, the local stores) of the Siversky region—the colours, the sounds, the smells—became intimately and even intensely familiar to the young Nabokov beginning at the early age of about six. His mother inculcated the virtues of sentimental remembrance in him, and he spent from four to five hours every good summer morning chasing butterflies in the woods, meadows, and bogs. The woods of North-ern Russia are beautiful (beautiful are the woods of Northern Russia). For Nabokov his love of a few particular places is so strong in some of his poetry of the 1920s that he does not fear even sentimentality, or, to put it another way, in the entire spectrum of his art it is only these early poems of place which glow with sentimental warmth and love.

The calendar and a large family supplied whatever Nabokov's own sensitivity and a happy childhood did not attend to. Though Nabokov's birthday (April 10 in the Old Style) fell in city season, his Saint's nameday, and his father's, too, of course, fell on July 15 (again, Old Style). In the Russian tradition the nameday celebration is a more important one than the actual birthday. Nabokov's mother and his sister Elena had their nameday on May 21, which fell at the beginning of the Vyra season. His brother Sergei's nameday was June 5; his sister Olga's, July 11. Moreover, V. D. Nabokov's birthday was July 8, and Elena Ivanovna's was on August 17. A summer then contained no less than six major family fêtes, which were usually celebrated with an elaborate festive picnic not unlike, Nabokov allows, those which are depicted in *Ada,* though there are some encrustations in the novel's picnics. And in addition to the fêtes at Vyra, there were also similar celebrations held at various times at Batovo and Druzhnoselie (another related estate a little farther off) to which the Nabokov children were driven.

Life in the city was quite formal, and there were restrictions of class and times. It was natural that first love should appear in the relaxed and much more open atmosphere of Vyra. That story has been told, and told very well and fully in *Speak, Memory* and Nabokov's first novel *Mary,* and there is no need to repeat it here. The romance lasted almost exactly one year, from the end of the summer of 1915 to the end of the following summer. Many years afterward the girl's sister appeared in emigration, and thereby some information as to the fate of his youthful love did reach Nabokov, but rather uncertain and secondhand.

She was one year younger than Nabokov, had at least a brother and two sisters, one a beauty very like her but slightly older and taller and slimmer. In 1915 their mother (the father was an estate manager who appears not to have figured very much in the life of his family at this time) rented a summer *dacha* for the family near the Rozhestvenskaya church. In the early part of the first summer Nabokov had his first encounter with a member of the family when he rode to the *dacha* together with his tutor to extend permission—at the same time declining to participate himself—for a soccer match that her older brother, then in officers' 103 school, wished to arrange on one of the meadows belonging to the Nabokovs. Unknown to Nabokov his future love sat high up in the branches of an apple tree and looked down on the three as they talked. Her Russian nickname, oddly enough, was the exact equivalent of the French name Lucette.

That autumn and winter Nabokov would meet her in the Tavrichesky Gardens, a park at one end of Sergievskaya Street, a handsome residential street where the family lived in a flat, perhaps belonging to some relative, for the Sh's are not listed in *All Petrograd*—no matter, Vladimir Vladimirovich never went there with her, and she never went to 47 Morskaya with him. In writing about his first romance and the at first scarcely perceptible decline that it suffered upon its transfer to St. Petersburg, Vladimir Vladimirovich seems not to have taken into account a simple term and phenomenon: summer romance.

A strange thing seems to have happened. As the two furtive young lovers went their rounds of the city's museums and parks and cinemas and other nooks of semi-privacy, the young man's love for the girl blended and evidently even got confused with his love for the cold and beautiful city without trees. The pale violet mists and light fogs of St. Petersburg, its smart trotting horses, the grey-blue of officers' greatcoats on promenade. Beautiful ladies of fashion, urchins and beggars, red-cheeked doormen and the sound of their brooms, a sombre policeman on a bridge. The cupolas of cathedrals sparkling in the pure blue and milk spring sky, and the slightly smaller churchlike edifices of the old-fashioned letter ѣ on the city's galaxy-like profusion of richly still illustrated shop signs —a laundress bending over with flatiron in hand, crossed rolls of crimson cloth, blacked boots, pineapple and grapes in an ochre chasuble, a horn of plenty, half-effaced with time, over a grocery store. The roar and clatter of the capital, the architectural patterns of frost and then the eventual victory of spring over granite and greyness, days which are clear and yet not clear, the elegant and smooth full stops of the city's squares, the creak of the barges on the splendid Neva as they press up against one another. I have decorated the preceding passage—a dreadful macédoine according to Nabokov—with pictures and images from Nabokov's early poetry. Nabokov assures me that he has **never** seen sombre policemen on bridges or heard creaking barges in St. Petersburg.

It has been said that Nabokov's generation was the most fortunate of all in the emigration. Those born even three years later than Nabokov were too young to have much of Russia to carry away with them. Those who had passed thirty had either a finished past behind them or an interrupted development which usually could never again regain its natural pulse and tempo. And the most unfortunate of all were those émigrés who had the ill luck to be born well and truly in the twentieth century (the talented poet Boris Poplavsky is the most notable representative of this grouping) and who among Russian writers constituted a pathetic and tragic lost generation. Nabokov was placed perfectly on the extreme edge of an incredibly fecund generation which experienced the loss of Russia more intensely and purely than did others and which was able somehow to use its love and its grief, its memories and its confidence to bear fruit in a void. His Russian past, Nabokov thinks, furnishes green fields behind his émigré prose. Nabokov and Khodasevich in literature; Stravinsky and Rachmaninoff in music; Chagall, Tchelitchew, and Goncharova in painting . . . What "real" country in the last half century can put forward artistic achievement significantly more important than that created by these seven in the great Russian diaspora? And behind them, an imposing corps of scientists, linguists, scholars, and lesser artists, some of whom are not usually even thought of or recognized as Russians.

What is clear beyond any doubt from an examination of Nabokov's published and unpublished youthful poetry written in the early years of the emigration is that the Russia of his childhood is everything to him—in one poem he speaks of Russia as being in the murmur of his blood and the riot of his dreams, and also as being both the goal and the beginning of his life, something which is always before him. If such poetry does little to increase Nabokov's stature as an artist, it does much to tell us where he comes from and who he really is. Churlish though he is about fate, Nabokov himself acknowledged the importance of his given moment in history to me in the strongest possible terms: —**If I had been born four years later, I wouldn't have written all those books.**

CHAPTER

4

For Pushkin the Lyceum at Tsarskoe Selo on the outskirts of St. Petersburg took the place of and finally was his family (so Pushkin himself reckoned); it was the place where Pushkin was happiest, and he attached particular importance to his memories and his friendships from those years throughout his life. Nabokov had no need of such a school experience, but it is also true that, notwithstanding the extremely respectful but somewhat supercilious way in which he refers to his school and its enforced democratism, his school was important to him, and it, too, can be found at various places in his art, furnishing, for example, the setting for the memorable soccer game in *Bend Sinister*.

Pushkin's Lyceum was one of the schools to which the young **109**

Nabokov might have been sent, but, its glorious past apart, it was now simply a school for the children of very conservative aristocratic families. It did not furnish a bad education. There were, besides, two other aristocratic secondary schools in St. Petersburg, one of which was the starting point for military careers, the other, to which V. D. Nabokov had gone, for careers in law. The only school in St. Petersburg which corresponded to the ideas and values held by Nabokov's parents was the Tenishev School, which had been founded only in 1900. Vladimir's two sisters were sent to a similar though less noted school for girls, the headmistress of which was the mother-in-law of the distinguished Russian philosopher Lossky. This was liberal St. Petersburg, and while the numbers of students were not large—a grade in the Tenishev School never contained more than thirty boys—the academic standards were high, and Nabokov is quite correct in stating that the course of study roughly equalled that of the American high school plus the first two years of college.

Prince Vyacheslav Tenishev (1844–1903) founded his school after two years of experimentation with a programme of secondary-school courses which he instituted in 1898. He gave slightly over a million rubles—a staggering sum for the times even by the standards of charitable families such as that of Nabokov's mother —for the construction of the school on Mokhavaya Street and its initial running costs. Prince Tenishev is an excellent example, from the generation preceding V. D. Nabokov's, of the dedicated and sophisticated liberal in Russian society. One of Prince Tenishev's other, more whimsical projects was the Ethnographic Bureau in St. Petersburg with branches throughout Russia engaged in the anthropological study of the Russian peasant. The Tenishev School was from the beginning very closely tied to the progressive but highly utilitarian theories, published and unpublished, held by its founding donor, and the aspects of school life which the young Vladimir found most oppressive—apart from the filthy communal towels (which are typical of the finest preparatory schools the world over)—were not chance manifestations of this or that teacher or current intellectual fashion, but rather they were some of the main principles for which the school existed. The first headmaster, Aleksandr Ostrogorsky, was a man whom Russians describe by that marvellous phrase *a luminous personality,* and he was at least as responsible as Prince Tenishev himself for the character of the school, though he did not direct it for a long time.

I have several prospectuses for the Tenishev School in the years both before and during the time Nabokov was a student there. The headmaster for most of the seventeen-year existence of the school was a certain Hermann Linstser—Nabokov had some uncomplimentary remarks to make about him to me—though in a single year during Nabokov's attendance there were two other heads. The most fleeting of them became involved in an acrimonious dispute when he accused a student of theft, and the incident flared to the point where an open manifesto written by the students, Nabokov among them, was addressed to the school's trustees; the other was the teacher of literature Vladimir Gippius, who was Nabokov's teacher. Among the early trustees and beneficiaries of the school I note a certain A. N. Strannolyubsky, the rather odd name by a strange coincidence of a completely invented minor character in *The Gift*. It seems evident, however, from the printed literature that the basic course structure and pedagogical methods of the school remained constant through changes of administration, staff, and trustees. What strikes me as a naïve though commendable passion for thoroughly modern teaching, together with perhaps a shadow of Prince Tenishev's ethnography, makes the descriptive material about the Tenishev School quite interesting reading. The student enrolment varied between slightly more than one hundred and slightly more than four hundred students towards its last years of existence. The number of students per year was held carefully in check, though the growth of the school did eventually lead to parallel classes in the early years. There were only twenty-two boys in Nabokov's class.

The class and professional background of the students' families for the school as a whole was as follows: more than a third were the children of engineers, architects, doctors, lawyers, and members of other professions; slightly over a quarter were the children of civil servants; and slightly more than a fifth of the students were the sons of merchants and factory owners. In sum, then, about eighty per cent of the students—in the literature, all of this is presented in chartly detail and with great precision—may be loosely categorized as belonging to Russia's putative middle class. There were always a handful of students who were the children of writers, painters, and teachers, never more than about the same number who were the sons of landed gentry *(pomeshchiki)*, Philistines (*meshchane*, roughly speaking, the lower middle class), and peasants. The tuition was 200 rubles a year for the youngest chil- **111**

dren, and then 325 rubles per year for semesters one through ten
—there were two semesters in each year—and 360 rubles a year
for semesters eleven to sixteen, which is the time (aged eleven and
a half) that Nabokov entered the school, in the third semester
(January–May 1911). For the times these fees were reasonably
substantial, but it did include a hot lunch, the costs of materials for
experiments in chemistry, physics, and the natural sciences, and
also the cost of the famous yearly Tenishev excursions, about
which more in a moment.

The figures on the religious backgrounds of the students are
most curious. The students of the Russian Orthodox faith—we are
told—accounted for 80.7 per cent of the total, while Roman Catholic and Protestant students totaled 10.1 per cent. But it is more
than possible that these particular figures have been given for
governmental eyes. There was strictly speaking no such thing as
an autonomous private school in pre-revolutionary Russia as all
schools were required to conform to strict governmental regulations. The most infamous of these regulations was the *protsentnaya norma,* or "Judaic quota," which fixed the percentage of
Jewish students who were permitted to attend institutions at secondary level and above at five per cent. And on page five of the
school regulations there is printed the statement: —*In accordance
with the order laid down by the Ministry of Trade and Industry*
(sic! the Tenishev School was technically a commercial institution,
and in fact some business courses were taught—this was another
stratagem devised in order to evade the infamous Minister for
Education of the period, Lev Kasso) *those of the Judaic persuasion
are accepted at a proportion of 5 per cent,* which is, however, a
footnote to the statement: —*The School accepts children of all
faiths and classes,* and is blithely contradicted by the figure of 9.2
per cent for Jewish students which occurs later on in the detailed
charts. Moreover, that figure itself is more than a little suspect.
Nabokov recalls that his class of twenty-odd boys would have from
twelve to fourteen Jews in it every year, and one of his close
friends at the school, who was an ardent Zionist (he is now an
architect living in Israel; Nabokov used to tease him for his Zion-
ism), would carefully keep count and bemoan the fact when the
number slipped to only twelve in any given year. Russian Orthodox scripture lessons were given twice a week in all grades, and
as a nominal member of the Russian Orthodox church Nabokov
had to attend these, but the Jewish and non-Orthodox boys would

go to the recreation hall during this hour, except for one Jewish boy in Nabokov's class who could not endure the noise and rough-housing and would beg the priest for permission to remain so that he could work or sleep during the lesson.

The school on Mokhovaya Street was built in a neo-Italianate style which would have been quite in keeping with many of the houses on Morskaya Street—St. Petersburg was, remember, the city of Rastrelli in its architectural tradition—and not unlike the fine Italianate buildings of the old turn-of-the-century Columbia College campus in New York City. Four stories high, the windows of the upper three stories were enclosed in extended arches which had non-functional iron-lace balconies at their bases on the (European) second floor. The building's face was (it still stands) divided into thirds by two of the nine window arches which extend to the first floor and thus give the building the appearance of a series of fine town houses. The courtyard side of the building is far less distinguished, and the three massive arches and some exposed girder arches to the side on the ground floor are rather what one associates with overhead passes and railway stations. The school's very strong emphasis on sports and exercise insured that the courtyard of the school remained perpetually trampled and brown. Above the playing field there was a sea of windows with Mondrian-like paning on the outside perimeters on three sides of the trapezoidal court, and one could see the squat dome of the school's astronomical observatory. The classrooms contained pedestal desks set at an angle with a narrow open shelf beneath and with fixed wooden seats set in paired rows. A notable feature of the school was one of the city's finest auditoriums, located on the second floor together with the student dining room, recreation hall, and a few classes. It was capable of seating slightly under five hundred people, and intellectual St. Petersburg often gathered there for concerts and important lectures. The Literary Fund with which V. D. Nabokov was so closely associated in these years held all its meetings there.

The system of examination and marking at the Tenishev School —there were oral examinations given on a continuing basis and class standing was announced in solemn assemblies with reports also made to the parents, of course—had a marvelous certainty about it which gave the school a certain flavour of eighteenth-century positivism. The over-all emphasis was not on grades so much as on scientific guidance. The school's handbook presents a 113 long and detailed essay, again replete with charts and figures, on the scientific method of classifying and guiding the young mind and body. Many of the ideas are drawn from the writings of such theorists as the social utopian Charles Fourier, elaborated and refined by German professors, and also to some degree from the works of William James (**Vilyam Dzhems**), a writer who was, by the way, much admired by V. D. Nabokov.

Personality, it is explained in the handbook, is influenced to a very large degree by body types, though these types as presented are vague enough and overlap sufficiently (Cellulose, Epithelial, Muscular, Nervous) so that, even if one is disposed to accept the classifications, there can be no easy deductions drawn, for example, about the very slender, very muscular, and somewhat nervous young Vladimir Nabokov. Temperaments were classified into phlegmatic (or passive-indifferent), sanguine, choleric, and melancholic, and basic character types were taken to be intellectual, active, emotional, and passive, which in turn are sub- and sub-sub-divided into a dizzying series of categories each of which contains up to seventeen traits and dispositions. The origins of this system are quite ancient; the modern part is the statistical analyses of the student body that follow in due course, and it is no surprise, given the class background of most of the students, that no less than 46.4 per cent of the student body—in some years more than half—are rated as basically "intellectual" in character. Very little was left to chance by the Tenishev School's liberal pedagogues—even changes in a student's handwriting are observed and taken into account. I hazard the guess that, if the mature Nabokov were temporarily his own guardian in some imaginary timelessness of the sort he is wont to write about, he would hesitate at enrolling himself in this institution so blandly and smugly dedicated to turning ten-year-old coarse egoists into intellectually alert, socially responsible altruists.

The school day lasted from nine until three and was divided into seven fifty-minute periods with half an hour for lunch. There was a forty-five-minute recreation break in late morning. When you were late for class, as Nabokov was quite frequently, he recalls, it was necessary to stand outside the door of the classroom with your arm up so that your hand showed through the glass door until the teacher deigned to admit you and your lightened or tingling arm. (This has been used by Nabokov in a novel.) In the Second

114 Class—the one in which Nabokov entered the school—the sub-

jects were chemistry, French, Russian, German, geography, physics, geometry, algebra, and history, plus Sacred History, carpentry, and drawing as minor subjects. The shop classes were taught at workbenches located in the school's basement. Nabokov recalls making many things from footstools to miniature helicopters and enjoying himself hugely amidst the odours of woodshavings and heady turpentine. Drawing was taught in a special classroom which had a ceilingful of hanging lamps with billiard shades. There was a skeleton for the study of anatomy, and when it was discovered that it was a young girl's skeleton one of Nabokov's classmates, whose motto had previously been "every man his own woman," declared himself in love with her. Frogs were dissected, mice were crushed in vacuum chambers (in other printed memoirs of the Tenishev School but not in Nabokov's memory), there was a constant smell of noxious gas in the chemistry rooms, the dust seemed to hang in suspension in the afternoon sun. It was, as Nabokov says, like all schools everywhere.

The poet Osip Mandelstam, the other illustrious alumnus of the Tenishev School, devotes a short chapter to his impressions of the school in his 1925 book *The Noise of Time*, and, oddly enough, the general tone of his remarks is in reasonably close conformity with the note of slightly sour affection which Nabokov strikes. The boys furiously playing soccer seem neither Russian nor even boyish to Mandelstam, but Cambridge undergraduates playing in England. The school costume was of an English character, and Mandelstam notes other very prominent English elements in the school such as assemblies which were conducted like miniature parliaments and a procession of Kadet speakers who, Mandelstam writes with gentle irony, *quietly whispered the constitutional poison.* Mandelstam looks upon the school and his classmates coldly and from afar (a boy from a wealthy mining family switched from dynamos to Wagner; another, *someone from the second portion of* **Dead Souls** *which Gogol burned*), but in conclusion he writes:

—*And all the same there were good boys at Tenishev. They were made out of the stuff of the children in Serov's paintings. They were little ascetics, monks in their own puerile monastery where in their notebooks, instruments, lovely glass flasks, and German books there was more spiritual sustenance and internal order than in the lives of the grown-ups outside.*   **115**

Mandelstam came to the Tenishev School once while Nabokov was there to give a poetry reading. These readings were organized informally by students rather than by the school's administration. Many if not most of the well-known St. Petersburg poets came at one time or another, including Nikolai Gumilyov, about whose death by Bolshevik firing squad Nabokov wrote a short poem in emigration, and Vladislav Khodasevich, who in the 1930s was to become a good literary friend of Nabokov's. The readings were frequently held in the hallways (which was only the slightest indignity to the arts—like the rest of the school the hallways were elegant and quite wide) with the interested students seated on wooden benches as the particular poet stood and recited his verse to them. But Nabokov, characteristically, never bothered to attend: —**I didn't go to Tenishev readings. I thought my own poems were better than all those poets.** The only exception allowed in his immature but still remarkable hauteur was Blok.

This same naïveté is the reason Nabokov gives for the private publication of his own poems in 1916 and then again in a collection together with the poems of a schoolmate, Andrei Balashov, which appeared surprisingly and belatedly in early 1919 just before Nabokov left Russia: quite simply, he didn't know anything about publishers. One of his poems was published in a "thick journal," the editor of which had once courted one of his aunts; he had simply mailed in the poem, and its appearance in 1916 marks his very nominal debut in the pre-revolutionary world of Russian letters.

Nabokov's study of literature at the Tenishev School began with lectures on the historical study of literature and the place of Russian literature in the European context. Much of that year was devoted to ancient Russian literature, the Byzantine influence, ancient chronicles, life in medieval Rus, *The Song of Igor's Campaign,* and the year ended with the study of the Petrine era and Kantemir, Lomonosov, and Trediakovsky. The study of writers was preceded by the traditional *Leben und Werk* pattern, and in this way the biographies and chief works of Derzhavin, Fonvizin, Karamzin, Zhukovsky, Krylov, and Griboedov seem to have been covered at more or less a university level of study. In the Fourteenth Semester—that is, in what would be called the Junior or Third year in most English-speaking secondary schools—Pushkin was studied in depth. The lectures included Pushkin's ties with Sentimentalism; his relations with contemporaries, particularly

Venevetinov and Chaadaev; an over-all analysis of the features of his prose; and, of course, detailed study of his masterpiece *Eugene Onegin,* and also *The Bronze Horseman* and *Boris Godunov.* The political and social implications of Pushkin's art are not unduly stressed, though Belinsky's pronouncements on Pushkin are studied. In the final year much the same sort of coverage was given to Gogol and Lermontov, following which Belinsky was studied in some detail; the year ended with a rather hurried potpourri consisting of selected poems and works by Tiutchev, Fet, Aksakov, Nekrasov, and Turgenev, which is about as far into the contemporary as the syllabus went. It will be noticed that both Tolstoy and Dostoevsky are missing from the syllabus, though some of Tolstoy's simple short works were studied in the lower-form years, which both verifies and explains Nabokov's seemingly incredible and capricious—to a Russian—statement years later in the presence of Bunin and Khodasevich (as recounted in the Berberova memoirs *The Italics Are Mine*) that he had never read Tolstoy's *Sevastopol Tales.* But Nabokov says he did read all Tolstoy's major works (and Russian poets from Derzhavin to Nadson) in volumes from the old Rukavishnikov library at Vyra, mainly on rainy days. And, in any event, one should not make too much of what Nabokov formally studied at school since he was taken up with other interests in his final two years and did not do as well as he might have.

Other aspects of the Tenishev curriculum are not particularly noteworthy. The French course—there were two streams, and Nabokov of course was in the advanced one—paid particular attention, among more or less modern authors, to Chateaubriand, Victor Hugo, de Vigny, and Musset. His long acquaintance with the work of Chateaubriand might conceivably be in some measure a contributory factor to the rather exalted position, puzzling to some, which Nabokov assigns that writer in his commentaries to *Eugene Onegin.* In the history course there was a detailed study of the English parliamentary system and of the rights and responsibilities of the Russian Dumas, a subject matter which may have been unique among Russian secondary schools. Going even a little farther than that, Nabokov recalls, the history teacher (who was, with Gippius, one of the most popular teachers because, like Gippius, he treated the boys as if they were adults) caused himself great difficulties when he assigned the essay topic "What Life in a Republican Russia Would Be Like," and some parents whose liberalism stopped far short of such possibilities dobbed him in. In the **117** end he was forced to resign. All things considered, it is strange that English was not taught at the Tenishev School, and we recall how Nabokov irritated his teachers by sprinkling his essays with foreign phrases. But the Tenishev School, for all its Anglomania, was a very Russian school in many respects, one of the causes of the difficulties which the young Nabokov, not then "sufficiently Russian" (that would come later, in England), had at the school.

Of important "influences"—culpable among politicians, expected among writers—upon Vladimir Nabokov from this phase of his life I am inclined to look, more than to the school or his schoolmates, to the fiery and red-haired teacher of literature, Vladimir Gippius, though, heaven knows, theirs was far from a serene master-and-disciple relationship. Nabokov vehemently objects and thinks it is bad enough that the Tenishev School inflicted Gippius upon him in the first place without having his biographer repeat the process over half a century later. In *Speak, Memory* Nabokov mentions his great admiration for him (not too many people Nabokov has met in his life have been singled out for this direct praise—the philosopher Whitehead is another who comes to mind), and also the savage mockery he had to endure when Gippius brought a copy of the 1916 book of poems to class and read selected passages aloud with commentary. Nabokov had a hard time with that little book. The important literary critic Kornei Chukovsky, who was friendly with V. D. Nabokov, was given a copy and wrote the boy a polite letter of praise, enclosing in the envelope as if by mistake, the *chernovik,* or rough draft of that same letter, expressing a rather less polite opinion.

Vladimir Gippius was an aesthete in his literary tastes, while in political matters he was extremely leftish. One of the essays Nabokov remembers writing for Gippius (it was an after-school punishment) was on the Decembrist revolt of 1825 and the February events of 1916. Gippius was in his late thirties when he first became Nabokov's teacher and just turned forty in 1916. In his youth Gippius associated closely with the mystical decadent poet Aleksandr Dobroliubov, a precursor of the Symbolist movement in Russia, about whom he wrote an excellent but awkwardly affectionate memoir-critique after that poet, as the phrase goes, vanished into the people. Gippius himself never enjoyed any success with his own poetry. The scattered poems by him which I have

118

been able to obtain do not justify Nabokov's preference for his poetry over that of his famous cousin Zinaida Gippius, Symbolist poetess and wife of another well-known poet and writer of the time, Dmitri Merezhkovsky. Not that he courted fame. He published his poetry under his own name and also two pseudonyms, V. Bestuzhev and V. Neledinsky, and thus his separate poems and four miniscule collections seemed to be the work of three poets. One of his collections coincided in its appearance with the death of his eight-year-old child, and he bought up the edition himself and presumably destroyed it. Through the literary salon of his cousin and her husband, Vladimir Gippius mingled with the poets —Blok, Sologub, Minsky—of the Silver Age of Russian poetry in the early moments of their fame; later, after 1909 when the Symbolist movement gave way to the Acmeist movement with its precise and concrete imagery, Gippius associated himself with that movement, but here, too, he remained not even a proper secondary figure but very much on the outskirts. His only moment of real notice as a poet came when he published a poem entitled *To Alexander Blok* in response to a poem by Blok, and Blok replied with a short poem titled *To Vladimir Bestuzhev*. Gippius then wrote a series of poems in reply to Blok's reply, but there the matter ended. My last bibliographical notation for him is in 1921, an article on "The Theater and the People." He died in 1941, presumably at the beginning of the seige of Leningrad, which is also the date on which his son Vasily Gippius, a scholar attached to the Pushkinsky Dom in Leningrad and the author of one of the best books ever written on Gogol, purportedly died. I should mention, too, that one of Gippius's ancestors is alleged to have engaged in speculation based upon deceased serfs and to have been a prototype for Gogol's Chichikov.

The strength of Vladimir Gippius was in his capacity not as poet or critic but more simply that as a custodian of literary taste, a passionate dilettante. His own taste had been formed in the propitious period when poets such as Tiutchev and Fet were being rediscovered and correctly understood for the first time. As a young man he was profoundly influenced, by his own testimony, by the work of Nietzsche and Dostoevsky. Between 1880 and 1920, from pure art to socially committed art, it would appear that there were few if any artistic currents of his time which did not touch Vladimir Gippius. Mandelstam wrote of the taste and manner of Gippius:

—V. V. Gippius [was] a teacher of literature who taught the children a much more interesting science than literature—literary malice. For what reason was he carrying on so before little children? Do children require the thorn of pride or the serpentine hiss of literary anecdotage? . . . He had a bestial relation to literature as though it were the sole source of animal warmth. He warmed himself by the side of literature, he rubbed up against its coat with his bristly red hair and unshaven cheeks. He was a Romulus who hated the she-wolf which gave him suck, and, hating, he taught others to love her. . . . Beginning with Radishchev and Novikov, Vladimir Vasilevich established even that far back a personal relationship with Russian writers, a malicious lover's acquaintanceship full of exalted envy and jealousy, light disrespect, and the consanguine disrespect which one is accustomed to find within families. . . .

Yet it should be noted that Mandelstam dedicated two of his essays to the memory of his teacher. Nabokov remembers him spitting out iambs, and always wearing two waistcoats (one grey, the other beige) overlapping one another. All testimony I have found agrees that Gippius was a difficult man who frequently quarrelled with his students over trifles. There were strange things about him. He was terrified of cats, and once a student drew a cat on the board before the lesson which sent Gippius bolting from the room.

It would seem that Gippius did not much like the young Nabokov. Once, when Nabokov was playing with a schoolmate in the halls, where the boys all played tag and other games, too, in the breaks between classes, their shouts and squeals and laughter garbled by the sections of wooden boardwalk laid down to protect the floors which could be manipulated to make the most interesting noises, Gippius came walking along at the wrong moment, and the small, nervous man was hit squarely in the belly by a disconnected chair disc with which Nabokov and his friend had been trying to behead one another. There was another equally serious mishap when, on a dare from another classmate (which was quickly turned into a ten-ruble purse), Nabokov misjudged both the width and the depth of a small decorative pond at the school and in he went, dressed, he recalls, as for a duel. The fountain contained large shiny goldfish whose sickly flesh was more white than gold. A moment later the headmaster came by. **—What have you been doing? —I fell,** declared the dripping poet and gamester, but

Nabokov was subjected to a summary trial at which it was decided that because he was a good skier he couldn't have slipped in the way he claimed, and he was sent home that day. The worst offence of all was probably the contents of his essay for Gippius on the February events, which infuriated the leonine teacher to such a degree that he simply said in a low voice and using the—in this instance—terribly offensive and familiar Russian form of address: —**Ty ne Tenishevets!** [—**You're not a Tenishev boy!**] And also, of course, there was Nabokov's refusal to take part in extracurricular activities, his tendency in his last years at the school to coast on his native intelligence and be satisfied with less than the highest grades, and in his final year the protracted and extremely suspicious, as far as Gippius was concerned (and rightly), absences due to illness necessitated by his romance of that winter.

It is my judgment—and nothing more than that—that Vladimir Gippius exerted as great a formative influence, and in much the same oblique and personal way, on the young Vladimir Nabokov as he had years earlier on Mandelstam. Perhaps I can better put it this way: If Vladimir Nabokov ever had a teacher in any traditional sense of the term in his life, that teacher was Vladimir Gippius. From Gippius, I submit, Nabokov learned a manner, a literary posture, which to a certain extent he has never abandoned. There was much about Gippius which Nabokov did not need or want, of course. But it does not take a very gifted ear or imagination to hear the soft echoes of Gippius's proprietarial devotion to literature and easy viciousness of judgment in much of what Nabokov has said and written about books and their authors.

The warm disdain with which Nabokov then and later, in *Speak, Memory,* reacted to much about the Tenishev School was as nothing compared with the anguish caused him by the school's obligatory yearly outings. The excursion had for a number of years been a popular fashion among the *gymnasia* and other secondary schools of St. Petersburg. They were at that time considered a necessary feature of a secondary education, but in practice they were simply very ambitious and farflung outings. The outing took place after the final examinations in early May, though there were also some excursions to points in and near the city held during the school year, and their attendance was obligatory for promotion from one grade to another. Some of the excursions went as far afield as boating trips down the Volga and to the Crimea, but they were all conducted with exceptional parsimony so that the cost **121** per student rarely if ever exceeded sixty to seventy kopecks a day. Discount tickets on railroads and boats were often procured for the group, and they usually passed the night sleeping in blanket rolls on the deck of a steamer or crowded together in a large room or two of a simple hotel. Students were expressly forbidden to bring any funds of their own. It was Nabokov's minor misfortune to fall into the long excursion to Finland.

The excursion for Finland left in early May. I do not have the precise duration of the expedition—they varied considerably from year to year—except that it was at least four days long and no more than ten days. The morning train left St. Petersburg for Imatra, and after Vyborg the two classes changed to a special car provided by the Finnish railways which was coupled to the train's rear. The trip lasted nearly six hours during which time the boys joked, jostled, and gathered together on the little rear platform of the train. Although a boy could be sent home for disruptive behaviour, the teachers' reports seem to indicate that high spirits and *èkspansivnost'* were the rule, and it was noted especially in Finland, where the boys' behaviour seemed to the masters to contrast with the constrained natures of the Finns, who, they thought, reacted to the troupe with a slight air of condescension. A lecture was given to the boys in Imatra, as it was at most places, but this did not take very long. A nearby waterfall was more interesting. For a small sum a man went over the waterfall in a barrel. From Imatra on the Russian border there was a forced march—the first of many —of about twenty kilometers to another town, and then a long steamship ride northwards into the heart of Finnish lake country. There were sporadic lectures on the ice age, the "Finnish question" (a delicate way of referring to a Russian imperial possession), and observations of Finnish peasant life.

Nabokov came with his butterfly net, but the beginning of May is a bad time for butterflies in Finland, so the trip was not very promising for him. Moreover, the net did cause him some difficulties. The escorting teacher was a naturalist, but his pupil's intense interest in butterflies struck him as a little bizarre. —He should have been rather pleased to have a young boy who knew everything about butterflies. He didn't like it. . . . It would have been all right if I had been a group collecting butterflies. But one boy who was totally immersed in collecting butterflies—that was abnormal. For this and another reason that Finnish expedition received no endorsement from Nabokov:

122

—It was a horrible trip, horrible trip. Horrible. I remember it was the first time in my more or less conscious life when I spent one day without a bath. It was terrible. I felt filthy. Nobody else seemed to mind.

The difficulty was that the early part of May in the Saimaa region of Finland where the group went was not only a poor time for butterflies, but still far too cold for anything but proper bathing facilities. Nabokov had a far more pleasant excursion to Finland in the winter of 1916 when his mother took him to Imatra for a short vacation to recuperate from his second bout with pneumonia. One of his more serious romances began there, with a young woman who was six years older than he, a romance which by chance was taken up again briefly in England some years later.

Of the friends Nabokov made at the Tenishev School the two who were closest to him were Samuil Rozov (the Israeli architect) and Savely Kyandzhuntsev, a fat, indolent, and charming Armenian, whose wealthy uncle, years later, was to sponsor the émigré newspaper on which Vladislav Khodasevich served as literary critic.

Rozov was the smallest boy in the class, but he was ferociously brave, and in soccer games he would throw himself upon their most feared classmate, P—. P— was the son of a carrier who had about a hundred St. Petersburg horse-cabs and lorries. He would occasionally amuse himself by racing through the streets of St. Petersburg astride a wagon which he drove standing. He had been left back more than a few times and was five to six years older than the other boys in the class whom, without exception, he terrorized, as, for that matter, he terrorized women teachers on the staff. Nabokov had several unpleasant encounters with P—, one of which was occasioned by the bully's hearing that he had been taking boxing lessons and demanding a premature exhibition. Eventually the boys were spared when P— ran off to fight in World War I in a Hussar detachment. Rozov was one of the most popular boys in the class and also the head boy academically. Nabokov recalls him in contemplation tugging at the corner of his mouth with one finger pressed against his nostril in such a way that it made one side of his nose turn white. He very frequently helped his classmates in various ways, and once a few minutes prior to an oral examination he helped Nabokov on a subject for which Nabokov had not prepared. As luck would have it, it was precisely the material which he had been listening to Rozov tell him about a few **123** minutes earlier that they questioned him on, and the examinee answered in such detail and at such length that the examiners had all they could do to shut him up. Years later Rozov visited Nabokov in Switzerland, and on a wet autumnal day in July the two old friends went walking in the mountains in Zermatt amid masses of wildflowers while behind them a German photographer snapped pictures seemingly without pause. It was on that walk that the picture of Nabokov smiling elfinly in a wet hooded parka, perhaps now the best-known picture of him, was taken.

Andrei Balashov, the boy with whom Nabokov published a book of poems in 1918, was not so close to Nabokov. Nabokov remembers his squint. Balashov, who died only a few years ago, also went into emigration (the overwhelming majority of Tenishev boys did, though an odd commissar or two did emerge from the school ranks). He fought in the Civil War, and the one collection of verse which he published subsequently consisted largely of poems devoted to his regiment. He was a bachelor, tall, slender, and with curly hair which retained its curl even when it went quite grey. Like Yury von Traubenberg he cultivated the air of the hussar-poet. He had no proper profession in emigration, but he dealt in antiquarian books. He died of consumption in Belgium. It was not an atypical émigré life.

Another classmate with whom Nabokov was rather friendly was the nephew of a very well-known historian. He spent the greater part of his life in emigration on the Ivory Coast in Africa, but Nabokov met him again in Berlin and then again in 1961 when he lay sick and drunk and dying in Nice. —**He told me many interesting things. —It wasn't interesting. —You weren't interested. But I had a good time with him. We played a lot of chess.** Forty-four years before Nabokov had been sitting at a table with that student at the Nabokov townhouse, and shooting could be heard in the background on Liteiny Street as they played chess.

The other boys have comic parts. A student who suffered so for the sophisticated sexual associations that were made with his name. Two other students, both of whom stuttered, though in rather different ways, and whom the boys liked to bring together for that very reason in order to enjoy the contrapuntal effect. One student was the joker of the class, the suitor of the skeleton and the master of coarse subjects. His gentle immaturity was untouched by time. Twenty years later Nabokov met him in Paris where he ran a movie house. He found that he had not changed physically in the slightest in all those years apart from a certain added tinge of blue in his complexion, and, as they watched films together, his former classmate would become frantic with excitement and suspense and even shout out warnings to the actors on the screen.

There is in Nabokov a far greater store of affectionate memory in connection with his Tenishev days than is apparent from what he has written in *Speak, Memory.* A long letter has recently come to light that Nabokov wrote in response to one which Samuil Rozov wrote him in 1937. Nabokov's reply was written on September 4 at the Hôtel des Alpes, where the Nabokovs stayed briefly before moving on to more permanent quarters for the winter at a boardinghouse in Menton. Written in ink in a small hand the letter closely covers three foolscap-size pages of thin stationery on both sides. In its length and its detail it is unique among the preserved letters of Nabokov's first émigré period in Europe.

Nabokov gently reproaches his friend for having written to him using the formal mode of address, for, he declares, he is one of the very few people with whom he would like always to remain on the more intimate informal form of address. Rozov's letter, which has not been preserved, was full of reminiscences of the Tenishev School, and Nabokov responds in kind, telling Rozov that he has always separated people into two categories, the rememberers and the non-rememberers, the former, of course, being infinitely superior to the latter. He remembers how the two of them used to be fond of visiting the recreation hall for the pre-school class where they would watch them twittering and darting about like little birds while the grey fluff of the master's head sailed up and down the aisles among them. Nabokov strains his memory in the very process of writing (the same stylistic trick he employs in *Speak, Memory* to bring back the name of the dachshund) and triumphantly brings forth the name and patronymic of that master, Nikolai Platonych. Nabokov sees the small and clear-and-bright-eyed Rozov as having been the school's Benjamin, and he confesses that he was a little bit envious of the way in which everyone loved him and how casually he reacted to this affection, almost as if he didn't notice.

Nabokov recalls their first laboratory experiments—the sprouting pea, grape sugar, blue starch, the wonder of litmus paper. And then in later years, the teacher whose demonstrations never worked, but who would always cheat to obtain the desired results. **125**

(This same teacher once astonished their class when on the day of a Russian victory at Przemysl in World War I he suddenly sat down at a piano and began to play the national anthem.) Another teacher is vividly remembered wiping the blackboard with a specially moistened sponge and then drawing with incredible care divinely rounded ciphers on the still-shining background. He also recalls another teacher, the geography master, who could not control his class and finally could stand no more—he went to the window, where he stood softly crying and rubbing the window with his finger like a small child. Nabokov says that he had no part in that, but there was an occasion when another geography teacher, whose manner displeased Nabokov, misspelled Nile (Nil) in Roman letters on the board, and Nabokov went to the board when he was momentarily absent and conspicuously made the correction. —Chto ty nadelal?! Ty ego obidel, his classmates reprimanded him. —What did you do?! You've humiliated him.

Rozov had in his letter recalled the taste of their constant cabbage and meat pies. Nabokov in his turn remembered other lunchtime details such as the classmate who had a passion for salt, and the yoghurt desserts which they ate with aluminium spoons. Once, he recalled, they were served a new variety of yoghurt, and while they ate a representative of the firm which promoted the dessert walked up and down among the tables observing the boys' reaction. They all, except Rozov, who grasped the situation and the man's anxiety, purposely made disgusted spitting noises as they ate it.

The two boys seem to have classified many of their classmates according to animal similarities. There was a fish. There was a good frog. Nabokov remembered how it was that he first heard of the existence of houses in which beautiful women give themselves to anyone who wishes. He even was able to recall the precise circumstances and place where this occurred, in a cab as they were passing the Singer Sewing Machine store in St. Petersburg. Nabokov's most vivid memory was of the bully P—, dressed in black and with pendulous arms, sloughing steps, and an ever-present odour about him, an odour of fate. He was a caveman worried by the reason for his very existence. Nabokov asserted that P— was the only person in his life whom he had been afraid of, and even twenty years later he sometimes saw P— falling upon him in nightmares. In the end, according to Nabokov, this student began (circa 1915) to behave extremely warmly towards him and oppressed him with this friendship, founded upon admiration for Nabokov's goalkeeping, even more than he used to with his belligerence.

Nabokov's recollection of football games at the Tenishev School—the feel of the ground underfoot, the sting of the ball, a particular player positioning the ball for a goal with his slender but incredibly powerful legs, the ball receding into the sky after P—'s explosive kick—are filled with emotion. He regrets that he has given too many details of his school life, the soccer games especially, to his art. Neither Nabokov's account of his life as a schoolboy in Russia in *Speak, Memory* nor the private letter, different though they are in emotional tone, need be discounted. In different ways they are both true records, and taken together they confirm at least that Nabokov has certainly never grown indifferent to his days (six days a week, from September 1 until May 15) at the liberal and strictly progressive school on the Street of Mosses. It is, however, also true, as Nabokov's wife was quick to point out, that: **—He has grown more reserved. He would never write a letter like that now.**

One of the older Nabokov servants, Aleksei, put the plate of meat, cold, on the table and then simply went away. Russia, the Russia of old at any rate, ceased to exist except as a golden source of inspiration and memory or an intriguing historical puzzle.

Nabokov's cousin Yurik came to live with them at 47 Morskaya. The house was still very busy, but the callers now had a grim urgency about them. The situation in Petrograd was very nearly out of control. Once one of V. D. Nabokov's sisters had happened upon Lenin haranguing an enthusiastic crowd of peasants, returned soldiers, and workers. **—Let him talk till he is tired, and then he will stop,** V. D. Nabokov told her with ill-concealed disdain. By November, of course, it became necessary, on very short notice, to send the family South. Had they remained in the city the two older boys would very likely have been conscripted into the Bolshevik Army. In the provinces of Russia the Bolsheviks were still far from in the ascendancy, and it is reasonably fair to say that at least half the population (probably much more) of outlying Russia had resisted the revolutionary intoxication of Bolshevik extremism and backed the Provisional Government of Kerensky. That is merely speculation—there was not to be an election to test **127** the mood of the nation. But in Petrograd there was in government circles only talk and tantrums—Kerensky himself was particularly given to these as a political device—and political posing. The real and potential splits even within the three liberal parties (one of the reasons which lead one to think that it was a chimerical hope to have expected the Kadets to join ranks that night in Berlin six years later) were serious enough that in my judgment the Provisional Government probably would not have had the capability of governing even if it had not been severely hampered by the inept leadership of Kerensky. While Russia writhed in the throes of revolution the liberals talked and talked, and when the Bolsheviks got tired of it they stopped their talk by force.

V. D. Nabokov was an exemplary figure in those days with his famous restraint and sense of order. He coolly risked his life, and his bravery is all the greater since we can clearly see from his own masterful account of the chaos that was the Provisional Government (in his posthumously published memoir *The Provisional Government*) that he himself knew how hopeless it all was. The Russian liberals were probably not first in fault, even if, as the saying went, they did not remove their white gloves in time to fight.

V. D. Nabokov finally made the judgment that it was necessary to join his family in the Crimea. There had been a search conducted at the house one day in his absence, and it was assumed (correctly, one of my sources confirms) that there was an order for his arrest. After a particularly perilous day at the Constituent Assembly he gave some instructions by telephone to the few remaining servants and made his way directly to the railroad station, where by a fantastic fluke of luck for those days he was able to purchase a first-class ticket to the Crimea, though he did not arrive there quite as easily as that. Because of the haste with which they had had to leave the city the Nabokovs arrived in the Crimea literally penniless. They did have some jewelry which was to stand them in good stead in England, but that was all. But it so happened that the daughter of Nabokov's friend and closest political ally among the Kadets, Petrunkevich, had married Count Panin, the owner of a beautiful and vast villa in the Crimea.

The Nabokovs were invited to stay in one of the two or three smaller villas which were a part of the Panin estate. The villa had courtly gardens similar to the gardens of large estates on the Riviera, but these gardens, Nabokov recalls, were even more spacious and green than their Mediterranean cousins. There were a large number of cypresses and other imported trees. However, for all the beauty of that particular estate's gardens and in general of all the gardens and parks of that coastal area with their Italianate vegetation, there was very little interesting butterfly activity in those low-lying regions. In his sixteen-month stay in southern Russia he made six sorties of varying distance into central and northern Crimea, chiefly in March and August 1918, and among the places he visited was the legendary Bakhchisarai, famed for Pushkin's mellifluous poem and the residence in centuries past of Tartar Khans.

The steppes of the Crimean peninsula, usually either parched or snowbound, gradually rise until they form a chain of mountains extending from the Cape of Kherson (near Sevastopol) to Theodosia on the other side of Yalta. Nabokov's most important collecting grounds were the rocky slopes of the mountain Ai Petri and the Yaila region, hilly pastures on the northerly side of it and the entire range. There were virtually no roads in the Yaila, and one had to ascend following trails upwards through pine woods. Southwards, on the rocky side, the ascent was more difficult because of the greater steepness. He had adventures in those mountains. Once he was taken for a spy in the guise of a naturalist. Some of these Crimean episodes, by the way, were significantly altered and incorporated in Nabokov's novel *Glory*, one of his three most autobiographical Russian novels in a thematic sense (the other two are *Mary* and *The Gift*). Though the author himself, somewhat to my surprise, I'll confess, invited me to mine material for the Crimean period of his life from that novel, he later withdrew his invitation. As it happens, we have a much more matter-of-fact chronicle of certain of those Crimean days because the seventy-seven species of butterfly and more than a hundred species of moth which he captured, in all literally hundreds of insects, formed the basis for his first published scientific paper on butterflies, "A Few Notes on Crimean Lepidoptera," which appeared in the English journal *The Entomologist* in 1923; and therein one may gather a great many specific if inert biographical details such as the fact that on June 3, 1918, Nabokov was on the summit of Ai Petri, where he captured a specimen of **Cupido minimus.** That is the sort of biography Nabokov much favours. . . .

At their residence on the Panin estate everyone was on edge because the region was, though loosely and confusedly, under **129**

Bolshevik control. V. D. Nabokov was living under the ingenious pseudonym Dr. Nabokov. The men often had to guard the house at night. Nabokov has written of this in *Speak, Memory.* On one occasion their house was searched by Bolsheviks, and fate played a trick even more ingenious than V. D. Nabokov's alias because one of the Soviet searchers was also named Nabokov. That search passed uneventfully because the Nabokovs' former chauffeur who had briefly joined the family —knew how to talk to him.

Then the Germans came, and after that the Crimea passed miraculously to the Whites. Life became gay again. That exuberant normalcy was the last flush of Russia's fatal illness, but few thought that at the time. A regional provisional government was formed, and V. D. Nabokov was named to the post his father before him had had in slightly simpler and better times, Minister of Justice. The post was in some respects a nominal as well as ephemeral one, because the Crimea was not so very normal in those final few months as to have an effective judicial system, but it was important to the Nabokov family because it meant that they had some money for the first time. V. D. Nabokov also received some financial help from two or three bankers who had managed their affairs rather better and who generously offered to loan him money simply because of the enormous amounts which V. D. Nabokov had had in their banks.

Because of his position in the regional government V. D. Nabokov was entitled to housing on the grounds of Livadia, which had been the tsar's estate in the Crimea. The governess Evgenia Khofeld, who was to be Elena Ivanovna's lifelong companion in Prague, was with the family and effectively in charge of running the household. There the young Nabokov had access to a sumptuous private library (with a librarian—a saintly librarian, says Nabokov—who was horrified at the prospect of the revolution leaving fingermarks on the books in his charge), and there, too, his Crimean butterfly collection remained when they left the Crimea. It is a collection which Nabokov thinks might conceivably have fared better than the more important one at Vyra and could today be part of a museum collection in the Soviet Union. Imagining another life for himself, one in which he had been forced to remain behind in Russia, Nabokov thinks that he would have lived quietly and even with a certain amount of distinction as an entomologist attached to some Soviet museum or institute.

130   Nabokov's first modest literary success came in the Crimea. He

translated the words for a song from German for a concert singer who was the wife of a friend of his father's, and the rendition was much praised in social and literary circles. His poetic activity had been disturbed but not disrupted by the events of the preceding year. One of the last things Nabokov had done before leaving St. Petersburg was a translation of Emile Verhaeren's poem *Les Voyageurs*, and he reworked his translation in the summer of 1918. It and some of his own poems of that time may well have been published in a Crimean newspaper. Nabokov has notebooks of poems written in St. Petersburg which, it would appear, he was readying for publication. The collection was to have been called *Open Windows* and was to have contained fifty-six poems. Scrawled in the back of this particular notebook is a careful auditing of the contents of the hundred and seventy-two poems which he wrote in the thirteen-month period ending in July 1917. There are thirty-one poems dedicated to his first love; thirty-nine poems dedicated to the young woman he met in Finland; twenty-four poems relating to events of the day; fifty-two, about nature; and twenty-six, about himself. The specific category of each poem has not been indicated, but Nabokov himself has not been about to aid in the identification. The list does conclusively confirm to me that a fair number of the early poems are *quite* autobiographical, though perhaps more in their conveyance of mood than in rendering specific incident. In his autobiography Nabokov has spoken of how he first felt the pangs of exile in the Arabian-night atmosphere of Southern Russia. In the notebook poems of this period there is an air of peace and rich colour. Nature appears wrapped in soft myths. In the long poem *The Crimea* which he wrote in London in 1921, the region is spoken of as a rose which has been presented to him by the Almighty, and a place in which Pushkin stood at his side and smiled at him. There is no sense of the war which raged around and finally throughout the area.

There was a lively café literary life in Yalta. There were concerts and even organized theatre. Nabokov himself acted (—**I may have been paid. I was certainly paid**) in a production of *The Betrayal* by the playwright Arthur Schnitzler. Letters were thrown in Nabokov's face, he fought a duel, and was killed. He has written in *Speak, Memory* of how, offstage, he continued his romance begun in Vyra by sporadic post while betraying his love in the loose and festival-like atmosphere in which he found himself.

Concurrently with the Russian revolution, Russian literature, **131** before that essentially a literature of two cities, benefited from an influx of vitality and warmth from the South as best represented by writers such as Yury Olesha and Isaac Babel. While he was in the Crimea the young Nabokov did meet on numerous occasions and become quite friendly with the estimable poet Maksimilian Voloshin, who was born in Southern Russia (in 1877) and who had been living for some years in the little village of Koktebel', which is a short distance from Theodosia. Voloshin was the Crimea's resident poet. A decade earlier his poetry had won him if not fame, at least distinction among his fellow poets, the Russian Symbolists, who congregated on Wednesdays at the famous St. Petersburg literary salon run by the poet-scholar Vyacheslav Ivanov. Though he is not usually identified as a Symbolist poet, Voloshin had strong ties with Western culture and was the first to translate writers such as Henri de Régnier and Barbey d'Aurevilly into Russian; he had travelled widely and for some time studied to be a painter; and in the period after 1917, which was when he wrote some of his most important poetry, he advocated acceptance of the revolution in a spirit of quasi-mystical quietude, and he also spoke for the brother-hood of all Russians in spite of the passions of civil war. There were those who counted him a great poet.

Nabokov met Voloshin through his father, who had been on friendly terms with him through his work on the Literary Fund in St. Petersburg. Voloshin entertained the young Nabokov as he did everyone. He was famous for his cordiality. He was a massive man but moved with great lightness and grace. He had the head of a friendly fury, masses of grey hair blowing in all directions in the often stiff Crimean breezes, and a beard which seemed to grow right up to his grey eyes. His Crimean house was a large but unpretentious sprawling seaside cottage. From the window of his study, Karadag, a mountain rising by the sea, looked very like a profile of his own head. Voloshin did not leave with the other Russians in 1919, and he accepted the harshness and finally the horror of life in the Soviet Union with quiet courage. When he died in 1932, Nabokov recalled, in a letter, that it was Voloshin who had taught him how to write poetry.

Nabokov recalls little of his Crimean meetings with Voloshin except that he was very interested in and kind to him, and that they spent many hours together, mainly in a Yalta Tartar café, discussing poetry and sipping wine. Nabokov remembers Voloshin
132   once declaiming in this café at night while the sea boomed only

a few yards away. And he does remember that it was through Voloshin that he first became acquainted with the metrical theories of Andrei Bely, which is important in Nabokov's intellectual biography. Bely was one of the most prominent members of the "younger generation" of Russian Symbolists, a wild and perhaps deliberately immature but always brilliant artist. (In more recent years Nabokov has ranked him beside Kafka and Joyce.) Bely was the son of a prominent mathematics professor, and his articles on versification are frequently illustrated with highly abstruse diagrams.

Nabokov acknowledges in his *Notes on Prosody* that it was Bely who first noted in a book published in 1910 that the half-stresses in a given poet's work may be connected to form geometric figures, and that these figures have a tendency to be repetitive for that poet. Bely's half-stresses become Nabokov's scuds in *Notes on Prosody.* It was only to be expected that Bely's theoretical works would appeal to the young Nabokov, vulnerable then as now to the ideal of joining fact and fancy, and in his poetic notebooks of the Crimean period one observes many of these diagrams on a page facing a poem. In Nabokov's case the usual geometric figure is a spaced series of triangles descending a line. To make them more impressive, his sister remembers, they were sometimes drawn in coloured pencil. In at least a few cases the secret figure is an important part of the poem—in an early poem titled *The Great Bear,* for example, the diagram of scuds forms a picture of that constellation. It is not at all unusual to find as here that even a scholarly work by the mature Nabokov has its taproot in his far-off youth.

The end of the little oasis of pleasure which living in the Crimea had provided was first signalled by Yurik's death. Youthful abandon and savage conflict had existed in close contiguity for so many months that it had almost come to seem that things might go on like that indefinitely. Even a severe toothache in May 1918 —the beginning of a lifetime of dental trouble—became the pretext for a poem in those heightened, slightly unreal times. There was no clear line of battle in Russia, and no one on any side really had sure knowledge of the outcome of the civil war.

Yury von Traubenberg relished the prospect of death in battle. As it happened he had just received his commission before he came to the Crimea, and his regiment was fighting in North Crimea. In one of his regiment's encounters a Red machine-gun nest 133 was decimating its cavalry, and the young Baron von Traubenberg made the request: —**Allow me to attack.** He galloped ahead, and his forehead was cleavered by a line of bullets. It was a senseless death, and it derived too directly from the Mayne Reid stories that he and Nabokov had so loved to read and enact a few years before, but in his own terms it was perfect. The death was a shock to the aristocracy and especially to the aristocratic youth of the province in peril, at a time when mere death and catastrophe had become mundane, essentially private matters. —**Your fine friend has been killed,** Nabokov says he was quietly told, in one of the two poems which he wrote in memory of his friend. He was a pallbearer. A large and very solemn funeral procession came from the church to the Yalta quay where there was a line of British soldiers (—**It was a nice gesture after all**) standing at attention. A first-rate military funeral band played. Only a few weeks before, a phalanx of Nabokov cousins, Yury among them, brought together for the first time in such numbers, had strolled briskly along that same broad quay arm in arm in the breeze.

Nabokov actually was in or on the very verge of being in the White Army, but it was only for a matter of days. Yury was killed, and then, anyway, the government fell a week later. Nabokov remembers trying on the army boots. When the decision to leave had been taken by V. D. Nabokov, accommodation for the entire Nabokov family and the rest of the Crimean Cabinet was obtained on a single ship, but they were taken off it at the very last minute because representatives of the French Government stationed there suspected—wrongly—that the Minister of Finance was taking governmental funds with him. To their credit the Ministers of the Provisional Crimean Government and their families were the last to board the ships. The money in question had already been used to evacuate personnel and minor officials on the first ships. In addition to the expected chaos, the Crimea saw a fair amount of corruption and bribe-taking in those final days. It was so close that the Nabokovs were all but abandoned to the Reds. The entire Nabokov family left the Crimea on a small boat called *Hope (Nadezhda)* to which they had been transferred by the French authorities from another vessel, the *Trapezund.* As the boat left Sevastopol it was actually under fire from Red troops who had just arrived at the shore.

Their trip across the Black Sea and into the Mediterranean was shared by tens of thousands who became part of that first "homesick million" of this century. There was nothing of particular note about it. There were inadequate sleeping facilities, and food tended to be either in short supply or odd profusion. The boats were often dirty, the seas were usually rough. Nabokov gave his wife's recollections of her departure from Russia by this route to his hero Martin Edelweiss in *Glory* and added a selection of his own experience on the *Nadezhda.* Nabokov's sister Elena remembers the lice, sleeping on an unhinged door, and eating dog biscuits. Nabokov winces at such obvious refugee clichés but allows that it very likely was something like that. There were two rubber baths between the three men, one shared between Vladimir Dmitrievich and Vladimir Vladimirovich, and the other used by Sergei Vladimirovich, who was if anything even more fastidious *(brezgliv)* than his brother or father. Sergei won a bet on the voyage by declaring that he could take a bath with a glassful of water. So still that mysterious appliance follows me—its slosh, its peculiar resiny smell, Nabokov even drew it for me once, but it looked rather like a diminutive World War II liferaft, and I cannot imagine how it functioned on so little water—and reminds me that if I cannot understand so simple a thing (one could *research* the matter in an instant, of course, but better not) how little a part of another person's life one may grasp.

His notebooks show me that he wrote poetry on the voyage. Not very good poetry, actually. The refugees were confined to ship, even on a stopover lasting four days in Constantinople, until the ship reached Athens. Although Nabokov has written that his sense of loss was not very real as their ship left Sevastopol, the full dimensions of his exile were soon enough drafted in his soul, and in a 1920 poem he refers to that trip into exile of the previous year as *sailing to nowhere.* The Nabokovs disembarked in Athens and spent the following few weeks in a simple hotel in the port suburb of Piraeus. In retrospect Nabokov was amazed to learn that he had in fact spent so little time there, for it seemed to him to have been a much longer stay.

Greece was an interlude of three romances (one had its beginnings on shipboard) and more poetry, mostly in the same vein as the Petrograd and Crimean poems but without their vivid sense of place. The country as such appears to have made little impression on Nabokov. One long poem, *Dream at the Acropolis,* which appeared in the collection *The Empyrean Path* in 1923, is an account of a sudden and intense recollection of Russia while inat- **135** tentively listening to a guide extol the Doric columns of the Parthenon. He returned there later, at night and during a glistening full moon, with friends and strolled among the columns holding hands with N——. Life had, however, changed considerably even since the Crimea. Everyone was passing through to some other place, mainly Paris and Berlin, where there were connections or friends and where, it was hoped, one could wait for the collapse of the Bolshevik Government in reasonable comfort. There was still military action in and around the Russian empire, but Nabokov did not believe in the so-called Gallipolician movement's chance of success in mounting an invasion (though his two brothers-in-law were officers in the movement, and he himself did contribute a poem to a journal published by the movement), and besides Nabokov felt that there were people in the movement who . . . —**were sometimes not gentlemen.** However that may be, Nabokov's presentiment was correct. The possibility of action, much less successful action, had slipped by.

The Nabokovs were bound for England, where it was hoped that Vladimir and Sergei could enter Cambridge, which had, anyway, been the plan for their university education even before the revolution. V. D. Nabokov's own closest connections were in England. One of the memoirs by V. D. Nabokov's sisters claims that while he was in England in 1914 on the delegation with Kornei Chukovsky and Aleksei Tolstoy, which is described in *Speak, Memory*, George V had taken such a liking to him that he had been invited to stay at Windsor Castle as a personal houseguest of the king. Many other Nabokovs also went to England, and, as has already been noted, V. D. Nabokov's brother was the *de facto* head of the diplomatic mission there.

They had left Russia on April 15 (New Style) and arrived at Constantinople two days later. They were in Greece from April 21 until May 18, when they boarded the Cunard liner *Panonia* bound for New York which took them to Marseilles on May 23. Had he remained on board the *Panonia*, foxtrotting his way across the Atlantic, Nabokov would have hastened his fate by twenty-one years, and, he feels, it would have been a good thing. On May 23 the family went to Paris by train, where they stayed for only three days before crossing over to London on May 28, which by coincidence is also the exact date on which Nabokov did land in New York in 1940. Nabokov pays careful attention to these coincidences.

136

The family stopped for a few months in London. I do not have too much information of interest about this interim at Elm Park Gardens. There was a purportedly supernatural occurrence involving one of the younger children, but the governess was much given to belief in these things, and thus that or a simple coincidence might have had something to do with it. It caused no particular notice in the family. Nabokov's mother had had these experiences, and so had his grandmother. Vladimir Vladimirovich encountered several of his contemporaries in London at this time, among them Rozov. He read his poetry to Rozov (who laughed at it) and played pool with him. This was in late June.

As it happened, Rozov, who was entering London University, was able to aid his friend in one important way. Nabokov had not taken his school record or even his certificate of graduation from the Tenishev School into emigration with him, and so, he had been told, he would have to endure —**the terror of an examination** to gain admittance to Cambridge. Rozov lent him his papers (containing all fives, the highest grade), which Nabokov showed at Cambridge, explaining that his was exactly the same, which was the truth but not quite the whole truth (Nabokov remembers that he had only a four in physics, and Rozov as a Jew had no grade in Sacred History in which Nabokov recalls he earned a five minus). Nabokov was granted exemption from the examination. There was a rule which allowed admission to the university to a Russian student who held a matriculation certificate entitling him to automatic admission to a Russian university, which Rozov's certainly did and Nabokov's did, too, so there was no great deceit, though Nabokov had the impression that the administrators with whom he dealt—to whom the Russian documents were meaningless— were under the impression that the papers were Nabokov's own.

Nabokov's college was Trinity. His lodgings, after the first year in rooms at Great Court, were slightly removed and to the side at the end corner of lame Trinity Lane (number 2, now 38 Trinity Street, a sporting-goods shop) down which I can dimly but falsely imagine a thin young Russian trudging his slippers towards the baths in an inelegant bathrobe of a grey morning. It was, Nabokov says, a beautiful purple dressing gown. He remained a little bit to the side throughout Cambridge. At least, no one espied greatness in him, though some did notice that he seemed to play the part of detached observer. Nabokov remembers that he was made **much** of in Cambridge. **137**

At Trinity Nabokov was an ordinary entrant, that is, a "pensioner" rather than a scholar. He began university as an ichthyology student (in subsequent years Nabokov's colleagues in entomology at Harvard's Museum of Comparative Zoology would be amazed that he had studied fish rather than butterflies), though he soon dropped that, explaining to his tutor after the first semester that ichthyology was seriously interfering with his (Russian) poetry. We have already seen that he had been writing verse prolifically for several years prior to coming to Cambridge, but it was there that he became a Russian poet in earnest. In *Speak, Memory* Nabokov describes his years at Cambridge as an attempt to make himself a Russian writer; in *Other Shores* this becomes simply an attempt to retain Russia; and in a sense the two things really were (are) the same for Nabokov. He has written that Russia was a lost kinswoman who had been insufficiently appreciated during her lifetime. And England? That, he told me, was a love affair which happened too soon. He was terribly unhappy there.

Nabokov studied Russian and French literature. A comparison with the Tenishev course of the set texts and general course of study for those years as given in *The Student's Handbook to the University and Colleges of Cambridge* shows that Nabokov did not have to exert himself excessively. It is well known that a lighthearted attitude towards scholarship is something of a tradition at Cambridge, particularly when distinction can be all the same attained as a kind of natural grace. But Nabokov recalls that he never missed lectures and took almost verbatim notes which helped him immensely while cramming for exams.

Nabokov's tutor in French literature seems to have left no trace upon his life or art and so can be passed over in this narrative, but his Slavonic Lecturer Alexander Goudy deserves mention in that he **has absolutely nothing to do with** the character Archibald Moon, also a lecturer in Russian at Cambridge, in the novel *Glory*. I had thought so because of that dipthonged nougat in the middle of their names. Goudy was an Irishman. He taught at Cambridge from 1905 to 1937 and died there in 1946. Nabokov remembers that he was only invited to Goudy's for tea once. (—I wasn't a hit.) His tutor, Ernest Harrison, who is mentioned in *Speak, Memory*, obtruded much more on Nabokov's undergraduate life. Nabokov had turned to him for assistance in obtaining further scholarship aid early in 1920, but he received none. Nabokov was frequently summoned to Harrison's room because of various misdemeanors.

The biographical commentary in Venn's *Alumni Cantabrigienses* cites Harrison's editorship of *The Classical Review* for twenty years together with an unattributed quotation: —*His scholarship was beautiful.* However that may be, in discussing Harrison with me Nabokov recalled him with some strength of conviction as —**an extraordinarily stupid man.** One day Harrison wandered onto the soccer field and asked Nabokov what the game was called, evidently under the impression that it was some exotic Slavic sport. In a letter which he wrote to his mother early in 1920 he calls Harrison a vile man. Harrison was known for his "pungent wit," and it seems that Nabokov had to suffer it at least a bit. At Cambridge in those years the tutor was really expected to act *in loco parentis*—a particularly absurd expectation in the case of a student such as Nabokov, of course—and a student was dependent upon his tutor in many small ways, requiring, for example, his permission to leave the college on weekends, something which Nabokov did more often than not because he was conducting several simultaneous romances. Harrison, it should be mentioned, was an homosexual, and so it is just possible that an attraction lay behind the unnecessary coldness with which he treated his most heterosexual charge; this possibility would explain Harrison's wholly unexpected gift of a copy of *A Shropshire Lad* (mentioned in *Speak, Memory*) to Nabokov when he left Cambridge.

In first term Nabokov found himself often in the company of another Russian student, who was subject to periods of dark Slavic moodiness, particularly as the year wore on and he had to face the prospect of being sent down. He attempted to acquaint Nabokov with The Protocols of the Elders of Zion, but apart from such exceptions, Nabokov remembers, he could scarcely abide the sight of someone reading and on several occasions made attempts to throw Nabokov's books and poems into the fireplace. Such sullen eccentricities aside, the fellow was charming in his way, and Nabokov remembers that they were romantic rivals on several occasions, and the friend's cousin became one of Nabokov's most important early romantic attachments; he very nearly married her.

Nabokov and this acquaintance and another, much closer friend (a Romanov prince) on occasion formed a secret band of three responsible for numerous sophomoric nighttime pranks. For the most part these exploits escaped the notice of the proctors, those maintainers of decorum, proof against the civil rights of the Cambridge undergraduate. Once a surprise counterattack was **139** staged upon the Russians' rooms by some other students. Another time a small fine had to be paid for some pastries thrown through a window. One day his weathered and raw housekeeper came to him in a state of excitement (—**A terrible thing has happened, sir —a terrible thing—I really don't know how to tell you**—), and—Nabokov wrote his mother—for a moment he thought the police had come for him. But it was merely that his football boots, left to dry by the fireplace, had somehow caught fire.

The Cambridge period does not stand out in very sharp focus in Nabokov's memory. In part this haziness may be due, as he complains in his autobiography, to the fact that he made the mistake of returning to Cambridge on a visit (in 1937) and thereby spoiled his memories. Also, from the beginning: —**There was a certain make-believe about it all.** There is a contradiction between several of the sources from Nabokov's own hand that we have for these years—primarily his cheerful letters to his mother and the downhearted, downright Dostoevskian article about Cambridge which he wrote for his father's Berlin newspaper in October 1921 —but that contradiction is more apparent than real. Though he was unhappy at Cambridge—**fierce unhappiness** was the way in which he once referred to his state of mind—he also had equally energetic fun at Trinity and in many respects was more a participant in the common life there than he had been at the Tenishev School. The style of life at Cambridge, not without its elements of strangeness and difficulty even for English students, was perhaps another reason (not the main one) why Nabokov was more Russian there than at any time before or after in his life. Ironically, this difficult span in Vladimir Vladimirovich's life seems to have been the most happy period in the life of his brother Sergei, who was enrolled at Christ's College.

The reason which Nabokov gives for never having availed himself of the library at Cambridge is simply that the library and soccer kept the same hours. In addition to soccer Nabokov also did a bit of boxing. Once, he remembers, he was knocked out while sparring with the son of a rajah who was in his zoology class and who was preparing for a match at Oxford. He played some tennis, and he spent a great deal of time in season in punts on the river. His letters to his parents are full of references to the joys and sense of timelessness of reclining in a punt observing crocuses and elms. Still, Nabokov did in some respects conduct himself with studied

140 ease in regard to academic matters at Cambridge. On one occasion in 1921 he coolly occupied himself with writing a poem while waiting for an examination to begin. And he didn't do badly. In that first part of the Modern and Medieval Languages Tripos examination in 1921 he obtained a First and was awarded a College Prize (a nominal £2, which, moreover, had to be spent on a fixed list of prize books such as *A Picture Story of Cambridge*). The most "difficult" question on his Tripos examinations—which he particularly welcomed, he remembers—involved giving a description of the garden of one of the landowners in *Dead Souls*. Other examination questions which he faced, such as translating passages from Dickens and Scott into Russian, needless to say, involved no effort on his part whatsoever.

Nabokov had at one point been considering quitting Cambridge. He found that he was prone to indulge his unhappiness over the events of recent years and to fall prey to spleen. A letter from his father, probably written in late 1920 or early 1921, sympathizes with his feelings and urges him to take heart and get the degree. He took the degree, but there seems never to have been any question of his entering any normal career such as journalism, teaching, or advertising (as his cousins did), for Cambridge was simply a much longer version of his Crimean stay, a place attractive and stimulating but above all strange from which, of course, one would very quickly move on. Nabokov has a charming habit of visiting his unused past, and, just as he once contemplated what would have happened if he had chosen to become a French writer (—**I might have been a great French writer**), he can consider what might have been had he not left England and see himself as an eminently respectable writer-don: —**I might have been knighted in England. . . .** Nabokov's life at Cambridge was sufficiently full and interesting enough to take him to diverse quarters of English society, country seats, long cycling expeditions, trips to London, dress balls, occasional visits to the lower classes. He went out with shopkeepers' daughters (—**Would you please introduce me to your cousin?** a proctor once asked Nabokov, and, after the spurious introduction had been made, he politely turned to the girl: —**Doesn't your father run a shop on King Street?**), and he knew a boy who subsequently almost became Prime Minister of England. But Sir Vladimir? It is my understanding that there were deep-seated reasons of character as well as chance causes why Vladimir Nabokov never became a tweedy writer of the English establishment or a uniformed member of the French Academy. **141**

On the other hand, the Nabokov I know and know about is a natural both as a Russian and as an American. It is largely a speculative judgment though, if I am correct, an important point.

After his graduation from Cambridge Nabokov went to Berlin. Because Berlin was the capital of the Russian emigration in the years immediately after the revolution, but also because he knew no German to speak of and cared nothing for Germany or German culture, and hence the environment was much better suited than were either England or France to the task of becoming a Russian writer. Many decades later Nabokov was somewhat surprised by and quite indifferent to a suggestion made by one of his classmates that he donate a set of his works to Trinity College, but he is recorded as having frequently worn his Trinity blazer during the years he lived in Berlin, where, because of its coronet on the handkerchief pocket, people would approach him in the street to ask if he was a British *Seeoffizier.*

CHAPTER

5

*G*ermany . . . *is a forward stopping place of the Slav and prepares the way for the Russification of Europe.* Nietzsche. Well, not exactly. From the Russian point of view it was rather Germanization which in Russia's modern history represented a powerful, constant, and insidious threat to both Russian interests and Russian ways. It is a commonplace that since the eighteenth century German bootmakers have wended their way to Russia to become tutors and schoolteachers. The industrialization of Russia in the nineteenth century (which hastened the end of serfdom) took place largely upon the model furnished by German industry and frequently with German capital. In Ivan Goncharov's famous novel the antithesis to the Russian Ilya Oblomov is a Russified **145**

German, Stolz. Historically Germans had been invited to Russia to help develop the country, and a German family related to the Nabokov family by marriage, the Falz-Feins, were perhaps the wealthiest of all russified Germans, the owners of the vast estate Askania-Nova in southern Russia the cattle and sheep on which were said to be innumerable, though it was known that there were in excess of one hundred thousand cattle-dogs on the property. The estate was also a sanctuary for many specially imported animals, and it has been preserved as such under Soviet rule. It was V. D. Nabokov's brother who married Lidia Falz-Fein—eventually they separated. Russians have worked together with and intermarried with the Germans more than with any other people since the time of the Tartar incursion, and, particularly among the upper class, there are few Russian families entirely without a German connection. For all that, the two peoples have seemed virtually proof against each other, and the tendency has been for personalities clearly identifiable as Germanic or Russian to appear or remain in families where recent intermarriage has occurred, which is amply demonstrated by the Nabokov family.

Nabokov did not at first have an active dislike of Germany so much as a profound indifference to it.—**I never wanted to set foot in Germany** was the way he put it to me, referring to his feelings about Germany in post-Hitler times. There were many reasons why Russians came to Berlin. Most obviously, it was not very far from Russia, and the hope of a rapid return stayed alive for many years. Then, too, however great the difference between the German and the Russian character, there was a strong interest in Russia and things Russian (though perhaps less so in individual Russians) in Germany, particularly so in contrast to the situation in France where the emigrants were looked upon with ill-concealed disdain and such necessities as working papers were not easy to obtain. It was relatively easy—but still difficult—to obtain work in Berlin, and, even more important to the majority of the hundred thousand émigrés who were of professional status, there were many German business enterprises which showed themselves willing to cater to Russian interests. The situation was particularly good in regard to publishing because the price of paper and printing were both very low in Weimar Germany, and Berlin was at that time, moreover, the largest publishing centre in Europe. The exceptionally good opportunities for widespread publishing activity in Berlin were certainly among the primary reasons why Berlin took precedence over Paris in the first decade of Russian émigré literature. There were, at least for a time, even high hopes that some Russian books published in Germany might be permitted to be exported to the Soviet Union. So great was the publishing activity in Berlin, in fact, that for a time there were more Russian-language books being printed in Berlin than in either Petrograd or Moscow.

The Russian population of Berlin tended to cluster in a few sectors of the city, and the complaint was voiced by many Germans that nothing was spoken on many streets of the city except Russian. Owing to the volatile economic conditions within Germany at this time, another of the attractions of Berlin for many Russian émigrés was the reasonable accommodation in quite decent areas of the city that could be had rather cheaply. Foreign currency was particularly favoured, sometimes even demanded, and the modest amounts of money which many émigrés had been able to bring with them were in dollars, sterling, or francs. Also, the refugee relief organizations received their funds in hard currency, which bought much more in inflationary Germany than in France or Czechoslovakia. Nabokov recalls that he almost always lived in the flats of German military men. **—They were the people who had lost the most and had the most rooms to rent.** The professional and intellectual Russians of Berlin lived for the most part in a kind of informally communal fashion. The permanently temporary *pension* life of Russian émigrés in Berlin—shabby but carefully tended furniture, politely distant landladies, lithographs which tended to repeat themselves throughout the city, creaking elevators—has been chronicled by several émigré writers and by Nabokov in *Mary, The Eye,* and *The Gift.* Russian Berlin was a provincial albeit cosmopolitan city, and the mood of most Russians there (but not of Nabokov) was neo-Chekhovian.

When Nabokov and his brother Sergei came to live in Berlin after their graduation from Cambridge it was arranged for them both to have jobs in a German bank. But the Eliotic phase of Nabokov's life was very short-lived indeed. His brother worked there five days, but Vladimir Vladimirovich stayed all of three hours. Nabokov recalls only that he wore an English sweater — **which didn't suit a German bank,** though surely the sweater must have been the least of it.

Nabokov was quite clear in his own mind that he wished to become a serious writer. The emigration could not really support 147 full-time professional writers (there were odd exceptions, writers who had been well-established prior to the emigration such as Ivan Bunin), but the reading audience in Berlin, Paris, Prague, the Baltic, and Harbin in Manchuria—these were the main centers of the early emigration, though there was no corner of the globe to which Russians did not roll—could and did at first modestly support talented young writers on a semi-professional basis. Even so, things were somewhat better and more promising in the twenties than in the thirties, though, of course, Nabokov's reputation was established by 1930 and so he was sometimes almost but never quite able to be self-sufficient on the basis of his literary earnings then. A cousin who went into advertising remembers visiting Nabokov in Berlin in those early years and urging him to do something "practical" or at least to switch to writing in another language in which there might be a future for him, but he was, the cousin recalls, obdurate and determined to remain a Russian writer.

The largest Russian-language publisher in Berlin was The Word (Slovo), which was owned by one of the largest German publishers, Ullstein, and managed by V. D. Nabokov's colleague and close friend Joseph Hessen. The daily newspaper *The Rudder,* which had the largest circulation of any Russian paper in the city, was an outrigging of this publishing arrangement, and the paper was edited by V. D. Nabokov, Hessen, and Avgust Kaminka. The arrangement came about because Hessen had had dealings with the Ullstein organization prior to the revolution. Ullstein was housed in a massive building covering a full city block. It had leather-appointed offices, its own huge library, and researchers. Business worth millions (of inflationary marks) was conducted there in an atmosphere of subdued gentility. The offices of *The Rudder* and The Word were located separately and were considerably more spartan, but The Word's capital allowed them to publish about twenty titles a year, and the circulation of *The Rudder* (I do not have any firm figures but it would seem to have been about forty thousand) was sufficient to employ a staff of twenty-two, most, of course, only part-time. *The Rudder* would pay the present-day equivalent of about one or two pounds for a poem and fifteen pounds for a short story. Nabokov says that he is not good at remembering prices, but he thinks that the rate was about one dollar (the purchasing power of which, of course, was considerably higher then) for a quatrain of poetry or three hundred words of

148

prose. The young Nabokov's poetry in *The Rudder* appeared virtually every week for months at a time in the period between 1921 and 1925. Much of Nabokov's early poetry is weak, and *The Rudder* certainly was an ideal place for the young writer to practise and grow. He used the hospitality of the paper to the utmost, and his contributions to it between 1926 and 1929 are already the work of a rather mature young artist. Nabokov's poems were also sprinkled through other almanacs and journals of the time such as *Northern Lights, The Spindle, Facets, The Future of Russia,* and *The Fire-Bird. The Fire-Bird* was set in elegant type on glossy paper and with brilliantly coloured illustrations, and though there were few Russian émigrés who could afford the furs and the expensive automobiles advertised in its pages, the very existence of such lavishness on the old scale bears witness to the energy and hopes of Russian culture in Berlin in those first years.

The first Russian poem that Nabokov published in emigration, in 1920, was signed V. V. Nabokov, but even while he was still at Cambridge Nabokov switched to the *nom de plume* Vladimir Sirin (pronounced *sée-rin*), which he kept through 1939. Nabokov has given no reason for his change to the name Sirin beyond the way in which the word appeared in his special vision:

—I saw Sirin with an "s" being a very brilliant blue, a light blue, the "i" golden, the "r" a wriggly black, and the "n" yellow. . . . I thought it was a glamorous, colorful word. . . . If you look it up in *Dahl* I think it is some kind of *oblastnoe slovo* [*regional word*]. The other meaning of the word is mythological, Slavic, pseudo-Slavic I should say. . . . The sirin, as it happens, is not Slavic in origin, but it is to be found in Russian engravings as early as the eleventh century, and in subsequent centuries the myth enjoyed particular popularity in Russia. The sirin is a kind of owl with particularly long tail feathers, a human face (usually male, but also female, and sometimes the bird was depicted with breasts), and three-fingered hands in human form. What is terribly interesting about the sirin is that it came into being as a result of a mythological metamorphosis of the siren, the harpy-mermaid creature. Nabokov thinks that there is probably no connection between the two birds. My information comes from a learned article on the subject in the St. Petersburg journal *World of Art* for 1899. In the Fifth Book of the exile-poet Ovid's *Metamorphosis* the mermaid-like siren has been granted an exchange of its fish's tail for feathers so that it may fly in search of Persephone, who has **149** been abducted by Pluto. Much later, the transformed creature traditionally carried a lyre, and there is a statue of one such humanoid bird in the fifteenth-century cathedral at Rouen. In Russia the sirin was, from about the fifteenth through seventeenth centuries, an enchanting creature, rather similar in some respects to the better-known Russian *Rusalka,* or water nymph. Whether by design or chance then, the sirin was an appropriate choice for the young Nabokov, connected as it is with the particularly entomological theme of metamorphosis. Another prominent theme connected with the sirin is its seasonal quest for the "daughter of the Earth," which parallels the theme of the quest for Russia in Nabokov's early verse, and finally, the creature is rather closely tied to the theme of the arts through the lyre which it carries. The pseudonym was also very well suited to literary usage inasmuch as the leading pre-revolutionary Russian publishing house by which virtually all the Symbolist poets were printed had been called, as has already been explained, Sirin. But I would guess that the primary reason for a pseudonym was simply the desire to differentiate himself as an author, especially in the pages of *The Rudder* where they appeared together (for too short a time), from Vladimir Nabokov his father. It was widely known from the start in Berlin émigré society that Vl. Sirin (the signature he first used) was the young Vladimir Nabokov.

While he was still at Cambridge Nabokov contracted to do the Russian translation of Rolland's *Colas Breugnon* for The Word. The novel is written in both an archaic style and metered, rhymed prose. One evening in London (in 1920 or 1921) Nabokov had made a bet with his father, who thought it couldn't be done, that he could translate the book in just the way Rolland (for whom he had no special affection) had written it. Nabokov almost gave up (he had exaggerated his progress to the publishing house), but a sly dig in a letter from his father made him see the devilishly difficult thing through to the end. Nabokov's first publishing house for his own work was not The Word but Facets (Grani), an enterprise directed by Sasha Chyorny. Again, while he was still at Cambridge, *The Empyrean Path,* his first émigré collection, was prepared for publication under the editorship of his father and Sasha Chyorny. In a letter to his son V. D. Nabokov urges him to be indulgent about their choice of poems. When the volume appeared, V. D. Nabokov was dead, and the poems were dedicated to his memory. Chyorny also published an almanac entitled *Facets*

(Grani) in which Nabokov published his long impressionistic article on the poetry of Rupert Brooke in 1922, and his whimsical
purported translation of part of a play by a nonexistent English
writer—part of the Pushkin pattern in Nabokov's life, for Pushkin
had done exactly the same thing—in 1923. We know from a letter
to his mother that at that time he was already at work on an
unnamed novel which he hoped to have appear in *Facets,* but that
project was abandoned (it may have been the novel *Happiness,*
which survived only as several fragmentary short stories), and,
anyway, *Facets* and its publishing firm (after publishing twenty-
two titles, for the most part of an indifferent character) had ceased
to exist. It was after that that Sirin's prose began to appear under
the colophon—the statue of Peter the Great on a rising steed—of
The Word, and Joseph Hessen's firm remained Sirin's publisher
until 1930, at which time that firm, too, was forced to close, primarily because of the economic situation in Germany and because
the center of the emigration had shifted to Paris. By then, as
Hessen recalls in his memoirs, Sirin had become the pride of The
Word, and after *The Luzhin Defense* in 1930 Nabokov was spoken
of (not by all, to be sure, but by some) as the outstanding talent of
the younger generation in the emigration.

The Empyrean Path and another, smaller collection of poems
which also appeared in 1923, *The Cluster,* did not meet with an
enthusiastic critical response. Both books were slated for their
sterile traditionalism, although the emigration had created a defi-
nite taste for the traditional. Those books and his appearances in
The Rudder did not herald a brilliant new star in Russian letters.
But all the same, Nabokov recalls, these old-fashioned poems did
add a certain supplementary aura to the already prestigious name
Nabokov among well-to-do parents, so that he was particularly
sought after among the many Russians who lived in Berlin by
giving lessons.

In Berlin Nabokov lived primarily by giving lessons. Nabokov
estimates that he must have had something on the order of forty
regular pupils during that decade. He gave lessons in tennis, boxing, and even prosody, but for most it was French and English
lessons. It was not an entirely easy life:

**—It used to tire me out terribly because it was necessary to go
from one corner of town to another. I always got up tired. I would
write all night. Then it was necessary to drag myself from place
to place for lessons. In the rain. They would give me dinner in the** **151**

houses. This was very pleasant. They would give me really astounding meals in one house. And with such enjoyment, so charmingly did they feed me. This has fixed in my memory. But then there was another type who would say, after an hour's lesson, excuse me, but I must go to the office, to the office, and then he would accompany me back to the Western part of the city attempting to make me continue the lesson all the way.

Many of the details of these lesson-giving years have been used in *The Gift*. In addition to Russian youths there were numerous Russian-Jewish businessmen —who wanted to learn to chat in French. Lightly, he would say. But there was no subject to chat about. One pupil turned out to be an agent (—It was in all the papers). Another student was the son of an adventurer who had died and whose widow had gone through a large sum of money but still wished to provide the best possible education for her son with what little was left, and so Nabokov was hired to polish his English and to play tennis with him.

On a few occasions Nabokov was engaged as a tutor of the sort that he himself had had in St. Petersburg and at Vyra. Once—this was after he was married—he was paid to take a boy to a Baltic resort. (Part of that resort was given to *King, Queen, Knave*.) When they arrived Nabokov was informed that there was no place for them at the hotel, and then a flushed fellow in the bar with a full glass in his hand indicated to Véra Evseevna that room might be found for her, however. Nabokov spun on his heel and caught the man's jaw with a hook, drenching both of them with the sticky liquid that had been in the glass. The pupil looked on with demure interest.

His most important steady pupil was a shy, attractive and intelligent son of extremely wealthy parents, to whom Nabokov gave daily lessons in English, tennis, and boxing. This amounted to a full-time job in terms of both time and salary (about one hundred dollars, or forty-five pounds, a week), and the position lasted for about two years. These were the first years of relative comfort and security for Nabokov in emigration, and it was in this period that he produced his first two novels, which in turn provided some leisure (and a butterfly-collecting trip) when Ullstein brought them out in German translations.

Nabokov would usually sleep very late in the mornings, often in fact sleep right through the morning, and then go to give lessons in the afternoon. But when working with this steady pupil he kept more regular hours. He would go to the boy's house every day at six in the morning for breakfast. After breakfast he would lead his pupil in a session of gymnastics, and the morning would pass into a succession of sports and language lessons. Nabokov was virtually a one-man finishing school for the boy, but essentially his job was to be companion to him. After lunch and lessons they would frequently go for strolls along the shore of the Schwarzwald in Berlin. He would return at about three in the afternoon, a nine-hour day.

—Then you had a cousin of . . .

—Yes, my darling. I had lots of girl pupils.

—And the other, *innaya,* was she a student?

—No, she was not. *Don't* bring up those names! He is going to *pounce* upon those, on all those names! Ladies who simply liked having lessons made up a small but important part of his livelihood, after students and businessmen.

From one advertisement which he placed in *The Rudder* offering lessons in his customary five subjects (English, French, boxing, tennis, and prosody) Nabokov obtained Mikhail Gorlin as a student of prosody. Gorlin subsequently earned some notice as a minor émigré poet in his own right. He published one book of poetry in 1936 and very shortly afterwards perished in a Nazi concentration camp together with his wife, the poetess Raissa Blokh. Gorlin was a tiny curly-headed chap who loved poetry in the passionate way that Russians can. He was something of a specialist on E. T. A. Hoffmann and also on the medieval Russian epic *The Song of Igor's Campaign.* Gorlin, Nabokov recalls, was working with Professor André Mazon in Paris on the Igor tale. Mazon was the first serious challenger of the tale's authenticity. —**He had adopted Mazon's theory, which, for all I know, may have been right . . . I can't make up my mind. I can't. There is no proof. But there are such *strange* coincidences. . . .** Nabokov gave Gorlin English lessons, too, and they studied Milton together. They met from two to four times a week for many months.

Whenever possible Nabokov would endeavour to be paid for his lessons in dollars. He never really had any more than barely enough money until the Ullstein translations, but payment in dollars made all the difference. Not only knowing no German but refusing to learn any and—according to his wife—being absolutely ungifted in regard to the German language, Nabokov's main German sentence was a variant of: —**Ich habe drei dollar.** He recalls that once he produced five dollars on the tramway (it was the 153 money he had just been paid for one of his first literary efforts, a Russian translation of *Alice in Wonderland*), and the conductor was so astonished—an American five-dollar bill would have rented a rather nice flat in Berlin even at that early date—that he stopped the tram to change it.

In spring and summer the relative importance of tennis lessons increased markedly. In April 1926 Nabokov was given free membership in a "good" Berlin tennis club solely on the basis of his play. He would get three dollars for a tennis lesson, and a sunny Saturday might hold ten lessons. —**I never had it, but it was a kind of possible dream.** Some of his pupils took combined language and tennis lessons, and there were times when he gave various lessons to different members of a single family. During this decade of his life Nabokov was extremely wiry. I have a snapshot of him at a picnic with one of his German landlords in which he does not look as though he could weigh even nine stone. He is accentuating his physique in the picture by comically flexing his biceps and throwing out his chest, standing on tiptoe. But neither his weight nor the hours he kept prevented him from playing soccer for his own amusement throughout his residence in Berlin. He played with an émigré team which competed with various German clubs in Berlin. His last soccer game was played in 1935, when he was thirty-six. His team was playing a team of very rough factory workers and did not do too well that day. Their goalkeeper, Nabokov, was knocked unconscious with the ball in his grip and had to be carried from the field. His head was rather brutally stomped on, he had two broken ribs, and —**there were other parts of my anatomy ill-treated that day, too.** Nabokov remembers that when he came to, the first thing he was aware of was a teammate impatiently trying to pry the ball, frozen in his grip, out of his arms.

His casual life afforded him the time to attend at least occasionally to other interests as well. In addition to composing a few chess problems for *The Rudder*—like goalkeeping, it was a highly specialized and essentially different aspect of the game which he cultivated—Nabokov played chess quite often of an evening, at home, in the flats of friends, and sometimes even in tournaments. He played the Grandmaster Nimzowitsch in one of those café tournaments where Nimzowitsch played against forty players simultaneously. Nimzowitsch moved very rapidly from board to board, and yet he still moved the pieces with extraordinary delicacy—like an entomologist handling butterflies, Nabokov thought

154

—and, while Nabokov did finally lose, he was one of the last to be defeated and held out from eight till twelve-thirty. He also played and lost very honourably to the World Champion, Alekhine, at that same Equitable Café. On another occasion Nabokov was actually on the verge of defeating the Grandmaster Nimzowitsch when a hand from the crowd suddenly reached out over his shoulder and moved a piece for him. It was evident in a flash to both players that the move was fatal, and Nimzowitsch struck instantly. Nabokov had to accept defeat, the victim of a bystander's impetuousity. The over-all opinion of Nabokov as a chessplayer seems to be that he is very erratic, but for that very reason and because of the extraordinary boldness and brilliance with which he plays he is capable of upsetting opponents of championship calibre. The Nabokov strategy.

In addition to the expected line that was drawn between the Germans and the Russian communities in Berlin (only the Baltic Slavs who spoke German fluently could really cross it, and even they were regarded as being more Slav than German), there were some lines equally sharply drawn within the Russian community itself. The division was not so much between classes—there were not that many peasants and workers in the Berlin emigration; there was a much higher percentage of lower-class émigrés in the Harbin colony in Manchuria and in the first wave of Russians who went to America—as between those who were disposed to place the idea of Russia above its system of government and those who knew, as the Nabokovs did, that mere patriotism was not enough to make possible a return to Russia without an enormous amount of compromise with oneself and even self-deception, not to speak of the danger. The former and the latter did not mix much either socially or in publications. Nabokov did not mix with writers of a pro-Soviet inclination such as Aleksei Tolstoy, Andrei Bely, Viktor Shklovsky, and Ilya Ehrenburg, though he does recall seeing some of these writers, and once he was sounded out about the possibility of return by a second-rate writer, Tarasov-Rodionov, best known for his short novel *Chocolate* and well known as a Soviet agent in the emigration.

Of course there was a degree of apprehension about the future among the émigrés and often a degree of uncertainty about each other. The unstable political and economic conditions in Germany frightened more than a few Russians who were considering whether to declare themselves émigrés into returning to the Soviet Union. The poet Sergei Esenin was among these. It surprised no one when Ilya Ehrenburg went back, but the return of Aleksei Tolstoy (who had once travelled to England with V. D. Nabokov in 1916) did surprise and shock some émigrés even though his opportunism was well known. In the Soviet Union, because of his background and life style, he became known as the "Red Count." Vladislav Khodasevich had been Gorky's literary secretary, but after a short time showed himself to be very much a part of the democratic emigration. On the other hand, Boris Pasternak, many of whose values were more suited to the spirit of Russian Berlin (there is one published source which claims Pasternak was very seriously flirting with the idea of emigration) and whose parents were already in emigration, went back. Others in the emigration such as the minor novelist Roman Gul' or the linguist Roman Jakobson, whose more radical political sympathies might have led one to look for their eventual return, did not. The critic D. S. Mirsky's famous and fatal flirtation with return is well known. Kuprin went back after several strokes, just before his death, to be welcomed and fêted. Others, such as Ivan Bunin and Igor Stravinsky, wavered about whether or not they should return to similar celebration. Nabokov recalls about Bunin: —It was a great temptation for him. A great temptation! But he withstood it.

During a period of three months in 1923 Nabokov was acquainted with one young Berlin writer who later returned. This was Aleksandr Drozdov, three years older than Nabokov, who edited *Northern Lights (Spolokhi)*, one of the better émigré literary journals in which a few of Nabokov's early poems appeared. Like Nabokov, Drozdov was a keen sportsman and an excellent soccer player. —He looked a little bit like Bill Buckley. That type. Pink complexion and blue eyes. In addition to his short stories, Drozdov published many —extremely patriotic and rather brilliant little articles. But patriotism turned to superpatriotism and then to attacks upon émigrés, and one of his articles caused Nabokov to challenge him to a duel. (The challenge was not accepted.) Drozdov had begun to do most of his writing for *On the Eve (Nakanune)*, a newspaper which was the primary link between the Bolsheviks and the émigrés, and then he was gone, back to Russia.

156   Another "change-of-landmarks" Russian (the label by which

those who went from White to Red were known), named Li-ubimov, whom Nabokov knew slightly, wrote *On Foreign Soil* in 1963. It was the first book on the emigration to appear in the Soviet Union in several decades. I happened to be in the Soviet Union at that time, and I recall a half-block line in front of the Writers' Bookshop on Kuznetsky Bridge in Moscow. Word of the Liubimov volume's arrival in the bookstore had spread by word of mouth among the Moscow intelligentsia—vivid testimony to the desire of Soviet intellectuals for any knowledge of the fate of the emigration. Nabokov was not mentioned in this book, but in 1966 he was discussed in another Soviet book, *Mirages and Reality— The Notes of an Émigré* by Dmitri Eisner, where he is described as a *lean and slightly decadent young man,* educated at Oxford, and an artist with no theme. . . .

Tarasov-Rodionov, the writer who tried to get Nabokov to consider return to Russia, left a note for him at an émigré book-store which he frequented—to browse, not to buy—asking that they meet. This happened about 1929 or 1930. A panorama of the splendid things he would return to see and write about (there is a comic moment which probably descends from this in *Bend Sinis-ter*) was spread before him: the Red Army, mass sporting events, collective farms, churches. —**Well, you know I must confess that sometimes I go to church, too,** he confided. Nabokov allowed that he wasn't much interested in such things. They were in a Russian-German café. Just then a man selling shoelaces—in fact, a former White officer—said something to them both in Russian. Tarasov-Rodionov was thrown into a panic, convinced that he was being spied upon. —**Oh, so that's what you are doing to me,** he told Nabokov, and that put an end to the recruitment to which Nabo-kov had gone out of curiosity. When Nabokov asserted that no Russian artist of any stature would return, Tarasov-Rodionov re-plied: —**Well, you are wrong. I've just talked to Prokofiev, and he is returning.**

The shadowy world of agents and double-agents and under-ground plots did exist in the emigration. Nabokov has written about this part of the emigration in his 1927 play *The Man from the U.S.S.R.* and his 1943 short story *The Assistant Producer.* But while there were hardly any oil magnates and only a few Russians with any money to speak of in Berlin (even a Soviet book such as *Mirages and Reality* admits this, though that is one of the first images of the Russian emigration which still comes to mind for **157** many Westerners), the political intrigues and the agents, though their existence was well known, did not often intrude upon ordinary life. Nabokov's pupil who suddenly and quietly turned out to have been an agent was perhaps typical in this respect. Nabokov also knew the noted popular singer Plevitskaya slightly—it is she who is the subject of *The Assistant Producer*—and once told me that he might possibly write an entire novel about her someday. For however atypical of émigré life these spectral activities and people were, they unquestionably obtrude upon the imagination.

A much greater portion of Nabokov's imagination and perhaps sympathy, however, was given to those real-life figures, sometimes agents but more often men of a quasi-mystical inclination, who journeyed to the Soviet Union and back with false papers and often in disguise. The hero of *The Man from the U.S.S.R.* is such a person, and Martin Edelweiss, the hero of his 1932 novel *Glory,* is about to undertake such an exploit. In one of his mature Russian poems, *To Prince S. M. Kachurin,* written in his American period, Nabokov imagines his own clandestine trip to Northern Russia. He did entertain the notion in his Berlin days. *Glory,* though his fourth novel in chronological order, was one of the first he began to work on. It began as *Happiness* (a portion of which at least, he recalls, was incorporated into the final novel), and then became *The Romantic Age,* which was the working title for *The Exploit* (rendered as *Glory* in English). Nabokov was attempting **—to write a novel which would give the brighter side of my life. In general *Glory* is my happiest thing.** It was also an attempt to put a positive face on the emigration. Nabokov also sounded this note in his 1927 article in *The Rudder* celebrating the tenth year of Soviet rule with thanks for the decade of total, unfettered freedom which History had granted to those in the diaspora. It did not pass unnoticed among the generation slightly younger than Nabokov's that his hero's name signifies "noble white." (In fact, the hero's name also refers to the edelweiss or Lion's Foot which happens to grow both in the Swiss alps and the Siberian steppe.) There were young Russians who took him as their own (as opposed to the values of their parents) in somewhat the same way that young Americans later were to admire Salinger's Holden Caulfield. Politically, Nabokov was the purest of the Whites, precisely because there could be no suspicion that lost principal lay behind his principles, and he never wavered, never was tempted except to dream.

There were various quasi-literary means by which one might supplement one's income in émigré Berlin, and at one time or another the young Nabokov had a hand in most of them. The most important thing, the Nabokovs insist, is that there existed possibilities in Berlin for them to earn more money, had they wanted to, but such considerations were always the farthest from their minds. The film industry was extremely active in Berlin at this time, of course, and a great many Russians, Vladimir Vladimirovich and Véra Evseevna among them (though they did not know each other then), were extras. Nabokov remembers one film in which he was prominently seen because he happened to be the only person there wearing evening dress (his old London dinner jacket), and so the camera focused on him during a scene showing an audience at the theatre. —I remember I was standing in a simulated theatre in a box and clapping, and something was going on on an imaginary stage (a real murder which the audience took to be part of the performance). . . . I don't think *that* film will ever be found. . . . The film would seem from the description of that scene to have been *The Dying Torch (Verlöschende Fakel)*, which was produced by Dewesti, one of the several Russian film companies in Berlin, and starred Mozzhukhin, a pre-revolutionary Russian film star who is mentioned in *Speak, Memory*, but the film itself may indeed no longer exist. —I got that little job through somebody who'd go there, and I went instead. You know, that kind of thing. The payment for such walk-ons was ten marks. Later Nabokov happened to see the picture with a friend and pointed to himself as he flashed on the screen, but the friend politely scoffed at him. And that episode, a year later, was incorporated into the first Sirin novel.

Once chance very nearly brought Nabokov onto the sanded screen in a more serious way. In July 1924 a "rising film star" with whom he was acquainted took him to her director. She told the director that Nabokov was an actor and had had a great deal of experience in southern Russia. He was walked around and looked over approvingly for two hours and then offered the lead role in a projected film project, but like so many plans in feverish Berlin nothing ever came of it. —I don't remember that girl. I would like to, but I can't remember her, darling. . . . —No, not——. That was earlier. You saw her as Salomé before you knew me.

Nabokov and Ivan Lukash, another aspiring young writer (they saw one another virtually every day for several years), worked **159** together on a series of film scenarios. There was a possibility of earning up to three thousand dollars for an accepted scenario, and Nabokov at one point in 1924 had requests from three different directors for scenarios. Nabokov grasped that the genre had its own demands, and he gave himself to the task with his usual determination. He had—has—a "filmic sense" and may be considered one of the earliest writers to have possessed this talent in the new genre. Though none of his scenarios was filmed—nor, for that matter, does it appear that any have been preserved—the most important of them, *The Love of a Dwarf,* became one of Nabokov's best short stories, *The Potato Elf.* That particular short story was Nabokov's first work to appear in the United States (in *Esquire* in 1939), and the translator, Serge Bertenson, who worked in Hollywood, records in his memoirs that it made such an impression upon the well-known Hollywood producer Lewis Milestone when he translated it for him many years before the translation appeared in print (Milestone had won an Oscar and the Best Picture award two years before for *All Quiet on the Western Front*) that he was on the verge of turning *The Potato Elf* into a scenario and wanted to bring Nabokov to Hollywood to develop "story lines" for other scenarios as well. Bertenson went to meet Nabokov on January 3, 1932, to talk with him about Milestone's proposals and recorded in his diary: *—He grew very excited at this. He told me that he literally adores the cinema and watches motion pictures with great keenness.* Nabokov's fifth Russian novel, *Camera Obscura* (later substantially altered and retitled as *Laughter in the Dark*), was just appearing serially, and Nabokov gave Bertenson the manuscript to read. But, in spite of the fact that the novel is actively concerned with cinema, Bertenson felt that it was too . . . *erotic* to be made into an American film, and besides, there wasn't a single positive character in it. Bertenson met Nabokov again the following week for lunch, and it was agreed that Nabokov would send him summaries of all his things which he considered suitable for film. It was only a matter of months before the American Depression belatedly brought Hollywood to a halt, and Milestone like many less successful producers found that there were no longer any funds available to produce pictures. Thus Nabokov's arrival in the United States was delayed another eight years.

Young Russian intellectuals and artists in Berlin frequently **160** worked together on various projects which promised some remuneration. Nabokov recalls working with some unrecallable girl on tour descriptions for a Berlin travel agency, and then later, when he had met Véra Evseevna, they worked together putting into decent English the Berlin dispatches of a Russian correspondent for a London paper. The articles (—his terrible, *terr*-ible articles . . .) were for the most part on Soviet and émigré politics. The payment for the work was quite good: —He paid me, what, about five guineas. —You. —You helped me, darling. Enormously. No, no, really. We were married then. That was twenty-five. Yes, we knew each other quite well. The correspondent was, Nabokov remembers, a very gentle and pleasant person, but he recalls one rather strange incident when he went to see him about something in connection with the translations. Nabokov arrived when the man was still asleep, though it was late morning, and Nabokov watched him getting up: —It was the first time and the last time in my life that I saw a man getting out of a bed completely dressed. Completely. He even had a hat on. It's true. It's true. He had his shoes on, even. It was cold in the room, so he didn't bother to take his shoes off. This was *very* Russian in a way. And this odd occurrence which Nabokov observed in the 1920s survived in his descriptive storehouse and eventually was, in his memoirs of the 1950s, used as a nonfactual but whimsical image to evoke the strangeness of his tutor "Lensky" in the early years of the century. For the tutor is described in *Speak, Memory* as coming *seemingly straight out of bed but already shod and trousered. . . .*

From time to time there would be work translating letters into various languages. The young German who so fancied watching executions from *Speak, Memory* first came to Nabokov because he had some letters he wished written in English to a cousin in America. On another occasion the Nabokovs were writing letters to India for someone when —we suddenly realized what was happening, and we threw him out, and his letters. Vladimir Vladimirovich and Véra Evseevna worked together on a Russian grammar, but, inasmuch as she did most of the work on it, he does not feel it should warrant a place in his bibliography. And there was a small dictionary, too, German-Russian and French-Russian, but there are differing recollections as to whether or not Nabokov had a hand in the French side of it.

All of these diverse activities would have provided a lean but quite satisfactory means of subsistence for Nabokov if it had not been for the need to give primacy to his writing. There was usually **161** enough money to live on. It was very casual drudgery which kept Nabokov in a state of cheerful tiredness. There was another source of modest income, too. Most of those Russians who had managed to preserve some of their wealth in emigration (generally speaking, those who had had overseas investments and foreign bank accounts, which V. D. Nabokov had refused to do for patriotic reasons) felt the need to share some portion of their wealth with others in the emigration who very often had previously been as affluent as they. Indeed even those who had very little themselves were frequently moved to share with their compatriots. Russian primary and secondary schools were established, there were special funds to aid those who had been wounded in the Civil War and the aged. There was also a special fund to aid writers, particularly older ones who had made their names in pre-revolutionary Russian literature and now had nothing to live on beyond those names and the thought of the memoirs they might still write but never did. Some young writers, among them Nabokov (—**Oh, I had them. Of course**), did receive these *"ssudy,"* or grants. One of the major contributors to the Berlin fund in aid of writers was the Falz-Fein family. Now the Nabokovs themselves contribute to a latter-day descendant of this fund, the *Litfond* in New York, twice a year.

One activity in which Nabokov invested a lot of time during 1924 and 1925 and which was supposed to pay—unfortunately, it did only irregularly, and in the end Nabokov had to threaten legal action: —**They still owe me money!** he told me with undimmed indignation—was the popular Blue Bird Theatre on Holzstrasse which was run by the talented director Ya. D. Yuzhny. It was a cabaret theatre of dramatic miniatures or skits and was loosely patterned after similar theatrical cafés in literary St. Petersburg. Nabokov and his friend Lukash were both active as writers for the Blue Bird. The Blue Bird miniatures were of a marginally literary standard, high enough at any rate so that young writers did not mind acknowledging authorship of their sketches in the programmes. It is unlikely that any of the Blue Bird sketches have survived, but I have seen some photographs of them. The dramatic vignettes were not casually executed affairs, for a great deal of care and skill have clearly gone into the scenery and costumes. In the photographs I have seen there seems to be some influence of Meyerhold's conscious artificiality in the staging.

In a letter to his mother (March 13, 1925) Nabokov describes how he spent the previous day. He got up at seven and went to the outskirts of the city for a film take and did not return till five. (The next day his eyebrows were still blackened from the makeup, which would not come off, and he was still seeing bright spots in front of his eyes from the blinding lights.) Between five and eight Nabokov had lessons to give, and after eight he attended a rehearsal of a pantomime for the Blue Bird's new programme; and doubtless later still that night he worked on his first novel.

On performance nights at the Blue Bird the show would begin at eight-thirty, and there would be ten to twelve miniatures in the course of the evening, none lasting more than about ten minutes. There were ten complete changes of programme in a given season. In addition to Lukash, Nabokov was particularly friendly with another writer at the Blue Bird, Yury Ofrosimov, a pleasantly but strangely old-fashioned sort of person, who wrote mainly children's stories and was also a director in his own right. In 1926 he staged *The Man from the U.S.S.R.* in Berlin. Ofrosimov had specifically asked Nabokov to write a play for his new theatre. A composer named Yakobson from Riga (who also still owes Nabokov some money, says Nabokov) worked with Nabokov and Lukash. The three collaborated on *Agaspher,* a ballet or staged symphony with, Nabokov's part, a poetic accompaniment (—**Horrible! If I have it, if I see it, I will destroy it!**) which was performed only once, in a provincial German city.

Nabokov wrote several Blue Bird miniatures as well as pieces for other theatres and cabarets in the city in conjunction with Lukash. Lukash had begun to write just before the revolution, and it had seemed to many that he bid fair to be one of Russia's important new writers. He was at first associated with the Ego-Futurist movement and published Whitmanesque poetry under the pseudonym Ivan Oredezh. During the Civil War he was a White officer. He finally landed in Berlin without any money, which was not unusual, but by then he was already married, to an Armenian girl, and then they had a child. Nabokov remembers the baby deposited on a window sill while Lukash paced up and down, imagining a routine on which they were working. Lukash, for practical reasons as well as those of literary ambition, was if anything even more prolific a writer than Nabokov himself in the early years of the emigration. In 1923, the year in which Nabokov published two books of poems, Lukash published three books of prose. He also published numerous short stories and sketches, **163** some of them in *The Rudder, Russian Thought,* and *Echo,* and, in all, eight books—those I have sampled are rather plain to my taste —which enjoyed a certain popularity among émigré readers, at least as much as the very early Sirin books. One of his books, an historical novel, was translated into English, and another, a novel about the life of Moussorgsky in St. Petersburg *(The Snowstorm),* was translated into French and greeted as a masterpiece by the volatile and influential French critic Léon Daudet. Nabokov described him to me as an exceptionally talented man with marvellous Russian and a feel for language, but he was also perhaps at somewhat of a disadvantage in the emigration because he was, Nabokov thinks, absolutely Russian and thoroughly divorced from any contact with West European culture. Nabokov thinks that he may have put something of Lukash into *Glory.* There would seem to be a fair bit of Lukash in the character of Bubnov in that novel. In life Lukash had somewhat the mature but childish appearance of a middle-level executive or administrator, particularly with the bow-tie he often wore (Bubnov has one, too) and his open face with widely spaced eyes, low-set, modest ears, and an exceptionally high (he was prematurely bald) forehead. Only the very extremity of his nose, which suddenly turned out in hesitant Tolstoyan bulbousness, was unmistakably Slavic. Of his friend's novels Nabokov says: —They are beautifully written. The style is superb. But they lack something, they lack some kind of compositional fire which he never had. Years later, in 1936, Lukash, who had had a bad row with the émigré newspaper on which he worked, wrote to Nabokov with discomforting candor: —I envy you. Everything is over for Iv. Lukash, which by then surely was an auto-epitaph on his once-promising literary career.

One of Lukash's most popular books was not signed by him. It was the autobiography of Nadezhda Plevitskaya, which he ghosted. Plevitskaya was not a cultured, much less an educated woman, but she had extraordinary tales to tell about her life (and, as it turned out later, even more extraordinary tales which she didn't tell), and her husband, Skoblin, invited Lukash to construct an autobiography from her words. Lukash became an intimate of the Skoblin household. The Lukash family even followed them to Paris. Later, after the kidnapping of General Miller in Paris, it was revealed that both Skoblin and Plevitskaya had been active Soviet agents in Berlin. It was then assumed among Berlin émigrés, according to one memoirist, that the guileless and talkative Lukash must have told Plevitskaya at least as much as he heard from her, for Lukash knew every Russian in literary Berlin, and the Soviets were very interested not only in wooing Russian writers, but also in keeping track of their activities in Berlin during the 1920s. One might reasonably suspect that something like this did happen.

No, I was quite wrong before. . . . However pointless the political and intelligence activities of the emigration seem now, and especially to those who did not live through it, they must have charged the atmosphere of otherwise shabby émigré Berlin; their interest certainly was far from confined to the romantic or literary imagination. The émigré cabdriver who indignantly ordered visiting Soviets from his taxi might turn out to be a Soviet agent himself. A quiet and intelligent young girl from a good family might have a part in an assassination plot which could have any one of a number of political hues. The Nabokovs remember the rumor that there was even a plot from the liberal centre of the emigration, which never came off, to assassinate Trotsky on a visit he made to Berlin. *The Rudder,* which was virtually a large family unit of Russian liberals most of whom had known and worked with each other for more than a decade in pre-revolutionary St. Petersburg, was nearly penetrated by the Soviet N.K.V.D. when a woman who worked at *The Rudder* and who was burdened with a seriously ill mother and no means to have her cared for adequately was approached by Ivan Konoplin, a young writer who had published three books in the emigration, with a proposal to make twice-weekly reports on the happenings in the offices of the paper. *The Rudder* was at that time printing many smuggled-out reports from within Russia, and the Soviets were presumably anxious to trace their sources. When Konoplin was revealed to be an agent, he vanished from the city. It is said that he became a major in the Soviet Army and died in a Stalinist concentration camp. There might have been something of this, too, in the eloquent, passionate articles by Nabokov's sometime editor Aleksander Drozdov fervently praising the Russian emigration and all it stood for (he was the only one before Nabokov himself to do this), written less than two years before his own return to the Soviet Union. No, the deception and use of Ivan Lukash by Plevitskaya—if that is what happened—would have been only an insignificant though sufficiently sad bit of misadventure in Russian Berlin.

Another interesting artistic contemporary, a poet with whom Nabokov was on much less close terms but who proved to be a **165** much stronger literary figure than Ivan Lukash, was Vladimir Piotrovsky. Piotrovsky first appeared in Berlin at a public poetry reading. No one knew who he was. He was very short and spoke with a slight Polish accent. He had a very self-assured air about him. He called himself Colonel Piotrovsky and said that he had taken a town single-handedly in the Civil War. Later, he began to sign himself Korvin-Piotrovsky (there does exist such a hyphenated family), claiming descent from a Hungarian King Korvus. The Russian-language 1956 history *Russian Literature in Exile* by Struve records that, after he had escaped from Nazi Germany, Korvin-Piotrovsky was active in the French Resistance and was captured and sentenced to death by firing squad, from which he was saved only five minutes before the execution by an exchange that was arranged for some S.S. troops being held captive by the Resistance, all of which has the ring of a tale from Korvin-Piotrovsky himself, though it could, ironically, also be what actually did happen. He died in California.

Nabokov would meet Piotrovsky at the Berlin Poets' Club, which was founded by his student in prosody Mikhail Gorlin. Most of its members were barely more than twenty, and by then— 1928—Nabokov had something of the reputation of a young *maître* in Russian Berlin. Nabokov would read his own verse with an authoritative air, and he would offer commentaries, with sharp humour and a certain amount of condescension, on the poems read by the younger members. It was customary for the young members of the circle to address one another by the honorary title of poet: Poet Gorlin, Poet Piotrovsky, etc. A memoirist who was a member of the circle and who subsequently became one of Nabokov's French translators has written that Piotrovsky was the only poet in the club whom Nabokov was willing to accept as his equal, in part because Piotrovsky (who was only three years younger than Nabokov) alone never took offence at his critical remarks and on occasion would even riposte.

In 1923 Piotrovsky had published a volume of poems and subtly pornographic short stories. They were not especially impressive, and his poetry and prose in the years immediately after held little promise. But in 1929 he published a cycle of unusual and quite excellent dramatic poems titled *Beatrice* which are the work of a real if minor poet. One of the most enthusiastic book reviews Nabokov wrote in his Berlin years was an appreciation of *Beatrice* which appeared in a Parisian émigré newspaper. The next book of poems which (by now) Korvin-Piotrovsky published was a collection which appeared in Paris in 1950. In this book he shows that he deserves to stand with and only a step or two behind Nabokov and Vladislav Khodasevich as a poet, and it is clear beyond any doubt that he has assimilated the drily bitter tone and simple metre of Khodasevich and occasionally, too, the sudden rich throb of Nabokov's Russian poetry. But by 1950, of course, émigré literature had expired, and so there could not be much hope of recognition of Korvin-Piotrovsky's talent, which was, anyway, not any more fashionable in character than Khodasevich's and much less so than Nabokov's. He left a small number of permanent poems (one, *There Is a Fear of Immortality,* is a favourite of mine), and Nabokov told me that if he does his anthology of Russian poets in English translation there will be two poems by Korvin-Piotrovsky in it. Nabokov remembers that after the war, in America, Korvin-Piotrovsky published an unpleasant poem about him in which he is, moreover, directly named, but I have been unable to find that poem.

The literary life of Russian Berlin was expressed in spoken form as much as in publication. There were many clubs and literary societies. Nabokov belonged to one called Arzamas, after the society to which Pushkin had belonged. On Passauerstrasse, one of the streets on which he lived in those years (others were Nestorstrasse, Luitpoldstrasse, and Motzstrasse), where there were many Russians, there was a Russian restaurant with something of a literary character where certain of the poets whose work appeared in *The Rudder* would gather, and also a Russian bookstore. As it happened some of the most regular literary meetings and readings were arranged by close friends of Nabokov's, the Tatarinovs. The meetings were held once a week, and the place of the meeting would change from week to week. The meeting place would usually be at a private house or a large flat. There was always a carefully followed programme. Someone would recite poetry or read his prose. Or there might be a performance of some kind. Afterwards there might be questions or comments from the audience. Then everyone went home. The evenings, Nabokov remembers, were sometimes quite interesting and at other times exceedingly boring.

There were also many private parties given in the great Russian tradition of the nineteenth-century literary evening. At one of these in the beginning of 1926 Nabokov had one of the first **167** successes of his literary career. He read his first novel, *Mary*, in its entirety in a three-hour sitting with one intermission. The company included *The Rudder*'s regular literary critic Yuly Aikhenval'd and the philosopher Grigory Landau. The novel was warmly received by all, though Madame Landau did register the reservation that the style of the novel was too polished. One of the guests that evening was a Professor Makarov who had only shortly before been in Russia and as it happened had stayed at a *dacha* near Siverskaya. After the reading he told Nabokov how he had at once recognized the region which *Mary* describes. The little book did not create too much of a stir in the critical press—Aikhenval'd wrote a rather lonely laudatory essay in *The Rudder*—but all the same it had a certain *succès d'estime* in émigré Berlin.

Yuly Aikhenval'd had established himself as one of the best-known literary critics in Russia prior to the revolution. His three-volume collection of impressionistic essays on Russian writers went through many editions. He was the son of a rabbi from the South of Russia who became a Christian not in rebellion or for social convenience but, some said, simply through a sincere belief that acceptance of the Orthodox faith might somehow bring him closer to Russian culture, which was the main love of his life. There was something impish in his manner. He was a very small man, and his face was folded in nearsightedness which glasses did little to correct. It was the death of him.

Aikhenval'd can lay claim to being the first important critic to grant recognition to Nabokov. Although he had not much liked Nabokov's early poetic efforts, he had spotted his talent even prior to *Mary* and clipped out and collected all the Sirin pieces which appeared in newspapers and journals. On the evening when Nabokov read his novel aloud at a party Aikhenval'd praised it to the point—Nabokov wrote his mother—where it became almost embarrassing. Looking back on Aikhenval'd's critical activity Nabokov told me: —**He adopted a strange method of writing an article on this or that author in the style of that author. That produced a stylistically pretentious effect. At the same time he had been responsible for demolishing two *frauds*, two puffed-up writers, Briusov and Gorky. I think he was a first-rate critic. The only thing I disliked about his style was this somewhat precious way he had of using the words and phrases of his author. His style was too sweet perhaps. But very honest. Extremely honest.** Aikhenval'd was a true Russian, or, better, he showed the Russian character at

168

its finest. Everyone seems to have liked him. He was well known for telling the story against himself of how he had once been snubbed by haughty Leo Tolstoy, and, although Joseph Hessen was the editor of both *The Word* and the newspaper for which Aikhenval'd wrote, there was one author published by Hessen whom Aikhenval'd simply refused to write about, and he could not be budged from his decision.

Aikhenval'd was the central figure in Madame Tatarinov's literary circle. The Nabokovs gave a little party in the winter of 1928, just after *King, Queen, Knave* had appeared (Aikhenval'd wrote a review praising the novel in much stronger terms than he had the previous one, and this time his positive review was joined by some others) and just before Aikhenval'd was about to go to deliver some lectures in Estonia. He was in an especially good mood that evening because he had received word from the Soviet Union, where his family had remained—Aikhenval'd was one of a large group of prominent intellectuals and philosophers who were forcibly expelled from the Soviet Union in 1922—that he had become a grandfather for the first time. There were about eight people at the party. Other guests included Raissa Tatarinov, Grigory Landau, and—Nabokov thinks but is not absolutely sure—Piotrovsky and his wife were there, too.

The Nabokovs' flat had two rooms which, as frequently happens with large urban flats which have been subdivided, were not proportioned in accordance with their nominal functions. One room was a living room; the other, a bedroom. But the living room was far too small to entertain more than two people, while the dimensions of the high-ceilinged bedroom far exceeded the space in which most people would sleep comfortably. The party was held in the bedroom. The beds were in one corner, and there was a large table from which tea and cakes were served. In another corner of the room there was a stove, and as it was a cold winter night and a cold room, Aikhenval'd and some of the other guests spent much of the evening talking animatedly and reciting poetry at the stove. The Nabokovs recall that it was an extraordinarily successful evening. The guests dispersed at about one in the morning. Aikhenval'd walked down the short flight of stairs, Nabokov following behind with the keys. Aikhenval'd somehow caught the cuff of his overcoat on an ornamental projection, and the young novelist had to disentangle the critic from a state of semi-suspension. On his way home Yuly Aikhenval'd had to cross the Kurfür- **169** stendamm and saw too late a tram clattering its way through the Berlin night. He died without regaining consciousness.

Sasha Chyorny, the poet who had helped Nabokov's father prepare *The Empyrean Path,* was another older writer who presided beneficently over the beginning of Sirin's literary career. He, too, was a tiny man (with eyes which have been described as luminous and extremely dark), and, like Aikhenval'd, he met his death prematurely in an accident (helping to fight a neighbourhood fire while visiting his son in provincial France, he had a heart attack). Chyorny—his real name was Aleksandr Glikberg—was well known prior to 1917 for his light satirical poems in *The Satyricon,* a magazine to which Mayakovsky also contributed. (Vladimir Mayakovsky acknowledged only Chyorny, who was the first to write "unpoetical" poetry in Russian, as an influence upon him.) In emigration Chyorny changed his manner and became a serious poet. Nabokov thinks very highly of Chyorny's émigré poetry and felt very close to him personally. Sasha Chyorny criticized the poetry of his young colleague and also **—helped me a good deal, in, I wouldn't say praising my verse, but in suggesting that you might send your poem here or there.** For all the sorrow of exile, there is sufficient evidence that in the first decade of the Russian emigration many older writers and critics such as Aikhenval'd and Chyorny helped to bring forth the new generation which some were sure would never arise in the unpropitious non-Russian air of Western Europe. That generation did appear. Nabokov was its greatest member.

Weimar Germany, the cultural historians tell us, was the fountainhead of some of this century's most brilliant and stridently anguished art. But whatever the world of the Russian émigré was, it was not the world shown in George Grosz's bitterly satirical anti-bourgeois drawings, because most of the émigrés, even if they had been subject to the dangers of *bourgeoisisme* before going into emigration, enjoyed some advantages as well as disadvantages of rootlessness. It was not the world of Bertolt Brecht—that style and those politics had had their time in Russia starting in 1914, and the emigration was hardly the place for this disposition, which was proving difficult enough to sustain even for Mayakovsky, the Poet of the Revolution. It was also not the world of Joseph von Sternberg's *Blue Angel* or Hesse's *Steppenwolf,* because the Russian émigré did not—and this was doubly true in the case of the émigré artist—really believe in the life he was living and hence either turned to the past or, as in the case of Sirin, treated the present far more calmly and disinterestedly than his German counterpart. And as for the Berlin of Herr Issyvoo, that, Nabokov briskly informed me, is —**the acme of vulgarity.** The Russians lived with each other in Berlin and marked time, hoping that history would allow them to go back even if it was not on a White steed. A feeling of decadent despair would come to a portion of the Russian emigration, and the seeds of it were evident in individuals (the use of dope was quite widespread), but as a general mood this occurred much later, in Paris.

The Russian artist in Berlin had something in common—and that only on the most superficial everyday level—with the ordinary beleaguered German who struggled against inflation and led a life which was in no way glamorous. The advantage of the Russian artist was that he did not usually care. The critic Viktor Shklovsky, who was living in Berlin in those years and who wrote a book, *Zoo, or Letters Not about Love,* which is in part about émigré Berlin, tells us that most of Berlin's Russians live in the area of the city contiguous to the Zoo, and they don't need to go anywhere else, Shklovsky explains, because Berlin is all the same to them anyway. In his 1929 collection of short stories and poems, *The Return of Chorb,* Nabokov has a work, "A Guide to Berlin," not quite a short story, not quite a philosophical article, which consists simply of five little pieces: on large sewage pipes which have been left on the street and are lightly covered with snow; the Berlin tram which, as Nabokov correctly forecast, will have vanished in twenty years; various ordinary workers going about their business in the city; the Zoological Gardens (viewed as a highly artificial paradise for the city); and a tavern. The city is seen from the future, when the most ordinary aspects of everyday life will acquire a festive and beautiful air. Thus Nabokov admits Berlin to his art, but a distance from it is all the same consciously held.

The Russian in Berlin rarely had the luxury of a routine day, and in this respect the number of parts which Nabokov played was typical of the lives of many more ordinary émigrés. A recollection of those years—there are unfortunately not so very many—recalls an acquaintance who delivered milk on a three-wheeled contraption with a large box for the milk, and in the evenings, in no way a "milkman," cut an elegant figure at dances and also acted in **171** many émigré theatrical productions. The Russians of Berlin didn't complain much. Russian restaurants closed and then reopened with new names and managements, but the metamorphosis was somehow never completed. As the inflation worsened, the lot of the taxidrivers—doctors, professors, engineers—grew harder. A well-known comedian had a line: **—I'm a Russian emigrant, and so I live on air,** which doesn't *sound* terribly funny, but one trusts that Russians laughed. Russians operated many of the city's tobacco and newsstands, miniature gypsy affairs on wagon wheels which were towed away at the end of the day, and in particular sections of town these booths always seemed to have a cluster of Russians discussing the latest news or gossip from the Soviet Union or sometimes perhaps even the literary reading or concert of the preceding evening. The thing which the Germans could not understand was why these newsstands never seemed to open until nine in the morning.

In later years, when Nabokov's reputation had been established, the literary reading gradually supplanted the lesson as a major source of income. He refers to this change in his life pattern, which began before they left Germany, as Phase II of his émigré life. In the early years in Berlin, although there were many literary evenings, they usually did not pay or pay very much, and the platform was shared by several poets. I have gleaned the following dates for public readings in which Sirin took part during the 1920s from émigré newspaper announcements and accounts: a reading on March 25, 1924, at the Flugerverband (Schöneberger Ufer 40); on April 18, 1924 (Fasanenstrasse, 78, am Kurfurstendamm); a reading at an unspecified place (of a poem about Pushkin which appeared four days later in *The Rudder*) on June 10, 1925; a reading on April 1, 1926, in the flat of Joseph Hessen; another reading at an unspecified place on April 9, 1926; in October 1926, at an evening when he was summoned from the audience and read impromptu with great success; on November 24, 1926, the place also unknown, but it was a large hall; a reading, of a poem about Joan of Arc, on November 18, 1927 (Fasanenstrasse, 23); on November 24, 1927, at an assembly marking the tenth anniversary of the Volunteer White Army; on November 28, 1927, at the Café Leon with Ofrosimov and another friend, Matusevich, who was an artist as well as a writer—Nabokov wrote a short review notice about him for *The Rudder* in 1931; at an Easter Festival on April 24, 1928; and at an evening celebrating the centenary of Tolstoy's

172

birth on September 12, 1928. After that Sirin begins to have the stage to himself, and prose makes its appearance. On March 3, 1930, Nabokov read his recent novella, *The Eye*, in its entirety in a large auditorium.

That chance list of readings must, of course, be a very skeletal remnant of the total number of literary readings in which Nabokov took part. He was a popular reader, and in those readings which I have discovered through press accounts the particular success enjoyed by Sirin is almost invariably singled out. On November 24, 1926, for example, during an evening dedicated to the theme of St. Petersburg, Nabokov read a series of sonnets on the city, and my source (*The Way* [*Put'*], No. 2, November 28, 1926) records: —*For a long time the audience held him on the podium with its applause.* In recalling his early readings, Nabokov said rather matter-of-factly: —**I always had a friendly audience, being a man of *tremendous* charm when I was young. I had, I . . . Really, darling, really!!** Véra Evseevna, who remembers attending his readings even before she knew him, smiles quizzically: —**And should I say 'Yes,' or should I say 'No,' or what? —I dunno . . . And humour. Charm and humour.** The company, led by Nabokov, breaks into laughter.

In 1924 Nabokov visited Prague for the second time—he had first gone there in 1922–23—to see his mother. When he returned he wrote (January 31, 1924) to her:

—*Today I transferred to the Pension Andersen, Lutherstrasse 21, III, and I am terribly pleased with my room which is spacious and light with an excellent desk and non-creaking cupboards, a bathroom where it is very convenient to unfold one's tub, a sofa which is not much to look at but wonderfully soft in composition, and finally, with an excellent comfortable bed on which I shall sleep till eleven, for in my pension they get up late and at all hours, which more than a little disturbs the landlady, a sallow and mustachioed Spanish woman from Chile with whom I converse in French. The food is excellent, and there is no trace of Germanic miserliness and primness, and all of this for four marks a day. I cashed my cheque through Borman in the Pikus office, and so I have no cares for about twenty days. If not today then tomorrow I shall receive in addition a pound from Korostovets for the translation of his first article in **The Times**, and since we have five articles in reserve I shall not have to struggle for my existence. My* **173** *deal will soon come off, and I shall know exactly how many pounds I can count on per month, and besides that on Sunday Lukash and I shall demand **in an absolutely firm fashion** $1,000 from Yakobson, in part as an advance and in part as payment for the completed pantomime which we have just been redoing and copying out again. Finally, through the charming composer Eilukhin we have penetrated the theatrical labyrinth and have been commissioned to do an operetta and a short play something on the order of our **Living Water** for which we also should receive an advance on the order of $100–$200. I have one other theatrical hope, which is, I fear, less promising than the others. Hessen is arranging a reading of **The Tragedy of Mister Morn** at which, by the way, Schmidt and Polevitskaya will be present, and the latter may act in it. Hessen himself proposed this to me . . . and generally he has shown a desire to help me in every way possible. In the course of all these days I haven't had a chance to touch **Mr. Morn** so the final scene still hasn't been rewritten, and the reading is going to be in several days. Aikhenval'd scolded [Lukash] for **White Flower** in **Today,** which hasn't improved his spirits. However radiant our joint theatrical future might be in the financial sense, after so many disappointments he cannot bring himself to cast his hopes in watercolour hues. This morning his daughter was christened. I visited Bobrovsky (at Friedenau) and found Tatyana Konstantinevna hugely pregnant. But both of them are in rather good spirits in spite of the forthcoming liquidation of their store. . . . As soon as possible I shall have you come here (by March), and we shall start to live as one ought. . . .*

But the firm conversation with Yakobson—not to speak of a subsequent correspondence lasting six months which a future biographer may find in some Estonian attic (Yakobson, by the way, is the drudge dramatist in *The Gift*)—did not realize Nabokov's hopes. Lukash was right to be wary of their radiant prospects in drama and the film. *The Tragedy of Mister Morn,* which is one of Nabokov's good unpublished early works, was not staged. The journal in the founding of which Nabokov was to have taken part foundered for lack of funds before its first issue. The work for English newspapers did not prove substantive or long-lived. The deal did not come off, and, as a consequence of all these ephemeral hopes, of course, Nabokov could not bring his mother and the children back to Berlin. The mark had just begun to falter then, and by August it was necessary to transfer to another pension because his landlady now wanted seventy marks per week.

In 1924 Nabokov began to write a great deal more prose, and fairly quickly he had amassed eight stories which he was considering publishing as a collection. These stories (a few of them were never published) appeared for the most part in the Riga daily *Today (Segodnya)* and the Berlin weekly *Echo (Èkho)*. —**Those papers, they were my wastebaskets,** which is not strictly speaking true because some of these stories which have only recently come to light —"Vengeance," "A Chance Occurrence"—are remarkably strong, though it is true that a few of the others—"Wingstroke," "The Gods—are overwritten poetic prose. In my opinion 1924 was the watershed year in the quality of Nabokov's writing.

Payment for his stories—never more than twenty-five to thirty-five dollars—could be very tardy, even from *The Rudder,* which was no longer as financially sound in 1924 as it had once been. The normal difficulty of finding a publisher was compounded by the fact that several of the important Berlin publishers had gone over to the new orthography with an eye to suiting the Soviet market; Nabokov preferred the old orthography, which he still uses when he writes in Russian. Everything stayed the same though a little tattier, but Nabokov kept on, with the boring work of his lessons which he now could give, he said, almost without thinking, and with the nighttime creativity which became more and more important to him. In 1926—he was already married then—he scraped together a hundred sixty-five marks, not without difficulty, to have a new suit made, blue with very broad trousers. (Of the two suits which he had had prior to that, the grey one was ripped at the elbows and the blue one glistened like the sun.) This new suit, necessary for, among other things, literary readings, satisfied Nabokov's modest material needs.

In his earliest Berlin years—beginning at the time when he visited Berlin from Cambridge—Nabokov was a very sociable and eligible young man. He has written that he looks back upon this period of his life as if he were a multiplicity of strangers. Several of his romances might have ended in marriage, but some essential detail always interfered just in time. He met a girl selling balloons at a ball in London with whom he had been in love and played in St. Petersburg when he was nine. He began to see a great deal of her, but she dropped him when by chance she learned of the other girls whom he was also seeing at Cambridge. Besides, she doubted **175** his prospects for the future and once told Nabokov that she wanted to marry someone who would —**leave something substantial behind, like a bridge!!** The family of another girl was dead set against the prospect of marriage because they viewed Nabokov's father as a dangerous "leftist liberal." Another girl accepted the proposal of a White officer. Nabokov tells tales about his youthful romances with impersonally good-natured amusement. Very occasionally in the course of recent decades he has chanced to hear of or actually meet one or two of these old girl friends. Once a matron advanced upon him with outspread arms and beaming face during an intermission in a theatre lobby. He suddenly realized who it was. —**Ah, Novikov!** she said.

In a letter to his mother in August 1924 Nabokov remarks almost parenthetically that it is time for him to marry and settle down.

Nabokov married Véra Evseevna Slonim on April 15, 1925. They have been and are very close to one another, and members of the family are united in their (unprovable, of course) belief that Nabokov would never have become the writer he is were it not for the balance and stability which Véra Evseevna added to his life. But Nabokov's wife is really a much, much more private person than he—Nabokov is an intensely private person, too, but he also struggles with counter urges—the sort of perfectly private person in fact who, so the tradition goes, deems it proper to appear in the newspapers twice, at birth and at death. That happy possibility has long since slipped by, for now she cannot escape attention. An interviewer from an Israeli magazine, only a little bit (because it is funny) above the sort of thing which Véra Evseevna must now endure several times a year, writes of her:

—Véra and Vladimir Nabokov come in like two famous mature actors, aware of their own importance. Véra is one of the most impressive women I've ever seen. Her black suit shows a nice and well-proportioned figure. She certainly has a "Jewish look." She talks softly and quietly. Her laughter is restrained, while his is rolling. Tears come down his cheeks, and he continually takes off his glasses as the laughter proceeds. A tall man with wide shoulders and a large balding head. He is 71, and she is all woman.

As we discuss the place of Nabokov's wife in his biography, Nabokov comes to the aid of his biographer: —**Darling, why don't** you say something? Why? —I don't think I should be represented. —You can't help being represented! We're too far gone! It's too late! Laughter. Tears. Glasses. He wipes his left eye with the back of his right hand. Hesitantly, unwillingly, and ever so carefully, Véra Evseevna begins to tell me a little bit of her story. But she softly warns me first: —I am terribly concerned about accuracy, that the facts be right.

Véra Evseevna's father, who was born in 1865, studied law as a young man in St. Petersburg, and he at first became an associate lawyer in the firm of his great uncle. It was the period when Russian Jews were entering into Russian culture for the first time, and it was also at just this time that the new laws laying down the *protsentnaya norma* for Jews in many fields of endeavour were enacted in Russia. Very many Jews nominally changed religion in order to avoid the often very difficult restrictions imposed by this most abnormal "norm." It was quite easy to do. But Evsei Slonim, who was not a practising Jew at all, thought such an expediency disgraceful, and instead he simply abandoned the law. For a while he toyed with the idea of leaving Russia and going to practise law in France, but his family circumstances were such that in the end he decided to stay in Russia and enter business. He was very successful. He made wise forestry investments—he taught himself forestry from scratch and never allowed a tree to be felled without another being planted in its place—and he had a partnership in a business which supplied the wooden support beams used in mine shafts. The Slonim timber was transported—in one location on a small railway which Slonim himself had had built—to the Western Dvina River, on which it was floated to Riga tied up into enormous rafts. He also served as a financial advisor to one of Russia's great fortunes.

Evsei Slonim traced his descent in a direct line from a celebrated (and abstruse) Spanish commentator on the Talmud who, in turn, could trace his descent directly from the ancient Judean kings. The Slonim family was multilingual on essentially the same lines as the Nabokov family: Russian, French, German, and English—Vladimir Vladimirovich recalls that before they married, Véra Evseevna was his only real "competition" for English lessons in Berlin. Véra Evseevna told me that at fifteen she did not consider herself a Kadet but a Socialist in spirit, but all that quickly changed, of course, after the revolution.

Shortly before the revolution Evsei Slonim bought up the   **177** greater portion of a small town in southern Russia. He wanted to make a model city complete with canalization and modern streetcars, a project which so enchanted his daughter that she was given a promise that she would be allowed to participate in the project when she grew up. At the time of the revolution Véra Evseevna, with her mother, two sisters (both of whom are still alive, one in Sweden and the other living in Switzerland), and one of their servants made their way circuitously to the South of Russia by train. Eventually her father joined them there, and the family sailed from the Crimea to Constantinople, from where they proceeded to Bulgaria for six or seven weeks before going on to Berlin. Evsei Slonim was quite fortunate in that one of his business associates, a Dutchman, was also a friend and business associate of one of the wealthiest men in Germany, Stinnes, and through this connection he was able to sell his considerable landholdings in Russia to Stinnes, who was purchasing Russian land quite cheaply on a speculative basis—the gamble seemed a good one—and even assisted some other émigrés to make similar phantom sales. Evsei Slonim was able to take up business activity (exporting farm machinery to the Balkans) in Berlin, but he was ruined by the German inflation and lost everything once again.

An offer was made to Evsei Slonim in 1923, which he accepted, to become a partner in one of the publishing houses (with Makovsky, formerly an important publisher in Moscow) which intended to produce English translations of Russian books for export to the United States. The publishing house folded without having published a single book. It was through this short-lived firm, Orbis, that Nabokov first met Véra Evseevna's father. He remembers climbing the stairs to the office with Gleb Struve, a friend from Cambridge (they first read Blok's *The Twelve* stretched out on an Oxford green together, the russet-haired Nabokov considerably less enthusiastic about the poem than his redheaded friend) and the son of the well-known Marxist-turned-conservative-liberal political figure and editor, Pyotr Struve. They were talking about how much they could expect to get from them for their translation of Dostoevsky . . . Nabokov recalls that Struve thought his estimate too modest and kept repeating: —**No, no, that's not enough! They should pay more than that!** as they climbed the stairs. They did not meet each other that day, though they managed to remember later that they had seen each other in the offices where Véra Evseevna was working. She was doing it in order to earn money for horseback riding in the Tiergarten.

Shortly after that first not-quite-encounter they met at a charity ball. Nabokov was away from Berlin working during the summer of 1923, but he wrote to her once that summer. They saw a lot of each other after his return to Berlin. (Nabokov often played chess with Evsei Slonim.) After they were married, Nabokov wrote to his mother about his father-in-law: —*He understands so well that for me the main thing in life and the sole thing which I am capable of doing is to write.*

Véra Evseevna had attended the Obolensky School in St. Petersburg. It was only chance that she and Vladimir Vladimirovich didn't meet there, because she knew many boys from the Tenishev School. Her upbringing was culturally advanced but very strict (—**When can I be free of my governess?** she remembers asking her parents in exasperation as a young lady. —**When you are married,** she was told), and she had plans to study physics. She was a precocious child and is today a very learned lady, in certain areas perceptibly faster than her husband, which is no small praise. One day, when we were discussing Nabokov's first novel, I asked if they could name another novel in Russian literature which is titled with a girl's nickname. Nabokov reared back in amused incredulity, as he is wont to do (—**What is this, an examination?!**), but Véra Evseevna almost instantly answered *Polinka Saxe*, a dusty and obscure nineteenth-century novel by Druzhinin, and she disqualified her own answer because the title contains a last name as well and just as rapidly named Turgenev's *Asya*, though she granted that it was not really a novel.

Although Véra Evseevna doesn't like to talk about herself, she won't be pushed into false modesty either. When I ask about her participation in butterfly expeditions, Vladimir Vladimirovich starts to answer for her (—**She is, but . . .**), yet finds there is no need: —**I've had wonderful luck. I've gotten many things he didn't get.** I ask whether this is something where one "wins," because I know that the Nabokovs very much believe in winning. The answer is yes and no. —**And once I saw a butterfly that he wanted very much, and he wouldn't believe me, that I had seen it.** Her husband still doubts: —**Yes, that's right, that's right. And on the side of the path you saw snakes actually jumping into the air. I think it was a dream.**

Véra Evseevna gracefully cedes the advantage to her husband in chess and tennis. They discuss their respective cases of *audition colorée:* —**She has different colours. And I don't think they are quite as bright as mine. Or are they?** —**You don't want them to be,**   179 she replies sweetly. She doesn't write, though in the early years of *The Rudder* she published some translations of a Bulgarian Symbolist writer. Here is the main thing: her enormous admiration and love for her husband's writing have never wavered, but at the same time her exceptional intelligence and critical independence have always been at play. She has always had quiet certitude about his artistic stature. And she has preserved all the publishing correspondence, including the many rejection slips over the decades.

Véra Evseevna was frequently at pains to stress that *her* biography is not the same as her husband's. **—We are very different, you know. Very different.** I reminded Vladimir Vladimirovich and Véra Evseevna that once before when we had discussed this question (**—Is he a behaviourist, darling?**) I had been told they were exactly alike, and I didn't believe it. **—Yes, we are exactly alike in one or two respects.**

Without drawing a portrait of Véra Evseevna myself I will say only that virtually all the printed descriptions I have read of her strike me as wholly or seriously wanting. In terms of simple description the would-be portraitists are so taken with her striking head of white hair—she had very light blonde hair which turned prematurely white—that details of her person which are no less evident are overlooked. There is, for example, her voice. **—Darling, he has something there which he put very cautiously and cleverly. There is something about the way you speak which is, well, there is a certain unusual refinement.** His wife rejects the notion. But I will not draw the portrait that is in my mind. . . . Another impression some have conveyed is far more serious. Since Nabokov switched to English and achieved fame she has often been charged with representing his anger (have I mentioned that Nabokov does have a temper?), in much softened form, to the outside world, particularly the publishing world, and people have made her bear the blame. She is in reality quite a different person. **—She has the best sense of humour of any woman I have ever known,** Nabokov says proudly of her.

They had two witnesses when they were married in the Berlin town hall. These were required by law, and Vladimir Vladimirovich and Véra Evseevna purposely chose two of their most peripheral acquaintances. As the foursome was coming out afterwards, one of their witnesses (**—and he was *echt deutsch*, real German**) said to them, referring to the porter or doorman of the Rathaus:

—He's congratulated you. Nabokov laughed loudly. **—I said,**

'How nice.' He laughed again. —We just walked out. I didn't have, you see, a *penny* in my pocket! We had to pay a certain sum. We had paid. That was all we had.

I would like to allude to the grace and the quietude which were a part of Nabokov's life in the twenties. We see it in Nabokov's comment in a letter to his mother (September 1924) about a pathetic letter he received from his former governess: —*I answered her at once. I have reached the original conclusion that if one performs at least one good act per day (even if it is nothing more than giving one's place to an elderly person on the tram) life becomes exceedingly more pleasant. In the final analysis everything in the world is very simple and founded upon two or three not very complicated truths. . . .* It is present, too, in the way he spoke to me of some friends of this period of his life: —**They were gentle people, delightful, innocent people, talented people. They never did anything mean to anyone.** The people with whom Nabokov and his wife associated most closely (I am drawing their names from the list of those to whom presentation copies of his first novel were sent), people such as the Hessens, the Tatarinovs, the Lukashes, the Kaminkas, Aikhenval'd, were, predominantly, essentially, people who could meet these delicate standards of judgment. The lives of these Berlin émigrés were not much cluttered with anything except literature, friendship, honour, and love for Russia. Once, when a Rumanian violinist who played at a café frequented by Nabokov and his friends was accused in court of having driven his wife to suicide and then showed up for work as though nothing had happened, Nabokov and his friend Mikhail Kaminka drew straws to see who would be the first to hit him. Nabokov won. When his turn came Kaminka took on not only the Rumanian violinist but the rest of the orchestra as well in a general melee. Their wives watched approvingly in the audience. For the next few days Nabokov and Kaminka remained at home waiting for the promised seconds so that the duel could be arranged. They never came. But this incident of rowdy chivalry was not at all typical of the sort of lives they led.

In his correspondence with his mother Nabokov returns repeatedly, and especially every March, the anniversary of his father's death, to the past:

—*We shall again see him, in an unexpected but completely natural paradise, in a country where everything is radiance and fine-* **181** *ness. He will walk towards us in our common bright eternity, slightly raising his shoulders in the way that he used to do, and with no surprise at all we shall kiss the birthmark on his hand. You must live in expectation of this tender hour . . . and never give yourself over to the temptation of despair. Everything will return. In the way that in a certain time the hands of the clock come together again. . . .*

From 1933 to 1937, the year in which they left Berlin, Nabokov and his wife lived with one of Véra Evseevna's cousins, Anna Feigin, the daughter of her maternal uncle. This is the same cousin whom they looked after in Montreux for many years. For two weeks after their marriage they had had to continue to live apart. Then they moved into two rented rooms in a larger flat. Over the years they never had and never coveted a flat of their own. Their best and most prolonged residence was her cousin's large four-room flat at Grunewald. The address was 22 Nestorstrasse. Both of Véra Evseevna's parents died in 1928, and her cousin, who had taught herself how to type doing the manuscript of *Mary*, became a kind of older sister to them both. They drank to her health every New Year's Eve in Switzerland while she was alive.

In early 1928 Nabokov was mounting a forced march to complete *King, Queen, Knave*. Nabokov went to a doctor, a lung specialist, and paid a fee to find out how to kill his heroine: —**"I have to kill her," I said to him. He looked at me in stony silence.** But whereas the characters in *Mary* had become —*real people, not characters invented by me. I know the odour of each of them, how he walks, eats . . .* (from a letter to his mother, October 1925), Nabokov complained that he was so bored without Russians in his new novel that he found himself tempted to lay it aside in favour of entomology, but he resisted the urge. Butterflies were one of the passions Nabokov sacrificed throughout most of the twenties. In 1926 he had visited the Entomological Institute at Dahlem on the outskirts of Berlin with a Russian friend. He became acquainted with the noted entomologist Moltrecht, a corpulent and red-cheeked scholar with a politician's extinguished cigar clamped between his teeth, who gruffly but delicately handled the butterflies and spoke of them (in a throaty Germanic Russian) so eloquently and with so much feeling that Nabokov was deeply moved. He went back, and occasionally he classified butterflies there. In 1925, while on his way to his regular pupil early in the morning, he saw an extremely rare large moth on the trunk of a linden tree near the Charlottenburg railway station. He captured it and took it straight to the astounded owner of a nearby butterfly store, to whom he sold it. Nabokov kept on with *King, Queen, Knave.* He had begun to think of the novel in August 1927, while he and Véra Evseevna were on that Baltic working vacation with a pupil. By mid-February Nabokov had written ninety pages; by April he had already reached page 330 and nearly had it finished. (His mother visited them from Prague, and he read the book to her in five or six successive evenings.) Nineteen twenty-eight and twenty-nine were good years. The German translation of his novel, which he had seriously doubted for a time would ever appear, was done, and then Ullstein published a translation of *King, Queen, Knave* as well. His collection of short stories and poems, *The Return of Chorb,* was published in Russian, and, what was most important, Ilya Fondaminsky, one of the editors of the main émigré publication, *Contemporary Annals,* made a trip to Berlin from Paris, one of the main purposes of which was to recruit Sirin's work for the journal, which he did with a vigorous Russian slap on his knee. Prior to that only some poems by Nabokov had appeared in *Contemporary Annals.* A long and generally happy association with the journal began with the appearance of his novella *The Eye* in 1930, followed by his first major novel, *The Defense.*

Standing on this little islet of security while the swiftly rising never-ending German inflation eddied and ripped around them, Vladimir Vladimirovich and Véra Evseevna were able to move to more comfortable quarters and even to put a deposit on a lakeside plot of land near Kolberg. The property they obtained was a sliver of land from an enormous estate which was being subdivided for weekend and vacation homes. Their friends Mikhail Kaminka and his wife spent time there with them. Vladimir Vladimirovich and Véra Evseevna used their lakeside land in the summer of 1929, picnicking and swimming; there was tennis nearby, too. Nabokov was finishing *The Defense.* It was their intention to build a little summer house of three or four rooms there, but it turned out that they were not that well off, and they gradually cooled towards the idea and finally relinquished the land, which was, however, subsequently developed and used in *Despair,* where that lake provides the backdrop for the murder.

The Nabokovs and the Kaminkas next had plans to leave Ger-   **183** many together. From Nabokov's point of view, though he was better off than before, Russian literary life had shifted from Berlin, various old friends were gone, there were no longer the literary journals and theatres. There was really nothing to hold him in Berlin. They had plans to immigrate to Australia and become sheep farmers, but the Kaminkas were having second thoughts, and there were other problems as well, and so that plan, which had been under active consideration in 1929 and 1930, fell by the wayside, too. Incredibly, the Nabokovs remained in Berlin for seven more years. It was far too long, and they were lucky to get out at all in the end.

CHAPTER

6

W e have only one portrait of Vladimir Nabokov
dating from his émigré period. It was done by Magda Nachman-
Achariya, a close friend of Anna Feigin, in Berlin circa 1935. (She
was the friend of the family who brought him case histories once
when he was ill, and Nabokov wrote a short review-notice of one
of her exhibitions in 1928. The Nabokovs described her to me as
a —tremendously sensitive person.) It is not at all certain that the
portrait, a crayon drawing, still exists, for it and portraits which
Nachman-Achariya made at the same time of Véra Evseevna and
Nabokov's mother were in a trunk of stored papers which was
either destroyed or stolen during World War II, but fortunately a
photograph of the portrait was preserved, and it was used as the   **187**

jacket photograph for the English translation of *Glory*. The picture has, to my eye, two striking characteristics. Nabokov, not only because his hair is shown slicked back and very close to his head, somehow appears wet in the picture, as though he has just emerged from the water. This is a matter of style, of course, and in the other Indian pictures which I have seen (Nachman-Achariya immigrated to India, where she had a certain degree of success as a painter) one sees this same air or posture of being a little out of place and very conscious of oneself in many of her subjects. It is a style which suits Nabokov's personality quite well. The other characteristic emanates from the subject: Nabokov looks at us in that picture not only as a man who knows precisely who he is and what he can do, but also what he has done. He is still a young man, but he has a different assurance about him. The snapshots of this period, mostly with tilted shoulders and patient smiles, do not capture this aspect of his personality nearly as well as Magda Nachman-Achariya's study.

Nabokov's second novel had been both structurally and emotionally almost a total reaction against the damp emotionalism (Nabokov's phrase) of his first. The warmth of feeling of *Mary*, which owed something to the influence of Ivan Bunin's poetic prose, is turned inside out in *King, Queen, Knave*, where all the pulleys and levers of the novelist's craft are purposely bared and emotion flashes into view only occasionally in the background. The two novels stand rather awkwardly beside one another.

His third novel, *The Defense*, following hard on *King, Queen, Knave* in 1930, presents something else again: a perfect synthesis of the two techniques. The virtuoso attempt to balance the so different potentialities of his first two works remains the key and the achievement of all Nabokov's subsequent books, and the failure to find this balance in the narrative and smooth swoop of pace is the primary fault of those works which in one degree or another fail artistically. The reception given *The Defense* in émigré literary circles was a hush of recognition. From the start émigré criticism had tended to assume that émigré literature, deprived of Russia, could not sustain itself. D. S. Mirsky, whose politics were leftist but whose literary opinions are almost always scrupulously fair and exact, wrote of the first years of *Contemporary Annals:*

—In literary terms **Contemporary Annals** is animated by the
inertia which pre-revolutionary Russia provided. The services of

Contemporary Annals before Russian literature are of course great. Like good conservatives its editors have preserved and are passing on to posterity everything which writers had not managed to write before the revolution. It may be that it was not worth while finishing such works later, but better late than never and even a work which loses something in the eyes of the present by its tardiness has, if it is really great, nothing to lose in the eyes of the future. It is for the future to judge whether Contemporary Annals has provided works of art which can stand above time.

And a short while later (on the eve of Nabokov's first novel in fact) Mirsky was ready to pass final judgment on the possibility of a further continuation of émigré literature in his 1926 English history *Contemporary Russian Literature:* —*The worst thing,* he wrote, *to be said about the émigré literature is that it has no healthy undergrowth: not a single poet or novelist of any importance has emerged from the ranks of the young generation outside Russia.* There is no question but that, for all the intense literary activity in émigré Berlin, Paris, and Prague, this sense of possible cultural foreclosure was present in everyone's mind. Nabokov himself had voiced it in a 1927 book review: —*Pray God that these years of emigration do not pass in vain for the Russian Muse.* Ilya Fondaminsky and many others as well saw *The Defense* as the first flower and justification of both émigré culture and *Contemporary Annals,* though, if the recollection of Berberova is correct, there were some who were surprised that that flowering should have come from the pen of V. Sirin.

In May 1930 Nabokov made his first trip abroad for a literary reading, to Prague, where he read several poems and excerpts from *The Defense.* The literary readings now assumed something of the formality of the professional lecture circuit. Invitations were given by local literary clubs, occasionally by universities where Russian was studied or there were Russian scholars. There might be anywhere from two hundred to five hundred people at such an evening, and the fee which Nabokov received for a reading could cover the cost of living for three months. Fees from literary readings and appearances in *Contemporary Annals* always exceeded the tiny and haphazard income from the Russian editions of his novels, which never sold more than a few hundred copies. (Nabokov received nothing at all for the Russian edition of *Mary* because it was arranged that, in order to defray the publishing costs, his **189** royalties would begin only after the first thousand copies, at slightly higher than the usual rate.) However limited the possibility of earning one's livelihood by one's pen in the emigration, there nevertheless was, at least in the early years, a very real audience. I have chanced upon the circulation figures for a Berlin lending library in the 1930s, and Sirin books (unfortunately individual works are not specified in the figures) were borrowed nearly three hundred times per year. That was not bad. Among living Russian authors Sirin was outdrawn in this particular library by Ivan Bunin, Dmitri Merezhkovsky, Ivan Shmelyov (whose reputation like Bunin's and Merezhkovsky's was established prior to the revolution), and the younger historical novelist Mark Aldanov, who remained the most popular among the younger émigré writers but whose books are of a much plainer and more accessible sort. Aldanov was the popular author whom Aikhenval'd always declined to review, probably preferring discreet silence to condescension. In Europe, as a young man of charm and possessing a sense of the histrionic, Nabokov's literary readings soon acquired a reputation and attraction of their own. I have seen Nabokov read in his American fame. His speech, distinctive enough in any case, grows a bit more mannered at the lectern. In a venetian-blind effect, the spaces between letters widen ever so slightly so that every word sounds as clearly and distinctly as "elocution" or "evolution" or "electrocution." In Russian his r's are permitted to roll and vibrate much more freely than in ordinary conversation; in English there is sometimes a soft echo at the end of a word so that a word like "much" is pulled along by a little steam engine. Nabokov otherwise reads in an understated fashion with only moderate volume, but he coaxes the text along and warms it with his breath so that the final lines of a poem or key points in a piece of prose are suddenly lifted on an upsweep of rhetoric. Then, but only for a moment, he partakes of the tradition of what Edmund Wilson termed (in his posthumous book, *A Window on Russia*) "Russian platform poetics," though in a quite different way than either Evtushenko or Mayakovsky. The words themselves are clearly more important to Nabokov than the delivery, and it is in part precisely this subtle deference which serves to make Nabokov such an unusual reader. When he was younger a bit more body English, elbows close to his sides, sometimes entered into his readings, but of late Nabokov's post-professorial technique is simply one of passion held in calm relief.

Nabokov's literary fame in the 1920s was confined to occasional and sometimes bizarre manifestations and allusions: one of his poems was parodied in the Soviet newspaper *Pravda* in July 1927 by Demyan Bedny, the poet who eventually became one of Stalin's lackeys, and *King, Queen, Knave* —**Such a good title!** —was borrowed by a minor German novelist for the title of his own book. However, by 1932 the author of *The Defense, The Eye, Glory,* and *Camera Obscura* enjoyed a solid reputation and had provoked considerable curiosity among the émigré reading public. When Nabokov came to France for his first literary reading there in November 1932, he was interviewed by a reporter for the Riga newspaper *Today.* It is the first interview ever given by Nabokov and also the last in his Russian period, thus it is historically quite important, though Nabokov feels quite strongly that the interviewer was a slap-dash reporter —**You may quote me** —and that his reported remarks cannot possibly be considered to be verbatim. Letters to his wife on subsequent reading tours refer to interview requests he has refused. (It was only after *Lolita* that Nabokov took up the interview game, with a vengeance.) The newspaper article noted the interest that Sirin's appearance in Paris had occasioned, and then he provided the following portrait:

—The curious will see a thirty-three-year-old young sportsman, very slender, nervous, and impulsive. His graceful manner and elegant speech with slightly rolled r's came to him from St. Petersburg; Cambridge contributed the look of a sportsman; Berlin gave him his good nature and a certain bagginess in his clothing—few people in Paris wear such macintoshes with button-out linings. [Nabokov notes indignantly that he was wearing an English trenchcoat.—A.F.] He has a long thin face with a high tanned forehead and distinguished features. Sirin speaks quickly and with enthusiasm, but a certain sense of restraint keeps him from talking about himself.

The reporter asked Nabokov about the charge of imitating foreign models which certain hostile émigré critics were beginning to level at him. He replied:

—That's amusing! Yes, they have slated me for being under the influence of German writers whom I do not know. I speak and read German poorly by the way. One might more properly speak **191**

about a French influence: I love Flaubert and Proust. It is curious that I felt my closeness to Western culture while I was still in Russia, but here, in the West, I have not consciously followed any Western writer. Here one especially feels the charms of Gogol and —closer to us in time—of Chekhov.

When the interviewer asked Nabokov why someone who is "physically and morally healthy" has such a predilection for characters who have gone astray, Nabokov answered:

—People who have gone astray? . . . Yes, perhaps you are right. It's difficult to explain this. It would appear that in man's suffering there is more that is significant and interesting than in calm life. Human nature reveals itself more fully. I think that this is what it is. There is something attractive in suffering.

All of this strikes the latter-day Nabokov as merely a reporter's commonplace paraphrase of obvious truths. And finally, Nabokov spoke of the manner in which he writes:

—Mood plays the main role in everything I write. What arises from pure intellect is put on a secondary plane. The plan of my novel comes to me suddenly, is born in a minute. . . . The first jolt is what is important. There are writers who look upon their work as a craft: each day a certain number of pages must be written. But I believe in an intrinsic sense and artistic inspiration. Sometimes I write for twelve hours non-stop. I grow ill when I do this and feel very badly. And sometimes one has to redo and copy out what one has done innumerable times—there are short stories on which I have worked for two months. . . . Sometimes it's necessary to rewrite and change every word.

When Nabokov next read in France, four years later in 1936, the evening was virtually the apogee of his émigré career. Another novel, one of his finest, *Despair*, had been published, and what was to be his major Russian novel, *The Gift*, was shortly to begin serialization in *Contemporary Annals*. The finest critics of the emigration—Vladislav Khodasevich, Vladimir Weidle, Alfred Bem, and (according to Nabokov, his best Russian critic) Pyotr Bitsilli—had all within the preceding two years written about Sirin
192 as a Russian and indeed European writer of the first rank. The

Parnassus of Russian émigré poetry was in the hall that evening (February 9, 1936). Nabokov shared the evening with Vladislav Khodasevich, who read first. Tickets for the reading in a smallish auditorium on the rue Las-Cases had been quickly sold out, and, though extra chairs had been added in the hall, people were still pressing in when Khodasevich had already began to read. Nabokov sat beside Ivan Bunin, who, deathly afraid of catching cold, kept his overcoat and a hat on and his nose buried in his collar. Georgy Adamovich, the important critic and head of the so-called Parisian school of émigré poetry, which was extremely hostile to Khodasevich and to a slightly lesser extent to Nabokov, too, was there, and Khodasevich read a poem about an imaginary poet which satirized Adamovich rather harshly. There had been an unpleasant incident prior to the reading when *The Latest News (Poslednie Novosti)*, the leading Russian newspaper in Paris and the paper for which Adamovich was literary critic, ran an announcement of the reading with Sirin's name printed in much larger type than Khodasevich's, and Nabokov had to complain on behalf of his fellow poet. *The Latest News* had been conducting a small vendetta against Khodasevich for some time. It is ironic and too bad that, once it had indisputably added something to the riches of Russian literature, émigré literature in its second decade turned significantly (there had from the beginning been waftings of it) more sour and sullenly querulous.

After the intermission Nabokov read three short stories (all of about the same length) which he had recently written: *A Russian Beauty, Terra Incognita,* and *Breaking the News.* Nabokov had a bad sore throat, but lozenges kept his voice sufficiently smooth. It was, he wrote his wife, one of the most successful literary readings he had ever had. When the reading was over, a large company of writers, some with husbands and wives, went to drink champagne at the La Fontaine café. Bunin, Khodasevich, Aldanov, Weidle, and Berberova were there; Fondaminsky and another editor of *Contemporary Annals* sat at a nearby table. The conversation was lively, and the group did not disperse until three in the morning. Berberova's recollection in her memoirs of how Nabokov shocked nearly everyone, and Aldanov in particular, by his curt dismissal of some of Tolstoy's early work as juvenilia and his assertion that he had never even read *The Sevastopol Tales* has been denied by Nabokov *(Supplement to Tri-Quarterly 17)*. Berberova writes: — *Aldanov had a hard time not to show his indignation;* but a letter **193** which Nabokov wrote his wife the next day indicates that Aldanov did voice his indignation, it did not really have anything to do with Tolstoy, and the conversation was considerably more interesting than Berberova recalls. Aldanov (Nabokov wrote his wife) screamed at him: *—You despise us all!* He then (real Russian stuff, this) called Nabokov the first writer of the emigration and demanded that Bunin take off his signet-ring and give it to Nabokov as a token in recognition of his superiority. The Nobel Prize-winner demurred, and then Bunin passed his affront on to Khodasevich, whom he did not like, by calling out: *—Hey, Polak!* (Khodasevich was half Polish.) Fortunately, however, the evening was on the whole gayer than these few awkward moments. The slightly corpulent, direct, and commonsensical Aldanov was quite correct (Nabokov was at that point the first writer of the emigration). And the gruff but just Bunin, though Berberova claims he could not hear Nabokov's name without having a tantrum, is credited in the memoirs of Galina Kuznetsova (who lived with him for many years) with having declared: *—Nabokov has discovered a whole new universe, for which one must be grateful to him.*

It seems to me in surveying old letters that poor Aldanov was continually finding himself in difficult situations vis-à-vis Nabokov. He wrote to Nabokov in deep agitation when it was discovered that one of the instalments of *The Gift* for *Contemporary Annals,* of which Aldanov was a contributing editor, satirized several émigré critics transparently and cruelly. And many years later in the United States, when Aldanov was the editor of *The New Review (Novy Zhurnal),* the journal which arose after the demise of *Contemporary Annals*—which closes a nice ring of the sort Nabokov likes because *Contemporary Annals* had many years before in Berlin been born from a short-lived journal called *The Future Russia,* which was also edited by Aldanov—a similar incident in which the roles were reversed took place. Nabokov ferociously took his old friend to task for having innocently published a fictional work by a rather famous Russian person (not, however, an artist) in which there were clear indications of anti-Semitism in the portrayal of several characters. Poor Aldanov, who was himself Jewish (his real name was Landau), was thrown into confusion as he tried both to defend himself against the charge—and it was not only made by Nabokov—of having soiled the pages of his new journal and yet somehow not offend the respected personage who had written the piece. The storm blew over, and Nabokov did contribute some Russian things which he had not had time to publish in Paris to the journal, because he and Aldanov were good and old friends and Nabokov knew that the mistake had been an innocent one, and because Aldanov was too stable and good a person to take umbrage for long. In *Speak, Memory* Nabokov refers to him as —*wise, prim, charming Aldanov.* On a simpler plane there is much about Aldanov's life and career which offers a fuzzy parallel to Nabokov's and explains why it was natural for them to like each other. In addition to his long series of historical novels in Russian, Aldanov wrote one book in another language, a French study of Lenin; he was an expert on Tolstoy, about whom, and many other writers as well, he wrote with a quiet but mordant wit; and finally, he was a chemical engineer by profession and published several learned papers on chemistry topics. It was Aldanov who, having received in 1940 an invitation to teach at the Stanford Summer School the following year, an invitation which was not convenient for him to accept (he felt, incorrectly according to Nabokov, that his English was not fluent enough), passed the opportunity on to his friend, thus finally smoothing the seas for Nabokov's immigration to America.

In the mid-thirties the circuit of Nabokov's lectures traced a loose web to and fro across Europe. He read in Antwerp and Brussels (an excerpt from *Invitation to a Beheading* and the short story "The Aurelian"), where he went without a visa, having been instructed by the Social-Revolutionaries of *Contemporary Annals* in how to disembark from the train at Charleroi and walk calmly across the tracks at a certain point in the underground station to the nearby subway system, as countless Russian revolutionaries travelling through Europe had done before him. He read again in Prague, but this time the Nazis were already becoming bothersome at borders (Nabokov enjoys telling how the flabbergasted Bunin was forcedly given a purgative and shaken out in a search for the jewels which it was evidently presumed a Nobel laureate might be attempting to smuggle away from the future German war effort), and so he went to Czechoslovakia by a roundabout route, carrying in his suitcase the manuscript of one of his sharpest satires on the Teutonic character, the short story "Cloud, Castle, Lake."

One of Nabokov's most fruitful lectures was given for the Russian Department of the University of Dresden, where he was invited by the talented philosopher of art Fyodor Stepun, who **195** taught there. There was a full hall for Nabokov's reading in the University's Arts Theatre, and afterwards the local Russian Orthodox priest, Father Pyotr, played chess with Nabokov on the stage. When the evening was over, Nabokov and Stepun strolled along the Mathematician's Walk to Stepun's quarters, where they had a wide-ranging discussion on questions of art that lasted till two in the morning. Stepun made a remark about someone's face resembling a cow's udder. Several years later that puckish observation furnished Nabokov with the description of Sebastian Knight's bad biographer: —*Mr. Goodman's large soft pinkish face was, and is, remarkably like a cow's udder,* which by artistic mutation in turn yielded, I judge, the important and now famous image at the end of the novel of the writer removing his black glove to reveal a multitude of tiny hands which spill about the floor.

After *King, Queen, Knave* there were no large sums of money forthcoming from translations. Ullstein did not take *The Defense* for translation into German as Nabokov had hoped. Life became slightly harder in some respects. The first doubts about the chances for a return to a democratic Russia were felt. They stayed in Berlin and lived something like a normal émigré intellectual life.

In 1931, when the novelist Evgeny Zamyatin was allowed to leave the Soviet Union after a personal appeal to Stalin, Nabokov, who was introduced to him through a cousin, saw him a few times. Nabokov remembers that Zamyatin, who was a naval engineer, was considered by most Russians who met him to be very reserved and something of an Englishman. Zamyatin did speak English—though, Nabokov recalls, somewhat strangely(—**Ewe half bean in Cambaridge?**), and there was something odd about the way he spoke Russian, too; he larded his Russian with what Nabokov took to be a Ukrainian dialect. On the whole Zamyatin kept quite aloof from émigré literature (he was not quite so anti-Bolshevik as people assumed, Nabokov remembers), and his social meetings with Nabokov were one of the very few literary acquaintanceships he had in exile. Zamyatin was, with Khodasevich, one of the first established Russian writers to speak of Nabokov as a peer. Like so many Russians at this time, Zamyatin soon went to Paris. Nabokov and his wife had long before this time obtained the essential green Nansen passport for stateless people, but still they stayed.

The 1930s were in many respects extremely happy years for Nabokov, but the steady, boring pressure of penury could not be waved away. Publishing offices either were closed or existed on the scuffed edge of the end; there were few lessons to be given any more. Nabokov's letters to his mother in these years return, simply and in passing but none the less strongly for all that, to the subject of their poverty. In August 1934, after the birth of their son, Nabokov wrote to his mother about her difficulties: —*I am now absolutely unable to help, and I don't know when I can help you (especially in a regular way); my affairs are in a terrible state now —debts and more debts!* In May 1935 he writes (the first part of the sentence is in English): —*I'm rather sick of being so hard up, but we mustn't lose heart,* and, a few months later: —*I am finishing a little story for* **The Latest News** *after which I shall get back to my English thing, or else to the novel with which I have been struggling for three years. . . .* In September 1935, after Nabokov was praised in print for the first time in the United States by Albert Perry, a professor of Russian literature, in a little article in *The New York Times Book Review* on émigré writers (Perry also wrote on Nabokov in Mencken's *American Mercury*), Nabokov wrote to his mother: —*In* **The New York Times** *they write "our age has been enriched by the appearance of a great writer," but I don't have a decent pair of trousers, and I quite don't know what I shall wear to Belgium where PEN has invited me to read.*

Much more important than any financial difficulties, however, émigré life in Berlin had at last become as uninteresting from a Russian point of view as German life there. But that is not the main thing. What is striking to me in looking at Nabokov's art from 1929 through 1936, that is, in the latter half of his Berlin period, is the overlapping pattern of his various writing projects (revealed to his biographer) which makes clear certain things which were puzzling to me (in my former part as his critic) when his work was considered from the point of view of date of publication. Nabokov's art in the thirties has, I believe now, a unity which is, however, not easily apparent. There is a cargo of personal detail in all the books, sometimes expressed in terms of openly biographical and near-biographical particulars as in *Glory* and *The Gift*, but more often posited in a fine mosaic of details which are quite independent of the plot. Thus, Luzhin in *The Defense* has nothing to do with Nabokov, but his name is made (incorrectly, Véra Evseevna insists; —**I am right,** says Nabokov) from the village of Luga which is near Vyra, and Luzhin is also the name of the hermetic hero (they both commit suicide) of the recently discovered 1924 **197** short story "A Chance Occurrence," which has a theme that was to be used in *Mary:* Luzhin, an émigré train waiter, finds himself on the same train with his wife, whom he believes to be still in the Soviet Union, but he doesn't realize it. Many small details in *The Defense* such as the skinned knee, for example (he told a Russian friend about this), do belong to Nabokov's childhood. His acknowledgment of this aspect of the novel is given in a letter to his mother written in October 1929: —*Well, I am very glad that Luzhin pleased you. Yes, if one really digs into it, one may find many of our little reminiscences.*

Glory is a direct telling of many details of Nabokov's émigré life in slightly altered form, and it would appear now that *The Gift* had its genesis shortly after the appearance of *Glory* in 1932, several years earlier than had heretofore been thought. Even such an odd and unautobiographical novel as *Despair* (a tale of a murder which goes wrong) may have initially come into being as a result of an event in Nabokov's Berlin literary life. In July 1926 Nabokov had a prominent part in a trial staged about Tolstoy's *The Kreutzer Sonata.* Such literary mock trials of characters, authors, or books have something of a tradition in Russian culture: when *Lolita* appeared some Russians held a mock trial over it in France. It was Nabokov's role in *The Kreutzer Sonata* trial to be Pozdnyshev, the murderer in Tolstoy's tale, speaking in his own defense (reported in *The Rudder,* July 18, 1926—he was quite good at it). His short story *Music* (1932) plays upon *The Kreutzer Sonata* as a theme, and also—is it not fair to deduce?—the form of the murderer's confession is used in Nabokov's art first by Hermann Karlovich in *Despair* and next by Humbert Humbert in *Lolita.*

—Until 1933 it was a rather democratic country. So at least thinks Mrs. Nabokov, though her husband in this instance does not agree.

In 1933 the Nazis stood ready to assume power, and the Nabokovs knew they should leave Germany even before Hitler took office. —We heard his voice. All democratic Russians in Berlin really felt a little uncomfortable after 1933, and this feeling gradually turned to fear. In Nabokov's case, however, it was something more like heedless disgust. George Hessen recalls going to a boxing match at the Sports Palace with Nabokov and an émigré newspaper reporter, Boris Brodsky, at which Nazi signs and announce-

198

ments were very much a part of the evening's entertainment, and on the way home either Nabokov or Brodsky (Hessen's and Nabokov's accounts differ) amused himself by playing with the flowers (or feathers) on the hat of a woman on their tram who was in obviously Nazi company. **—I was scared, and he was glad,** said Hessen. Whoever actually played that reckless game that evening, it is not out of character with other things which Nabokov did do. Hessen, for example, used to get telephone calls from Nabokov in those dangerous days asking unnerving questions such as: **—When will our Communist cell meet?**

In January 1934 émigré Berlin fêted Bunin for the Nobel Prize which had been awarded to him a few months earlier. Nabokov and Véra Evseevna, then six months pregnant, attended the festivities, one of the very last émigré celebrations in Berlin. The Nabokovs use as an example of the Russian's congenital failure to observe the fact that, although they continued to lead their normal social life until the eleventh hour, only George Hessen among their acquaintances knew she was pregnant. Hessen affirmed that that was so, but he gallantly defended the Russian's powers of observation, pointing out to me that Véra Evseevna's dress and posture were both extremely artful—for certain Russians showing a pregnancy is a very bourgeois thing to do.

Véra Evseevna was by this time working very hard as Nabokov's literary secretary. Nabokov's time was now wholly devoted to literary activities, and Véra Evseevna provided a small supplement to her husband's literary income by occasionally working as a translator or interpreter. She had first taken a full-time job at the French embassy in Berlin—that was in order to pay off debts contracted at the time of her father's prolonged illness and death —and some years later she took a part-time job with a German firm which acted as legal advisors to that embassy. She also took down French speeches in shorthand at international conventions and acted as a guide-interpreter for American tourists. Once Nabokov's wife was an interpreter at the Einsteins', who were then involved in an international pacifist movement (Véra Evseevna winced, and Nabokov winces even more so, wanting it made very clear that it is his biographer and not he who is "dropping" the name of that man whom he respects neither as a peacemaker nor as a physicist!!), and once she was shorthand reporter at an international wool Congress, this latter job having been offered to her by the Nazis: **—I am Jewish,** she told them. **—Oh,** 199 but it does not make any difference to us. We pay no attention to such things. (Véra Evseevna laughed—it is her favourite story). In May 1934, when their child was born, Vladimir Vladimirovich played chess with George Hessen's half brother until three in the morning, when it was time. The child, Dmitri Vladimirovich, was born two hours later at a private clinic near Bayerischerplatz, not too far away. Even before the physical dangers involved in remaining in Germany had become absolutely clear—Jews were being beaten up on the streets, the city seemed to grow unusually still at night, Russian émigrés found that it was no longer safe to have literary meetings after darkness fell—Nabokov and his wife felt (he has written about this in *Speak, Memory*) the strong danger of contamination affecting their child, and the manner in which Nabokov talks about Berlin in this period suggests that he feared more than simple germs. Berlin was no longer suitable as a backdrop for their life.

Nabokov received an important gift in 1934. A good friend named Nikolay Yakovlev, who was an historian and Avgust Kaminka's son-in-law, provided him with a list of the names of aristocratic Russian families which had died out. This list with names like Cherdyntsev, Barbashin, Kachurin, Sineusov, Revshin (—**I must have used more than half of them**) served to furnish the names of characters for almost all the rest of Nabokov's émigré writing. In 1936 he received another important gift, the inheritance of a few hundred dollars, which was his portion of the sum received by the descendants of the Graun family when the German courts set about freeing entailed property. That little bit of money helped a great deal. After the first Nazi attacks on Jewish shops, Nabokov walked the streets of Berlin with a non-Jewish acquaintance, making a point of going into all the Jewish stores which were still open. It was time. Nabokov had gone on his lecture tour in 1936. In 1937 the entire family visited Prague to show Nabokov's mother her grandchild for the first time (it was also the last time Nabokov saw his mother; she died not too many months later). Just before the Nabokovs left Berlin—forever, they say, and their lips tense slightly—whimsical fate thrust into their pockets two princely advances of forty-two pounds each for the English publication of two of Nabokov's books to help speed them on their way.

In the conclusion to the long letter which he wrote to his friend Samuil Rozov in 1937, Nabokov declared:

—A struggle with poverty has been my terribly banal concern for all these years, but other than that my life has proceeded happily. We are now living (I am married and have a three-year-old son— to say that he is entrancing hardly describes him) in Cannes, and I have absolutely no idea what is going to happen next: whatever happens, I shall never return to Germany. It is a loathsome and terrifying country. I have always been unable to abide Germans, the swinish German spirit, but in their present state of things (which, by the way, suits them rather well) life finally became absolutely unbearable there for me, and I don't say this simply because I am married to a Jewish woman.

That was before the real horrors. Afterwards, in America, he touched briefly on the theme of German savagery in *Pnin* as well as in several of his last émigré and first American short stories, but he told me that he is far from done with the subject and is now even prepared to return to Germany. I have never heard Nabokov speak more feelingly on anything: **—Oooloo, ooo!!! There is a sense of responsibility about this theme which I think I will tackle one day. I will go to those German camps and *look* at those places and write a *terrible* indictment.** . . .

Nabokov's first protracted visit to France since his childhood trips to the Riviera occurred during the summer of 1923 (there had been a few crossings from Cambridge, of no particular importance). Solomon Krym, who had been the head of the Crimean government and who was a friend of V. D. Nabokov's, managed a large estate in southern France in conjunction with Prince Gagarin which was being run as a serious agricultural enterprise. It belonged to the Bezpalov family. Nabokov had the idea—a **marvellous** idea, as he warmly recalls that time in his life—to apply to Solomon Krym to work on the estate as a farmhand during the summer. The estate, called Beaulieu, was located near Soliès-Pont not far from Toulon. A small river flowed in a U-sweep around the manor house in which Nabokov had an attic bedroom. From its window he looked out on the orchards near the house and the wooded clump of hills across the river.

Solomon Samoilovich Krym was a Karaite Jew (in Russian, *karaím*). **—These people don't have what is called Jewish blood. But they belong to the Jewish religion. They look absolutely like Tar-** **201** tars. Most of them wear Tartar dress. He was a tremendously influential and wealthy man, a winemaker. And he emigrated like the rest of us, went to the south of France. He didn't speak a word of French. He went to a boys' school and learned French there. Then he passed an examination in viniculture. Vladimir Vladimirovich here undertook to give me some instruction in the tenets of Karaism, which was, he explained, a form of Judaism which follows only the Talmud. Véra Evseevna uncertainly (but correctly) disagreed: —On the contrary. They didn't accept the Talmud, but they accepted the rest. I don't know exactly how it worked. They are not quite Jews. Solomon Krym, Nabokov remembers, was himself a poet and a wit, and a man who was at one and the same time both an extremely cultured Russian and full of fascinating Oriental lore. They became very good friends, and Nabokov remembers that, though Krym was not a butterfly collector, he understood very well his young farmhand's urge every now and then —to chuck the whole business of farming and go collecting butterflies. Once, when Nabokov was afield doing his farmwork, an old Englishman came by on horseback, dismounted, and asked him to hold his horse. The old man, who had a butterfly net and was in pursuit of a two-tailed Pasha flying around a fig tree, was startled when the bronzed young *paysan* dressed in blue denim pants inquired in taxonomically perfect Latin about what species he had been able to find in the region, which nicely parallels what happened to Nabokov himself some twenty years later, while collecting in the mountains of Utah, when he was offered a lift by a young truck driver who breezily called out: —Hop in, entomologist! Have you gotten a Magdalena?

On the plantation there were groves of cork trees, and the orchards consisted of peach, apricot, and cherry trees. Nabokov was very fond of the peaches and apricots, to the point where the songbirds and sunsets on the estate came to have a peach-apricot flavour in his mind. Nabokov worked the rows of the vegetable fields, picking asparagus and sweet peas and corn. He also was a cherry-picker, though with more enthusiasm than professionalism. —Picking cherries is quite an art, quite an art. The first time I worked quite fast and took the ripest cherries and put them inside this basket which was lined with so-called American cloth, oilcloth. I hung it on a branch. It tumbled down and all the cherries were spoiled. I had to start all over again. He would get up at six, work through the morning, drink wine, go swimming and sunbathe in the nude at about one, then return to work.

One incident at Beaulieu, which took place a few days after Nabokov's arrival, seems (to me, not to him) to have furnished Nabokov with the setting for the seminal scene of the Burning Barn—it is not actually shown in the novel—in *Ada* (Chapter 19); at least, while the date of the fictional scene is questioned by one of the novel's narrators (—*July 28? August 4?*) what would be approximately the correct date for the Beaulieu barn fire, June 10, is mentioned on the preceding page. Nabokov awakened in his attic room in the warm night to cries of what he gradually realized was *Feu! Feu!* being shouted everywhere. He became aware that he had been left alone in the house by mistake as everyone ran to fight the fire in the barn and that everyone was outside dipping and passing buckets from a kind of pond. He came out of the house to help, was confronted with perfect horror and pandemonium all around him, and, being new to Beaulieu and not familiar with the grounds, he stepped into the water and suddenly found himself swimming. If my connective inclination is to be given any credence, then it further demonstrates how a chance remark or incident may, perhaps even subconsciously, appear in quite different form and context *decades* later.

Nabokov's second visit to France lasted four and a half months —from February 8 through June 24, 1929—and was paid for by the Ullstein translation money. It was the first opportunity in a decade Nabokov had had to devote himself seriously to butterfly collecting. Sometime after the scientific vacation was over he published an article, "Notes on the Lepidoptera of the Pyrénées Orientales and the Ariège" (signed with his Cambridge spelling, Nabokoff) in *The Entomologist*, the same journal in which he had published his first article on butterflies in 1919. When Vladimir Vladimirovich and Véra Evseevna returned to Berlin with the hundreds of butterflies and moths described in the article, Nabokov did much of the classification work at the Entomological Institute at Dahlem and the Natural Science Museum in Berlin. Sometime later, in 1932, they acquired, not too dearly, at auction, a massive eight-foot-long butterfly case with lovely glazed drawers in which they could store their butterflies spread, pinned, and labelled.

On their way to the Pyrenees in 1929, they travelled in luxury by sleeping compartment to Paris and then took the night train from Paris to Perpignan. During the night Nabokov had a dream **203** (his first recorded dream, a trifle incongruous in *The Entomologist* perhaps) in which he was offered something which —*looked uncommonly like a sardine, but was really a tropical moth, the mimic—mirabile dictu—of a flying fish*. From Perpignan it was a thirteen-mile trip by motorbus to the village of Boulou and another mile to the Hôtel Thermal du Boulou. It was only a short hike to the Spanish border, and Nabokov did much of his collecting on that road. At that height in the Pyrenees, spring is a gusty affair, and Nabokov complained in his article that the foliage of the cork trees tumbled to and fro and the wind blew from both Spain and France at the same time, which was an unpropitious state of affairs from the entomologist's point of view. Nabokov climbed mountains, and at night he waited patiently by the hotel's outdoor night light for moths while the hotel's other patrons on the verandah discussed their queer fellow lodger, who took long hikes, descended into ravines—the man with a butterfly net does often seem odd, and so one had better concentrate one's attention instead on the world Nabokov saw and the way in which he not only captured but entered into it:

*—On the same day I saw in a leafy tunnel pierced by a sunbeam a **Libythea celtis** poised wings spread on a twig, and a few **Colias croceus** gen. **vernalis** were flying along the roads. Three days later near a brook I took a beautifully fresh **Ch. caliginearia,** male, silvery grey and pink, which fluttered weakly out of a bush, and when in the net crawled about with its wings held rather in the manner of a **Hypena**. Subsequently I got other male examples by beating bushes, and also found a pathetic wing in a spider's web. . . . On March 13 **Callophrys rubi** var. **fervida** appeared at sallow —fine specimens of a milk chocolate colour. It soon became extraordinarily abundant, remaining so till the end of my stay, though by then very worn. On certain days when the wind was exceptionally furious this game little creature, with perhaps a few **cleopatra,** was the only butterfly on the wing, flickering among the broom and gorse on the slopes.*

On April 24 the Nabokovs transferred to Saurat, a large village at an altitude of two thousand feet nestled among mountains rising to six thousand feet on all sides, and on these mountaintops and the luscious meadows below the collecting improved markedly, and in one spot, in an elevated birch wood, Nabokov —*was charmed to see together two insects that are rarely met with in the same place—the Southern* **P. aegeria** *and males of* **Aglia tau,** *so remindful of boyhood and spring in northern Russia.* But when the summer's first brood of butterflies started to cover the region in bright wind-tossed confetti, it was time, *heart-breaking* time, to return.

When Nabokov came to France for the fourth time, in 1936, to read from his works as he had four years earlier, his visit was a tour by an acknowledged albeit still young master not only for Russian émigrés in Paris but also to a certain extent for literary Paris as well. A French as well as a Russian evening was held in February 1936. Though Nabokov was a replacement speaker, as a result of which there were only about ninety people present, the evening was also spectacularly successful. One of the ninety was dignified James Joyce. The noted philosopher, dramatist, and Kierkegaard expert Gabriel Marcel, who had taken a particular interest in Nabokov's writing (he first learned of Nabokov through close mutual friends), spoke for nearly an hour in introducing him. The lecture on Pushkin (it was the centenary of the poet's death) later appeared in the *Nouvelle Revue Française.* In the course of the reading that evening, he wrote his mother *applause came like bomb explosions.*

Nabokov (my authority for these judgments is his wife) writes perfect French, and his pronunciation is also quite exact. But when he is simply speaking French, as opposed to reading from a prepared text, he speaks in a slightly flawed manner, his worst fault apparently being a tendency to confuse the gender of nouns. Nabokov here protested softly, but Véra Evseevna promptly recalled such a slip which he had made the preceding day, adding: **—And it's not the first time. Sergei spoke much better French than Vladimir, but his English was much less rich than yours.** Be that as it may, Nabokov was one of only two Russian émigré writers (the other was Aleksei Remizov; Russians such as Sarraute and Troyat do not count because they never were Russian writers) who were adopted and fully accepted by French avant-garde circles in Paris.

When Nabokov was in Brussels he became very friendly with the Belgian French writer Franz Hellens, whose aesthetic views (Hellens is noted for the technique of *réalité fantastique*) are in some ways rather close to Nabokov's and who had, moreover, a Russian wife. In 1971 Nabokov contributed a little note of homage to a Belgian volume in honour of Hellens, at the age of ninety the **205** greatest living Belgian writer. He had known Hellens' books for several years before he met him and had admired in particular his 1925 novel *OEil-de-Dieu,* which is, like Nabokov's *Despair,* in part a parody of a detective novel. Hellens had written to the influential editor of the *Nouvelle Revue Française,* Jean Paulhan, warmly praising Nabokov's story *Mademoiselle O.* In Paris Nabokov met Jules Supervielle, then considered (by a few) the hope of French literature, who was one of the leading contributors to the *Nouvelle Revue Française;* and, having also been given *Mademoiselle O* to read, Supervielle, too, recommended Nabokov and his work to Paulhan (it was Supervielle who told Nabokov of Hellens' letter). The story appeared in *Mesures,* another journal with which Paulhan was connected, and, as already mentioned, his Pushkin article was published in the *Nouvelle Revue Française.*

I especially wish that there were more to be told of Nabokov's meetings (there were at least three, and they were very friendly) with Supervielle, who is a poet and writer I like very much and who evidently was a good person, once described by his friend René Etiemble as —*the most unassuming and the least **arriviste** of men.* But there are times when, as Nabokov puts it: —**the tape recorder of memory forgets to be turned on.** Nabokov remembers him as a tall gaunt Spaniard with a charming old world manner (—**which I also have**), though when Nabokov met him, through his cousin Nicholas, the composer, he had aged greatly and was in a state of disarray and utter confusion prior to leaving for Uruguay. He had a flock of daughters and a wife who looked like the eldest of them. Nabokov translated some of Supervielle's poetry into Russian, and Supervielle, who knew many languages and, I believe, some Russian, paid him a considerable but characteristic compliment: —**I am sorry I can't translate my French into your Russian.** He was a man, Nabokov recalls, to whom simple neighbourliness and trust meant a very great deal in life.

Nabokov gave Gabriel Marcel the manuscript of the English translation of his latest novel, *Despair,* which he had done himself in Berlin. Feeling just a shade unsure of himself in regard to the finest nuances of English style at that point in his life, he had attempted to get professional help for the final draft of the translation. Véra Evseevna called the English embassy and asked for the name of a translator —**who would be an experienced man of letters with a fine style.** And they said: —**Would you like** H. G. Wells? to which Véra Evseevna replied: —**I might.** Someone else appeared, and they started to go over the text together. —You remember what he said: "I'm sorry, I can't do it because this is"—I don't know what epithet he used, but it was to the effect that it was *ob-seen*. Yes, yes. I remember his eyes. Green eyes. When the translation was prepared for submission to the English publisher John Long, Nabokov received an English lady's long list of nits (on the order of "compared with" corrected to "compared to") and, worse yet, "suggestions" about the novel proper. But by this time Nabokov was no longer troubled by whatever degree of insecurity had bothered him before in regard to his English, and he sent instructions to Véra Evseevna in Berlin which stand very well as his final attitude towards the notion of "correct" usage: — *All of this stuff is completely insignificant, for any Russian reader can find just as many birth-marks on any page of any of my Russian novels, and any good English writer commits just as many grammatical imprecisions as your Englishwoman has noticed. Please, don't upset these British majors and old maids, but simply send the copy prepared by me to England without a single one of the corrections prepared by other hands.* The novel was printed by John Long exactly as Nabokov wanted it, and that first English translation (Long published a translation of *Camera Obscura* the preceding year, but it was not done by Nabokov) is important in Nabokov's biography because it is a part of that process of metamorphosis which was in a few years to produce *The Real Life of Sebastian Knight* and then make him an English writer. After he had done that translation, he knew he could do it.

The logical choice of a country and language, Nabokov told me, was certainly England and English, but he had those not particularly happy years at Cambridge, and comfortable and drowsy England did not seem particularly eager to furnish Nabokov with either an academic position (—*Your application will, however, be filed for future reference,* wrote the Vice-Chancellor, B. Mouat Jones, M.A., with regret, after Sir Bernard Pares had made attempts to obtain an academic appointment for Nabokov at Leeds University) or with any recognition for his art. But France was flirting with him, and Nabokov was for the first time half considering a dalliance. He had considerable hope that Gabriel Marcel's interest in *Despair* would do much to expedite a French translation of the novel.

Up until that time only one Sirin novel had appeared in

French, though extremely favourable critical sketches on his art had appeared in several French magazines. There were problems, which, as I see them, were more cultural than linguistic. Historically there has existed a special relationship between French and Russian literature. Perceptive French critics such as Jules Goncourt had bitterly accused nineteenth-century Russian writers, and not without cause, of borrowing French themes and innovations, exaggerating them, and in the end receiving critical adulation for this in Paris. Nabokov says simply: —**All Russian novelists, beginning with Karamzin, borrowed a good deal from the French.** Ironically, for a Russian writer so evidently "Western" and "European," Nabokov lacks, notwithstanding brief parodistic bows to Flaubert and Proust in places, this historical umbilical cord to French culture, and a strong case can be put (to the detriment of neither) for a basic incompatibility between French literature and Nabokov's literary personality. Gabriel Marcel could read only the made-up epigram to Nabokov's most "philosophical" novel, *Invitation to a Beheading,* an aphorism from Nabokov's equally imaginary favourite philosopher, Pierre Delalande: —*Comme un fou se croit Dieu, nous nous croyons mortels.* Nabokov wrote Véra Evseevna that Marcel had rather charmingly termed himself "allergic" to that whimsical quotation from Delalande. That formulation, from a man who greatly admired Nabokov's art, is perhaps a rather nice statement of the problem which Nabokov would certainly have faced to a much greater degree than he eventually did in America had he elected to become a French writer. There is reason to think that the French writer Sirin-Nabokoff would have found himself in much the same position as his friends Hellens and Supervielle, recognized and brilliant writers who have somehow all the same never been seen at their true value or taken to the heart of their culture. But that, of course, is simply another way of speaking about what Nabokov himself has termed the fear he felt at that time in his life of being *enveloped* by French culture.

Nabokov knew other prominent French writers. He knew Edouard Dujardin. He did not know Jean Cocteau, but his brother Sergei was very friendly with him, and once Cocteau spoke to him on the phone briefly, thinking it was Sergei, and warning him that his phone was being tapped. He was invited to lunch by Edmond Jaloux, the tactful and kindly but overly polished critic, who, André Gide wrote, was more comfortable in a tail-coat than ordinary

TOP LEFT: *The Nabokov coat of arms*
BOTTOM LEFT: *D. N. Nabokov, Minister of Justice under Tsars Alexander II and III*
ABOVE: *Nabokov's grandmother, Maria Nabokov, neé Baroness Korff*

TOP: *Maria Nabokov and her children,
St. Petersburg, circa 1880*
LEFT: *V. D. Nabokov with an unidentified
young lady at a masquerade ball,
St. Petersburg, 1889*
ABOVE LEFT: *V. D. Nabokov, Berlin, 1919*
ABOVE RIGHT: *Vladimir Nabokov. American
passport photo*

LEFT: *Nabokov with his mother, St. Petersburg, 1900*
BELOW: *Nabokov with his brother Sergei (left), at Vyra, 1906*

ABOVE: *Nabokov in his final year at the Tenishev school*

RIGHT: *Nabokov (center, tuxedo) at a family wedding, Berlin, 1923*

BELOW: *Nabokov on the streets of Berlin, 1934*

LEFT: *Nabokov with his brother Sergei, St. Petersburg, 1916*
BELOW: *Nabokov with Ivan Bunin at dinner honouring Bunin for the award of the Nobel Prize, Berlin, 1934*

ABOVE: *Nabokov in the 1940s* (Collie Smith)
BELOW: *Nabokov teaching at Wellesley, 1943* (Courtesy of
Wellesley Alumnae Magazine)
OPPOSITE PAGE, ABOVE: *At the Agassiz Museum, Cambridge, 1947* (Photo:
Joffe. Copyright © 1947, 1975 by the Condé Nast Publications, Inc.)
OPPOSITE PAGE, BELOW: *Nabokov with his brother Kirill and sister Elena,
Switzerland, 1959*

ABOVE: *Nabokov with his wife, Vera, and his son, Dmitri, at the piano, 1960* (Wide World)
RIGHT: *Nabokov, 1959* (Magnum)

clothes and whom Nabokov described to me as —**totally second-rate and terribly influential.** Nabokov tumbled into laughter as he remembered Jaloux and the lunch: —**I think that even in this repulsive little *Larousse* . . . ye-e-e-s, he should be here. Good old Jaloux,** and Nabokov read the Larousse entry aloud, punctuating it with snorts of laughter, and appending to its end: —**He was as fresh as a peach, I remember, and a com*plete* mediocrity.** The lunch was saved for Nabokov by the presence of champagne—he loves champagne—which Jaloux always had for lunch.

Despair was translated into French, but it did not appear until 1939, rather late, and there was no particular critical response to the novel apart from Jean-Paul Sartre's ill-tempered little piece complaining that M. Sirine was a rootless person, and had read too many books to boot. Still, Nabokov might have been a French writer, even a great French writer, who knows? If the course of World War II had followed a different pattern and France had not fallen. If, before that, his friend Raissa Tatarinova (Tarr) had succeeded in obtaining for him the post she was trying to arrange as a book and drama critic on a French newspaper. But after the first flush of the French flirtation, the simple fact, according to Véra Evseevna, was clear: —**There were no opportunities for a career for him there.** The experiences which he had had, or not had, in both England and France were to be one of the factors setting off his sometimes too boisterous devotion to America, where things went very much better in many ways.

Nabokov met James Joyce in Paris, but it was another wholly disappointing great meeting for literary history. They had mutual friends, Paul and Lucie Léon; Léon was at this time something of a legal and business secretary for Joyce. Lucie Léon has written of the dinner they had, but there is a great deal of information about the goose that was cooked and nothing about the conversation, for Mme. Léon confesses that she spent much of the evening in the kitchen. She recalls that Nabokov seemed unusually stiff and formal, but Nabokov feels that by inclination and nature he has always missed being the life of the party. Nabokov remembers nothing whatsoever of the three or so hours of conversation he had with Joyce; Véra Evseevna remembers that Joyce was very interested in the ingredients of *myod*, the Russian version of mead. Mme. Léon recalls that Nabokov had told her husband that he would like to meet Joyce, but in one of his letters to Véra Evseevna from Paris (February 24, 1936) Nabokov tells his wife how, after

Léon had surrounded his proposal that Nabokov come with him to meet Joyce with a great many warnings on what he should and should not say, Nabokov finally begged off, saying that he was busy and there was no real point to such a meeting. He continued in the letter:

—Joyce and Proust met only once, by chance. Proust and he were together in a taxi, the window of which the former closed, where-upon the latter rolled it down, and they nearly quarrelled. All in all it was rather tedious, and anyway, in these new things of his [Work in Progress], the abstract puns, the verbal masquerade, the shadows of words, the diseases of words . . . in the end wit sinks behind reason, and, while it is setting, the sky is ravishing, but then there is night.

Certainly a degree of the unmemorableness of the meeting, when it did take place two years later in 1938, must have owed something to Nabokov's Russian mistrust of the possibilities inherent in such occasions.

Nabokov continued to meet Joyce from time to time after that in the offices of the *Nouvelle Revue Française.* Nabokov first perused *Ulysses* shortly after it appeared in 1922 when his tall Trinity classmate Peter Mrosovsky (who closed doors with a grace-ful swing of his heel against the top corner) came into his digs with a copy fresh from France to show him the dirty passages; he read the book seriously more than ten years later and admired it enor-mously; but by 1936 Nabokov, who had just entered his prime, was right to feel that Joyce was past his, though both the judgment and the judge might have seemed strange to all but a few at the time. In the 1950s *Ulysses* was studied intensively by Nabokov for his lectures at Cornell University, and publication of these lectures (revised) has been promised.

So Nabokov was simply a Russian émigré in Paris as he had been a Russian émigré in Berlin. In his approximately three and a half Parisian years Nabokov, now himself the recipient of phan-tom fame, associated with all the most famous Russian writers in exile in a way that he had not done in Berlin (though he and Bunin had spent some time together in their last Berlin year), but all the same Nabokov felt —Life in the Russian colony in Berlin was perhaps more interesting than in Paris. Life had changed in that decade. —The thirties were pretty hopeless. . . . I think that in the middle thirties we had just given up the idea of going back. But it didn't matter much because Russia was with us. We were Russia. We represented Russia. . . . What had we lost? What had we lost? We had lost . . . Vladimir Vladimirovich's sentence trailed off and was left unfinished. Two years later he wanted to complete the sentence: —. . . **a few sounds and smells, the sun at the end of a leafy avenue, the backdrop of a magic childhood.** Even hallowed Paris itself, the literary cafés and the Eiffel Tower in its lace panties, did not have any effect upon Nabokov. He found it somewhat dingy.

Only when he came to America, in June 1940, did Nabokov see a justification for the French phase of the emigration. Then he published six paragraph-long philosophical sketches (an uncharacteristic form for him) under the title "Definitions" ("Opredeleniya") in the New York émigré newspaper *The New Russian Word (Novoe Russkoe Slovo)*. One of them is a definition of France from the point of view of the émigré artist:

—A bright, intelligent, endlessly delightful country, where every stone is full of nobility and grace, where any cloud above a hillock overgrown with chestnuts is in itself a work of art—this is the way the émigré has been used to feeling about France, and no temporary disasters can alter this feeling. Whoever may be at fault for her fatal helplessness, the fragility of a country does not always count as a fault, in the same way that power is not always virtue. For after all, this was the country where it was best and easiest to think about Russia. Paris served as a suitable mounting for Russian recollections. And I know people who would not have exchanged their cheap nocturnal vigil behind an empty glass in a corner café for any wonders of any other places.

In his long Russian poem *The Paris Poem*, written in Massachusetts in 1943 (Nabokov has never stopped writing Russian poetry, but after he came to America his output became very occasional, one every few years), Paris, despite the title, is a very conscious irrelevancy. Even the line *Wondrous at night is gaunt Paris* is, as Nabokov takes pains to inform his English readers in the notes to his translation in *Poems and Problems,* really not a tribute to Paris so much as a parody of Gogol, and the specific image of Paris, her gurgling *pissoirs* at night, is a private metaphysical echo and joke. Some of Nabokov's most important Russian work was written in **211**

France; for the most part, however, it concerns Berlin émigrés, or the setting doesn't matter. As England had been a hallway to maturity and emigration, so France was another passageway, this time to America, English, and worldwide fame.

When Nabokov came to Paris in 1936 he lived in the apartment of Ilya Fondaminsky on the Avenue de Versailles, a splendid flat of about eight rooms, some of them quite large, with a luxurious bathroom (Nabokov remembers that especially well); Nabokov had a very comfortable small bedroom there for several weeks. Fondaminsky, it is agreed by all memoirists (with the single exception of Berberova), was a consummately intelligent, sensitive, and idealistic man. In *Speak, Memory* Nabokov credits him with having done more for émigré literature than any other single person. A man of independent means, who had resided in France prior to 1917 because of his part in revolutionary activities against the tsarist regime, Fondaminsky both furnished and found financial support for *Contemporary Annals* and saw to it that the contributors were paid modestly well. He also provided the funds for the first serious and professional émigré attempt since the 1920s at maintaining a theatre, the short-lived (three seasons) Russian Theatre, which was founded in Paris in 1938 and for which Nabokov wrote two plays, one of which, *The Event,* was the theatre's most successful production and the other of which, *The Waltz Invention,* was being prepared for production when the Parisian period of émigré literature ended. Many of Nabokov's literary readings were part of a series of such evenings organized and sponsored by *Contemporary Annals.* Finally, *Contemporary Annals* had a subsidiary publishing house, and many of Nabokov's works were published by it in book form after they had appeared in the magazine.

But it would be wrong to infer that Ilya Fondaminsky was simply a wealthy patron of the arts. He was a deeply democratic and cultured revolutionary—a rather rare combination. Fondaminsky had had an older brother, Matvei, who in 1886, when he was twenty, was sent into Siberian exile for belonging to a revolutionary circle and who took part in a famous uprising of prisoners three years later. Matvei was seriously wounded, recovered, remained in more extreme imprisonment, and finally died there of tuberculosis in 1896. It was against this background of anger and idealization that the young Fondaminsky became a committed revolutionary. But he was also an expert on the Italian

212

Renaissance. He took part in the first, unsuccessful revolution of 1905, speaking (under the name Bunakov) at scores of factories, and was arrested for his leadership of the July 20 naval uprising in Revel, one of the few fronts of the 1905 revolution which all but succeeded. It was expected by other members of the Social-Revolutionary movement that Fondaminsky would be executed, but he was unexpectedly released by the Revel military court and unofficially one of the judges whispered to his wife, Amalia, that she should take her husband abroad at once. The (unfortunately apocryphal) story that was reported in the Russian press was that the Fondaminskys had left the courtroom, hailed a cab, and that Amalia Fondaminsky had cried out: —*Driver, abroad!* But it is true that they did go into emigration almost immediately. Fondaminsky stayed in France for many years and returned to Russia in 1917 when he played a part (he knew V. D. Nabokov) in the Provisional Government. When he had to go into exile once again, his flat in France was waiting for him. He also had a villa in Grasse, and many writers stayed there as his guests.

After so many years on French soil Fondaminsky grew to feel himself a part of France in a way that most Russians never did. For this reason and two others (the heavy blow he felt at the death of his wife in 1935 and his religious and philosophical interests, which had become particularly deep in the 1930s) Fondaminsky elected not to flee France for America at the time when most of his associates were leaving. Since he was a Jew this choice was tantamount to electing to go to a concentration camp. He is supposed to have died in Auschwitz in 1942 and to have been saintly in what he did for others while in the camp. Fondaminsky had lingered at the verge of conversion for more than twenty years but only became a Christian in his last days in the camp. Nabokov remembers the touching way he had of attempting to steer a conversation to a religious theme and then asking whether one would be interested in reading a certain saint's life.

Fondaminsky was an historian, but his writings are not as forceful as his personality evidently was. He was a man who would give himself to everything he undertook with wholehearted commitment, and yet he was not an aggressive person. At first he did not even want to be on the editorial board of **Contemporary Annals,** but when he had agreed to be one of the editors he made the excellence of that journal one of the primary tasks in his life. He was fond of saying: —*When they ask us what the justification of* **213** *our émigré existence was, we shall point to the volumes of Contemporary Annals.* The other four editors of the journal did not possess quite this degree of quasi-religious faith in the endeavour (self-doubt and a feeling of futility were always close at hand among the émigrés), but in my view there is no gainsaying the fact that the seventy volumes of *Contemporary Annals* (1920–1940) can stand beside English-language journals such as *Horizon* or the best years of *Partisan Review,* and it surpasses in quality the ordinary run of the two notable nineteenth-century "thick journals," *The Contemporary* and *Annals of the Fatherland,* in honour of which the Paris journal had been named. Two of the most important ways in which Fondaminsky guided and shaped the character of the journal were his belief that culture and art were essential formative, independent means to any justifiable social or revolutionary end, and, secondly, that, although the journal was to have basically a "Socialist" viewpoint, its pages were to be open both politically and artistically. There were few people of any intellectual or artistic distinction in the Russian emigration who did not at some time or other appear there. When Fondaminsky solicited Sirin's work for *Contemporary Annals* in 1930, he told Nabokov: **—Why, we like your work so much. We simply can't understand why you haven't, why you aren't publishing your work in *Contemporary Annals.*** Nabokov handed him the manuscript to *The Defense* which he had completed not long before and said: **—You're welcome. . . . And he bought it there and then without having read it.**

When Nabokov came to Paris for his first reading, in October 1932, for about a month, he visited Fondaminsky virtually every day and towards the end of his stay was invited to transfer to their flat, then on rue Chernoviz. The Fondaminskys extended themselves to the utmost for the young writer but did it all in such a way, Nabokov remembers, as to make it appear effortless and natural. He had a book-lined bedroom with a bottle of mineral water always at his bedside. Elegant scented toilet articles were laid out for him. Amalia Osipovna attended to the distribution and sale of the tickets for Nabokov's reading, and she also typed a portion of the manuscript of *Despair* for him, while Nabokov smoked (too much—in later years he feared he had been a difficult houseguest) and the Fondaminskys' stout Siamese cat (who reminded Nabokov somewhat of a kangaroo) warmed itself by the hearth. Nor did it matter when Nabokov came in very late one night shortly after his transfer to their flat and lit all the lights in the house trying to turn out the hall lamp, which had been left on for him; and then, after lying awake awhile, fearful that he might not have corrected his awful blunder, he went back to double-check his error and ended by Pninishly committing it once more.

Nabokov recalls with particular pleasure the time he spent with Fondaminsky and his friend and political associate Vladimir Zenzinov when he came to Paris in 1936. Zenzinov was the man who was selected to assassinate his friend Azef for the Social-Revolutionary Party in 1914, when it was discovered that Azef was a secret tsarist agent (the assassination attempt did not succeed), and another Social-Revolutionary whom Nabokov met there was the actual assassin of Father Gapon, the priest who played a prominent role in the 1905 revolution but also turned out to be a tsarist agent. —There he was sitting in front of me at the tea table. . . . I looked at his red freckles, his red hands. He was supposed to have *strangled* Gapon with those hands. . . . Those Social-Revolutionaries were terrorists. They were also metaphysicians and intellectuals. . . . But they were rather naïve in a way.

Nabokov got to know Aleksandr Kerensky, the former head of the Provisional Government, quite well at Fondaminsky's because Kerensky also lived there for a time. Kerensky had not been on particularly friendly terms with V. D. Nabokov in St. Petersburg, and so the families had never been in social contact, but he and Vladimir Vladimirovich grew quite fond of one another. Years later they occasionally still saw each other in New York. Nabokov remembers, as a boy, sitting in the first row of a large auditorium with his father while Kerensky made a speech, and when he said: —I swear on the heads . . . , two little boys came running out from the wings, and Kerensky placed his hands on their heads as he finished his declaration. —There was something theatrical about him. Pleasingly theatrical apparently. . . . He would deliver a speech on any pretext at Fondaminsky's. Nabokov found it very pleasant to hear him talk about the Imperial family or his adventures, or to listen to his views about Russia generally.

Fondaminsky held open house, a kind of informal literary salon, every Saturday, and Fondaminsky's Saturdays and the café located near his house at the end of the rue de Versailles where writers and poets, Nabokov among them, spent many hours constitute something like a spiritual centre for the culture of the Russian diaspora. It was there that Nabokov met most of the Russian writ- **215** ers whom he had not known before, though Nabokov did not attend Fondaminsky's Saturdays because, he says, he dislikes group discussions. It was Fondaminsky's special gift to be able to draw together on a relatively amicable basis writers as far apart as the reactionary Dmitri Merezhkovsky and the (tragically) Sovietophile Marina Tsvetaeva, or the religious poetess Mother Maria and the decadent Georgy Ivanov. It wasn't always easy. Nabokov met Teffi, the author of fine short stories in a humorous Chekhovian vein about the non-intellectual middle-class emigration, who was a woman with something of the Dorothy Parker wit. Nabokov remembers how once she was complimented on how young she looked, and she replied sweetly: —**To the eye, not to the taste.** He met Sergei Sharshun, a talented minor novelist, and once by chance overheard him discussing the reading he had just given, a moment which it would seem (he says no) Nabokov used in *The Gift*. He met the aphoristic poet Baron Anatoly Shteiger, and came to know him and his sister, who was also a poet, rather well. When I remarked that, though he had never produced much, Shteiger seemed to me to have been very original and talented, Nabokov said: —**I don't think he was.** He said this rapidly and lightly, like a wineglass falling down a marble staircase and landing miraculously unbroken: —**His talent has been greatly exaggerated. He was a very minor poet. *Very* minor poet. With a very limited gift and with a very limited emotional life. A nice person. A charming person. A well-bred person. That's all.**

He met Shteiger's close friend and poetic mentor (though their styles are quite different), Marina Tsvetaeva, on three or four occasions. Tsvetaeva had started as the Poetess of the White Guard, had changed her politics (her husband turned out to be a double agent, too) and generally kept aloof from other émigrés. She had her own entourage. Because I knew that Tsvetaeva did not much like Nabokov's writing, and that he respected her poetic talent but was not terribly fond of her work either, and since politics (another natural subject for these people) would have been even more awkward to discuss than art, I wondered what they talked about. —**It would be just the same as if** [a sometime friend was named] **were here. I just wouldn't talk about Vietnam.** Nabokov recalls a literary stroll he had with Tsvetaeva on a rainy grey Paris day discussing writers whom they mutually liked or hated.

He met David Knut, a talented Jewish poet who fought in the Resistance (his wife perished) and eventually immigrated to Israel and became a Hebrew poet. Knut published four books of poetry in Russian. Mother Maria, another Russian poet who perished heroically in a German concentration camp. The frizzy-haired blond Dr. Vasily Yanovsky, who had been ridiculed by Nabokov in one of his Berlin book reviews years before for an ineptly described soccer match in one of his novels, and who now struck Nabokov as a —*delayed* **enfant terrible.** (He wrote in English, too, and many years later his writing was highly praised by W. H. Auden.) A poet and critic who seemed to Nabokov —**vaguely similar to Chichikov.** Nikolai Berdyaev, well known to English readers as perhaps the foremost post-revolutionary philosophical opponent of Communism, an extremely intelligent man who had a horrible speech affliction—after every few words his tongue would throw itself out of his mouth, and he would have to replace it by hand. The dean, by age, of the émigré writers, Boris Zaitsev, for whom Nabokov remembers he suddenly felt pity as he watched him being tormented by Khodasevich. Nabokov laughed as he remembered that scene.

But the writers whom Nabokov saw most frequently at Fondaminsky's and elsewhere were those who were, like himself, quite independent of any group or school or "note"—Bunin, Aldanov, and Khodasevich. Of the four writers only Bunin was more or less immune to snipes and attacks from various artistic factions, particularly the Parisian poets who followed the cues of Georgy Adamovich, the regular literary critic for *The Latest News.* Bunin, Khodasevich, Aldanov, and Sirin were conspicuously absent from the pages of the excellent periodical *Numbers,* founded in 1930 in implied opposition to *Contemporary Annals,* and in the cases of Khodasevich and Nabokov, in particular, strong attacks upon their art and even their person were mounted from this journal. This crafty and determined attempt to cut down the tall poppies on the field of Russian literature in emigration cannot be said wholly to have failed. A fairly large and articulate group of readers was cultivated who were ready to affirm that Sirin was an "empty" and even a "middling" writer, and as for Khodasevich, he was virtually forgotten as a poet (Nabokov remarked upon this fact when he wrote a memorial article on Khodasevich's death in 1939), which certainly had something to do with the bitter silence which eventually fell on him.

But both Khodasevich and Nabokov were quite able to take care of themselves. Khodasevich was the regular literary critic for **217**

Renaissance (Vozrozhdenie), a smaller circulation émigré paper which competed with *The Latest News*, and he wielded a deft scalpel for the sake of strict literary standards. Nabokov fought somewhat differently, obliquely, but with more spectacular results, such as the time he tricked Adamovich, who always dismissed his poetry, into wild praise for a poem which he published under a pseudonym, Vasily Shishkov, and then wrote a short story, "Vasily Shishkov," which he purposely published in *The Latest News* to rub the critic's nose in his mistake, or the short story "Lips to Lips" in which Nabokov both sadly and savagely satirizes the editor and one of the wealthy patrons of the magazine *Numbers*, in whose pages the patron's pathetic attempts at writing were published. It should be noted that Nabokov flips a dart *en passant* at Adamovich and Georgy Ivanov in *Pnin*, too, long after, one should have thought, it mattered, but Nabokov was quite firm with an émigré friend who rebuked him when *Pnin* appeared, holding that it was the duty of the present to put these things down in print for the future. On another occasion, that of Nabokov's Shishkov parodies, Mark Aldanov had asked Nabokov in anguished perplexity: —*It's war! War! How can you waste time on such trifles?* Khodasevich understood.

There is no doubt in my mind that the imaginary dialogues between Godunov-Cherdyntsev and the poet Koncheev in *The Gift* represent the aesthetic positions of Nabokov and Khodasevich discoursing as spiritually friendly peers on the summit of Russian literature. Nabokov denies this emphatically, indignantly. I have had access to the meticulously kept calendar of Vladislav Khodasevich (which unfortunately stops at 1935) from which it would appear that Khodasevich and Nabokov first met on October 23, 1932, and that they were together at least twice in the weeks which followed. The few letters I have from Khodasevich to Nabokov exude a rather more chatty atmosphere of naturally shared assumptions and prejudices than does the dialogue in the novel, which really is imaginary. In one letter (January 20, 1938) Khodasevich tells a delightful story on Pavel Miliukov, informs Nabokov about a forthcoming article on *our friend Georgy Ivanov*, and, having just read an instalment of *The Gift* in *Contemporary Annals*, he congratulates Nabokov on the novel and especially on his parody of Adamovich (the same one which so upset Aldanov): —*Mortus was, as you observed, furious, but this is useful.* When

218 I asked Nabokov about his meetings with Khodasevich he replied

(I wonder if he noticed it? evidently not) with almost a direct quotation from the novel itself: —**We only talked about routine trifles.**

Referring to his generation of Russian writers and poets, Khodasevich once wrote: —*One was allowed to be possessed by whatever one liked. The only requirement was that one be totally possessed.* Nabokov belonged to the end of that same generation, and to the extent that Khodasevich's proposition is correct it helps at least partially to place and explain from an historical point of view certain aspects of Nabokov's character. They had other things in common as well. In 1936, however, Khodasevich must have been somewhat closer to the Koncheev of *The Gift*, for Nabokov wrote Véra Evseevna after he had paid a visit to Khodasevich, who was ill and reminded him somewhat of Pushkin: —*He was in very good form and served me some of his playful poison.* Khodasevich's face was long and bony, really more like a starving Pasternak than Pushkin, with that same shock of hair sheaflike across his forehead; but whereas Pasternak's Mongol features seem to me to have had an intimation of comfort and display about them, Khodasevich's angular face had simply the tired wariness and indifference to his appearance of the professional gambler (which he was). In his last years, we know from several émigré memoirs, he became obsessed with the idea of absolute, relentless honesty in everything, and he thereby further increased his already considerable store of literary enemies and set himself quite apart from the world, ready to meet posterity. Nabokov remembers him coming to tea at their flat and removing his dentures and placing them on the table before starting to eat. Towards the very end he yellowed to the colour of old parchment. At his death—he was fifty-three—a lock of Khodasevich's hair was sent to Nabokov by a mutual acquaintance. It was immediately disposed of, which is surely what Khodasevich himself would have done in the same circumstances.

At Fondaminsky's Saturdays there was one servant girl. Nabokov remembers that she was —**a girl of incredible, theatrical beauty, deeply devoted to her gentle employer and married to an authentic apache who could be sometimes seen in the kitchen devouring bananas or ironing his silk shirts. Fondaminsky the old terrorist and new mystic was fascinated by that elegant hood. At his Saturdays she seldom served, the host and his guests taking over.** Fondaminsky did his best to prevent a collision between **219**

Adamovich and Georgy Ivanov (they often travelled in each other's company) and Nabokov or Khodasevich. In 1936 when he was first introduced to Adamovich, Nabokov wrote to his mother: —*I said something so caustic to him that he will not forgive me.* . . . Nabokov remembers Fondaminsky asking him not to enter the living room during those meetings, and particularly when Adamovich and Ivanov were there. Once there was a meeting of a group of writers which included Gippius, Merezhkovsky, and Ivanov, and Nabokov, who had an appointment somewhere else, passed— *just by chance*—through the living room. He stopped and shook hands with everyone in the room except Ivanov, whom he left in a half-rising position. Fondaminsky was very nervous and kept repeating: —*Will you have some tea? Will you have some tea?* A short while after that Nabokov passed Ivanov on the street, and they both turned their heads away from each other.

Georgy Ivanov had made his name in Russian poetry prior to 1917 as the most promising of the very young poets who trailed after the Acmeists Akhmatova, Mandelstam, and Gumilyov. His poems were saturated with a sense of St. Petersburg (much more so than is the case with the first poetic efforts of Nabokov, who was four years his junior), but when he left Russia there occurred a drastic change of tone in what he wrote. Though a clear line of descent from the decadent Acmeist Mikhail Kuzmin can be seen —Ivanov was always imitating someone to one degree or another —he wrote poetry in an understated but totally pessimistic voice of a sort which had never been written in Russian before, poetry in which the hopelessness and worthlessness of everything after Russia (which, he insisted, no longer exists) is his main theme. The primary features of his face were his heavy, dissolute eyes and his ripe, almost swollen lips: he cultivated that look and that spirit in his poetry. In many respects Ivanov represented a perfect contrast to Nabokov, as can be shown vividly enough in Ivanov's attitude towards Pushkin. —*Pushkin's Russia, why did you deceive me?* he once wrote. —*Pushkin's Russia, why did you betray us?* For Nabokov, of course, Pushkin represents the primary "gift" of *The Gift*. That Ivanov was in many respects an exceptionally unpleasant person would probably be granted even by many who admire him—as I do—as a poet, though in the case of his quarrel with Nabokov it must at least be said that when he wrote his scurrilous attack on Nabokov in the first issue of *Numbers* he was (covertly) counter-attacking for a stinging review of a book by his wife which

Nabokov had written. But they would, of course, have quarrelled eventually even without that.

No, one could not say that the 1930s, particularly the late 1930s, represented a fellowship of Russian artists in exile. The term of émigré literature was now nearing twenty years. Hope of ever returning to Russia had finally been surrendered by most of the émigrés. (Vladimir Vladimirovich told me that he had given up this hope by the mid-thirties.) The literature existed, but it had no resonance, or at best one so circumscribed that it could be calculated not even in thousands but in hundreds of readers. The old combinations by which a livelihood might be put together in ways more or less directly connected with literature were less possible now. Pavel Miliukov's *The Latest News* (it was, with *Contemporary Annals,* the other major source of income for most of the well-known émigré writers) made a move to "condense" one of his short stories. Nabokov refused and protested loudly, claiming that *The Latest News* was seeking a pretext —*to free itself of me.* The paper claimed that its first obligation had to be to a handful of workmen-authors who had entered into an agreement (refused by Nabokov) to turn out two stories a month. Good Aldanov repaired the breach as usual. Nevertheless, Nabokov never had a very high opinion of Miliukov, the editor of *The Latest News* and the man whom his father had died shielding. The fact that Nabokov was more or less obliged to turn to Miliukov's paper at least from time to time for a portion of his income, and that that newspaper spent a certain amount of its time trying to belittle his work, was not a very happy situation. According to the letter Aldanov wrote him at the time they were all very angry with Nabokov in the offices of *The Latest News* over the parodies in *The Gift.* After its first few numbers Miliukov also became one of the editors of another journal in which Nabokov's work was appearing, *Russian Annals,* a kind of supplementary journal (the contributors were almost identical) to *Contemporary Annals. Contemporary Annals* itself seemed to have an uncertain future, for after about 1936 Fondaminsky was drawn more and more to his religious and philosophical interests, and he took less part in the editing of the journal. By 1937 the journal was being effectively edited by only one of the five original editors, a man whose primary commitment was to social rebirth through religion. This shift in editorial balance surely must in part explain the now famous rejection of the Chernyshevsky chapter in *The Gift.* Rudnev, the **221** *de facto* managing editor, wrote Nabokov several letters expressing virtual ecstasy over *The Gift*, but he explained that one of the five editors was threatening such a row over that chapter that it would have to be bypassed. Nabokov wrote to Fondaminsky seeking his intercession and suggesting that the dropped chapter be printed in *Russian Annals,* but Fondaminsky was evidently in a very awkward situation and chose not to act. The impending war was to make the question purely hypothetical, but the future of émigré literature seemed to hold out ever more thorns, few if any roses.

After spending the greater part of 1937 and 1938 on the Riviera, the Nabokovs came back to Paris. Their flat in Paris, from early March 1939 to spring 1940, was at 59 rue Boileau. Several other émigré writers lived on that street. Two doors down lived the noted playwright and director Nikolai Evreinov (Nabokov met him only once), and also Aleksei Remizov, one of the most famous writers to go into emigration, a queer little simian man with medieval and Dostoevskian inclinations in his writing. Many ranked Remizov alongside Bunin. Nabokov did not. —**He detested me. We were very polite to each other. . . . The only nice thing about him was that he really lived in literature.** Nabokov would from time to time meet Remizov in the offices of French journals. Once Nabokov was talking to Joyce at the *Nouvelle Revue Française,* and Joyce asked him whether he knew Remizov. —**Why, yes, why do you ask?** Nabokov responded in perplexity which he re-enacted for my benefit. —**Joyce, you see, was under the impression that Remizov *mattered* as a writer!!** Both Nabokov and Véra Evseevna will not hear a good word said about Remizov's writing. When he still lived in Berlin, in fact, Nabokov's strongly negative views of Remizov's artistic stature involved him in a very unpleasant and all too traditional Russian scene. An old and fat and lonesome and talentless Berlin painter named Zaretsky, upon hearing the young Sirin make a scathing remark about Remizov's writing, wrote a rejoinder which he read at a private literary *soirée.* In it Remizov was compared to Pushkin and Nabokov to a notorious writer who was in the pay of Tsar Nicholas I's police. Nabokov calmly told the old man that were it not for his age he would slap his face—more than that, the Russian word for face which Nabokov used was the one ordinarily only applied to an animal—whereupon Zaretsky tried to call him out before a literary Court of Honour. Every Russian literary organization had one, and there are few major Russian writers who have escaped the temptation of summoning or the irritation of being summoned before such a "court of peers." But Zaretsky was not Nabokov's peer, nor for that matter were the people who were to sit in judgment of the dispute (one of the two judges, still alive, is now an East German journalist), and so Nabokov, characteristically, simply declined to take part in the farce, though he did of course offer to fight if called out.

In 1936 and 1937 life was slightly easier from a financial point of view than the preceding two years had been. There was still nothing approaching comfort, needless to say, but *Camera Obscura* (rewritten and retitled *Laughter in the Dark*) had been sold to an American publisher, there were various stories and plays either already completed or in progress which would appear in *Contemporary Annals, Russian Annals,* or *The Latest News,* and then *The Gift* would appear as a book. They were able to transfer to the Riviera. While they were there they received official permission to remain in France but without work permits, which was to cause them some hardship towards the end.

Nabokov and his wife spent the month of June 1937 in Marienbad. In early July of that year they went to Paris but departed for Cannes in mid-July, staying at the Hôtel des Alpes there until mid-October, when they took up residence at a boardinghouse, Les Hesperides, in Menton. Nabokov remembers that another Russian in the boardinghouse with them, a man of mystery, was very nice to Dmitri. In early July 1938, they transferred to the Hôtel de la Poste in Moulinet, and the next month they went to Cap d'Antibes, where they stayed at the House of the Union of the St. George-Cross for Disabled Veterans. In mid-September 1938, they took their first flat in Paris, on the rue de Saïgon. They sometimes used both this and the later flat on rue Boileau as *pied-à-terres,* for even in 1939 they travelled in the summer to Seytenex in the Savoy mountains and then to a Russian pension, Rodnoy, at Fréjus.

Nabokov did a lot of writing in this period of his life, and also, he and Véra Evseevna were able to resume collecting once again. When they returned to Paris those butterflies and moths were kept in their Berlin storage cabinet, which was housed in Ilya Fondaminsky's flat. Their stay in southern France was extended from a few months to well over a year because they received a large sum from Bobbs-Merrill for *Laughter in the Dark.*   **223**

The Bobbs-Merrill money provided a respite, but only that. The second phase or decade of Russian émigré literature was fast coming to a close, and what came after was to be something quite different—an émigré "literature" with no new names, no new movements, with absolutely no possibility of even reasonably supplementing one's income with one's pen (oh, there were a handful of journalists for the two or three surviving émigré newspapers), with ever fewer possibilities to print books except at one's own expense, with nothing in fact to look forward to . . . and to look back on?, only a Russia hopelessly blurred by decades of separation and an émigré existence which few survivors could profess to understand and still fewer take pride in. Seen from a distance by a detached observer, even the unpleasant querulousness of the Parisian period of émigré literature was, all the same, a sign of life and creative energy.

The flat on the rue de Saïgon was between the Etoile and the Bois de Boulogne; it recalled some of their Berlin habitations in its proportions but was far larger—one gigantic room, with a large kitchen capable of also serving as a dining room to one side and a very large bathroom to the other. The flat was (still the Bobbs-Merrill money) rather attractive, but it was intended to accommodate a young man on the town, not a family of three. Because the flat's one huge room was perforce not only the living room but also the bedroom and nursery, it was necessary, when Dmitri was sleeping, to entertain company in the kitchen, and Nabokov wrote most of *The Real Life of Sebastian Knight* on a suitcase placed across a bidet in the sun-filled bathroom with chessboard tiles.

The last year or two in France was one of the most difficult periods in Nabokov's life. The difference now was the child, that and the fact that neither Nabokov nor his wife were legally entitled to take any kind of job in France. Both Véra Evseevna and Vladimir Vladimirovich were sensitive and talented parents in their way. Though they were perhaps never terribly well off while Dmitri was very young, they saw to it that this made no difference where he was concerned. When Nabokov pressed a snapshot of his two-year-old son upon everyone during his 1936 reading tour, people would ask if he was five, or even six. The boy had toy cars, boxing gloves (and lessons from his kneeling and pummelled father), and the Mercedes racing car with pedals (*Speak, Memory,* Chapter 15) which he would navigate quite wildly but expertly among the pedestrians when his father took him for a late-after-noon stroll, an intimation of the professional racing driver he was to become during one period in his life.

It was now no longer possible to be casual about one's empty pockets and speak of poverty as though it were a chosen way, as Nabokov had in the old days of his Berlin youth (—*my golden poverty*, he had called it in a 1925 poem). Towards the end of 1939 and the beginning of 1940, when plans had begun for the migration to the United States, things became more and more difficult. At the last they simply did not have the means to exist on a day-to-day basis, and they needed some money for the trip besides, so Nabokov had to ask various friends for loans. One woman kept asking him: —**Are you sure you're going? Quite sure?** It was a matter of about fifty dollars.

A year earlier the composer Rachmaninoff, whom Nabokov had never even met but who admired Sirin's writing and who lent an occasional helping hand to émigré literature in the manner of Fondaminsky (the most talented painters and musicians in the emigration had, of course, a huge career advantage over their fellow artists and countrylessmen who were writers and poets), sent Nabokov the following brief note:

Dear Vladimir Vladimirovich,

*Only today, May 28, did I learn of your letter to L. L'vov [a journalist who had formerly been on the staff of **The Rudder** and now worked on the Paris paper **Russia and Slavdom**] of May 10 in which your two words **ghastly destitution** (**dikaya nuzhda**) stunned me. I am sending you 2500 francs by telegram, which you may repay me when those words no longer apply. And if this should not be soon—though God grant that this is not the case—it doesn't matter. The mere thought that I have been able to help you in a moment of need is sufficient repayment.*

*I am afraid that the question of the publication of **The Gift** must be put off for a time.*

Under the Vichy Government, a Russian émigré was mysteriously transformed into a *prestataire, n.m., a person liable to prestations, n.f. payment (of a toll, etc.; taking (of an oath, etc.).* It was a decree which no one could understand, though it was clear to all what its potential dangers were. Denunciations were being made, and many Russians were being called before committees of 225 émigré fascists and reactionaries for questioning about possible Jewish blood.

The emigration, like most other social groups in Europe, was dividing into four segments. There were those who were going into the underground to fight the Germans (numerous contributors to *Contemporary Annals* were in this group; the very term Resistance was given to the movement by Russian émigrés, who were specially honoured for their heroism by the French Government when France was finally freed), those who chose to collaborate with the Germans (surprisingly, there turned out to be one or two *Contemporary Annals* people in this category, too), those who for reasons of age, family circumstance, or religion had decided to flee Europe and had been able to obtain passage, and, finally, a very large group who decided or simply had to sit and pray for the best. All of that came some weeks after Nabokov's departure in May. His choice then was simply to go or join the French Army. The fact that his wife was Jewish did not make the prospect of remaining any more wise than attractive. The Nabokovs were given invaluable assistance by friends, and a Jewish rescue organization directed by a lawyer named Ya. G. Frumkin, who ironically was almost a perfect double for Nicholas II (he is still living, in his nineties, in New York), not only remembered V. D. Nabokov's passionate defence of Beilis—Frumkin was an old friend of V. D. Nabokov's—and his scathing attack upon Russian anti-Semitism, but also remembered it well:—**We were given a first-class cabin. I had a lovely bath every morning. It was marvellous.** Nabokov had been able to borrow money to pay half the fare. But before they got on that boat, Nabokov had to go through some harrowing red tape to procure the family's exit papers. Nabokov remembers the experience quite vividly: —*The two-month ordeal of going from office to office and from guichet to guichet ended with a lucky bribe that made the last rat in the last rathole finally disgorge our visa de sortie.* And that experience neatly closed the circle of Nabokov's first experience when he applied for entry to France in 1936. An official at the French Prefecture on that occasion blandly told Nabokov that he had lost the application papers which he had been given. He held Nabokov's frayed and tattered old Nansen passport in his hand. —**What do you need this old piece of scrap paper for?** he asked and made a motion as if to throw it out the window behind him. —**You give that back to me!** Nabokov instructed loudly and sternly, and in the end this time no bribe had to be given.

On the eve of their departure from Paris Nabokov went to say good-bye to Ivan Bunin and found Zinaida Gippius and her husband Dmitri Merezhkovsky there. They were both very much a part of the Adamovich circle. Gippius (she preferred the original German form Hippius, which seems, however, particularly lugubrious in English) had made demeaning remarks about Sirin in *Numbers* and elsewhere, and Merezhkovsky had given a lecture in Paris in 1935 entitled *With Jesus or Sirin?*, but Nabokov came to know them at Fondaminsky's, and in the end he was on rather amiable, or at least tolerably speaking, terms with them. Nabokov told me that he thought Gippius could never quite live down her prophetic pronouncement to V. D. Nabokov in 1916 that his son would never, never be a poet; and the Merezhkovskys were, it seemed to him, miffed at the fact that he did not pay them due deference (Merezhkovsky had been tipped by many to be given the Nobel Prize in preference to Bunin) or attend their Sunday salons, which vied in popularity with Fondaminsky's. Of course there were few views held in common between them, but still, towards the end of the Paris period Gippius seemed willing to acknowledge the talent of Sirin, and Nabokov for his part never allowed other considerations to cloud his appreciation of her artistic stature. **—I don't think he was a bad writer, but he hasn't written things that will endure. His wife, on the other hand, has written at least three or four poems which will always remain, shining like precious gems in the history of Russian literature.** (Here Vladimir Vladimirovich began to recite some Gippius poems by heart.)

Zinaida Gippius had once been a beauty, but her beauty had matted with age (Nabokov says: **—Replace by: now she was a painted hag**).

—She would speak in a very, very squeaky voice and ask idiotic questions, idiotic questions which I don't even remember. And is it really true that you also write in Dutch? That kind of question. Thus circumstances, which had led to that awkward lunch with Bunin at the Parisian Russian restaurant Kornilov's, which is described in *Speak, Memory*, and perhaps a bit of Nabokov's sensible fate which avoids great meetings between great writers, prevented once again any memorable discourse between Bunin and Nabokov at that parting. Bunin sat deep in a stuffed armchair, a very little man (he was of average height) with round eyeglasses, and watched his visitors (Aldanov had once remarked that watching Bunin and Nabokov talk was like watching two movie cameras **227**

aimed at each other) while Zinaida Gippius plied Nabokov with her usual questions. —**You're going away to America? Why are you going? Why are you going?** Nabokov answered shortly. It was, of course, a silly question, when Hitler was advancing on Paris. Long before, in Berlin, an acquaintance had asked the same question and had volunteered the advice that it would be better for their souls to stay and suffer. Then Gippius began to insist at great length that they must go by bus to Calais. There was a rumour that the trains had been taken over by the French Army for troop transport. Nabokov said his good-bye to Bunin rather perfunctorily and descended the stairs with the Merezhkovskys, she still continuing to impress upon him the necessity above all of travelling to Calais by bus. It was a bright and gusty spring day.

Nabokov's real good-bye to émigré literature was in the last issue of *Contemporary Annals*, which had appeared only weeks before: Sirin was represented in it by three pieces—a poem, a book review, and the first portion of his next Russian novel, *Solus Rex*, the novel which was never to be completed but was to be more than superseded by *Pale Fire* twenty years later. It was time. The ship they sailed on, the *Champlain*, was the very last one to leave France before the full terror and conflict began.

The last of Nabokov's six *Definitions*, written in his first days in New York, concerned émigré literature:

—in the purity of its designs, the strictness of the standards it set itself, in its ascetic, sinewy strength, it has been, in spite of a small number of first-class talents (anyway, in what times have there ever been many?), worthy of its past. Material poverty, printing difficulties, the lack of responsiveness of the reader, the barbarous ignorance of the ordinary émigré crowd—all of these things were compensated for by the incredible opportunity, which had never before been experienced by Russia, to be free from any state or social censorship whatsoever. I use the past tense, for an active twenty-year European period of Russian literature has ended as a result of events which have disrupted our lives for a second time.

CHAPTER

7

There were no reporters waiting for Mr. Nabokov at dockside when the *Champlain* landed in New York that misty morning of May 28 as there were to be when he sailed back to Europe nearly twenty years later after *Lolita* had been published in the United States. In fact there was no one at all; an old friend from Cambridge, Count Robert de Calry, and a cousin, Nathalie Nabokov, were going to meet the Nabokovs, but there had been a mixup about the landing time. Their first hour on American soil was extremely pleasant, and Nabokov would maintain later that that first impression was a tune which was to be sustained during his American years.

One of the keys to their baggage had been lost. (It was discov- **231** ered much later in Véra Evseevna's pocket.) Nabokov stood bantering with a diminutive Negro porter and two quite large Customs men until a merry little porter arrived and opened the lock with a simple thwack of his iron. Unfortunately the locksmith-by-luck was so pleased by his simple solution that he kept playing with the lock until it snapped shut again. Lying on top of everything when the trunk was finally opened were two sets of boxing gloves. The two Customs men grabbed the gloves and began a mock sparring session, dancing around Nabokov. (—**Where would that happen? Where would that happen?**) The Nabokovs felt quite at ease, unlike the hundreds of their fellow passengers milling around them, almost all French and German Jews, who had no English. He made a telephone call to the Tolstoy Fund (directed by one of Tolstoy's daughters, one of the agencies which was most active in resettling Russian immigrants) and asked Véra Evseevna, in English, he remembers, where she thought he could get a newspaper. One of the men said: —**Oh, I'll get one for you,** and he returned in a moment with a copy of *The New York Times.* Then they hailed one of those bizarrely painted yellow checkerboard cabs of the period and set out to his cousin's apartment on the East Side. It was not very far, though it seemed like the end of an epic journey to them. —**Then we looked at the meter, and we saw nine, o, oh God, ninety, ninety dollars. —We had a hundred. —Yes, we just made it. . . . So we gave the hundred dollars to the cabby.** And the good New Yorker laughed and told Véra Evseevna: —**Lady, I haven't got a hundred dollars. If I had that kind of money, I wouldn't be sitting here driving this cab. . . . Of course the simplest way for him would have been to give us the ten dollars' change and call it a day.** Again, it was the kind of good-humoured and lucky episode of the sort which, Nabokov avers, might never have happened in Europe.

There were a surprising number of friends and faces whose presence had followed Nabokov along some part of the way from Russia to Germany to France and now to the United States. Nathalie Nabokov; De Calry, the friend from Cambridge; another good friend named Bertrand Thompson, who was an American efficiency expert whom he had first met in Berlin, and his wife (Thompson, who died in retirement in his nineties only a few years ago in Uruguay, could speak more interestingly and knowledgeably on virtually any subject than anyone he has ever met, Nabokov thinks); his very close friend since the 1920s, George Hessen;

Mstislav Dobuzhinsky, who had given him art lessons as a boy and whom he had known in Berlin; Roman Grynberg, one of the last of Nabokov's European pupils in Paris, a well-to-do businessman who was a lover of literature and a publisher of occasional Russian almanacs; and there were others as well. But how many had been left behind. How many had perished. The overwhelming majority of those who might be loosely termed his peers had stayed behind, died, returned to the Soviet Union, or simply ceased to write. Aldanov was in New York. Korvin-Piotrovsky was in California, but that was much later. Nabokov was, really, the only major Russian writer or poet in America with the possible exception of Aldanov, and Aldanov was to return to Europe after several years. Aldanov's quarterly, *New Review,* which began in 1942 and which he co-edited (later it was edited by a professor of Russian history at Harvard, Michael Karpovich), had contributions from Bunin, Gippius, Ivanov, and other writers still in Europe, but somehow the tone of intellectual urgency and freshness in *Contemporary Annals* was never recaptured by the new journal, which was dominated by writers whose names had flashed only occasionally in the previous journal and by many people who weren't writers at all. Some fine and important things appeared in the journal, but that was the general impression which it produced. There simply was no possibility that émigré literature could continue on its old terms in America. And the size of the country and the fact that many Russian intellectuals soon drifted out to teach their native language and sundry subjects on far-flung American campuses dissipated whatever cultural cohesion there might otherwise have been among Russians in the United States.

Nabokov never made any terribly close friends in America, but he was quite friendly (much more so than he ever had been with West Europeans during his first period of exile) with many people during his twenty-year residence. After years in the country he still perceived the same jocularity among Americans that he had so enjoyed that morning on that pier. It always puzzled and some-times annoyed his Russian acquaintances. Five years later—by then he was living in Massachusetts—when Nabokov and his wife went to receive their citizenship papers, they took with them, as the two sponsors, Miss Amy Kelly, a very charming older woman and estimable scholar who taught English at Wellesley College, and Professor Karpovich. Just before the examination time Karpovich said to Nabokov: —**Now look here, I want to ask you some-** 233 thing. Don't joke, please don't joke with them. This is quite serious, you know. Don't joke. —O.K., Nabokov agreed, but it was not to be. The examiner (—of Italian origin apparently, judging by his slight accent) gave Nabokov a phrase to read, *The child is bald,* which seemed a little silly to Nabokov, but he read it. The examiner corrected him and said: —No, it is not bald. It is bold. Nabokov replied that babies don't have very much hair. The examiner acknowledged the fact with mock interest and next asked Nabokov a question on American history. Nabokov didn't even understand the question, but within a moment the two men were kidding each other and roaring with laughter, while the apprehensive Karpovich stood looking at them as if they were both madmen. —You passed, you passed, the examiner gasped at last. Nabokov remembers the day with great affection: —I had a wonderful time becoming an American citizen. That was an absolutely wonderful day. He cites this incident as an illustration of the Russian lack of a sense of humour and also, by implication, of his own innate Americanness. —That's very characteristic, you know. This rather prim Russian who wants to be very serious, and this easygoing American way of settling things. He saw at once that I could read English. It was very soothing, very soothing.

In their first weeks in New York the Nabokovs stayed for a short time in his cousin Nathalie Nabokov's apartment. Subsequently they arranged to rent for two months the apartment of a niece of Countess Panina, the woman who had given the Nabokovs first sanctuary in the Crimea, and then they accepted an invitation to the Vermont summer home of Michael Karpovich, whom Nabokov had known in Europe. They occasionally stopped there in the summer during the forties. That summer house in West Brattleboro, with its endlessly arriving and departing émigré guests, is given its literary memorial in *Pnin.* Suitably surrounded in birches, it was the very last capital of Russian culture in exile. In fact, Nabokov says that he considerably magnified and embellished the memorial in *Pnin.*

When they returned to New York they were rather hard up, but there were prospects. The job that he could have had (through the good offices of the Tolstoy Fund) as a bicycle delivery boy for Scribner's Bookstore didn't suit, but a less risible and more serious attempt was being made by a friend to get Nabokov an appointment as the head of the Russian section of the Voice of America. He was taken there and introduced to all the staff members

(—everyone bowing, I thinking: I will never take this job . . .), and a complete security check was done on him with interviews of all his relatives and acquaintances in the United States, but at the last minute the plum was snatched by one of the referents for himself. —Isn't it strange that your mother was only thirteen when you were born?, the interviewer from the FBI asked Nabokov. He had made a mistake in writing the year of her birth. Nabokov was to have a great deal of contact with the FBI over the years as friends of his came up for similar jobs which required security clearances, or when he was teaching at Cornell and checks were being made on students who had applied for government jobs. It will be understood, I trust, that this particular aspect of American life was not one which the Nabokovs, from the vantage point of their particular experience of the world, objected to in any way as so many other American intellectuals did and do. Nabokov even became quite friendly with one agent in Ithaca. He was a sad man who had a feeling that because of what he did for a living no one liked him. —And I'm a Catholic, and that makes things even harder, he told Nabokov.

In spite of their financial hardship in 1940 and 1941 the Nabokovs were pleased with virtually everything in America. Except perhaps the ways of some of their fellow émigrés in America. Nabokov received advice in 1940 from a very well-known Russian, presumably intended to help him "get on" in the new country, warning him that all Americans were completely uncultured, credulous fools. He was introduced to a Russian who taught at Columbia University and was immediately complimented: —All one hears here are Yids. What a magnificent aristocratic pronunciation you have! There were other such unpleasant incidents in those early years in Russian New York. Nabokov found the conversation at one émigré party at which he was the nominal guest of honour so offensive that he was forced at last to turn on his heel and walk out, his host at the door plaintively imploring him to return. In May 1941 Nabokov wrote to his friend Hessen, who was having some trouble getting settled: —I am convinced that you will find work here without difficulty. This is a cultured and exceedingly diverse country. The only thing you must do is deal with genuine Americans and don't get involved with the local Russian emigration.

In the winter of 1940 Nabokov plunged with new zest into research at the Museum of Natural History in New York classifying **235** butterflies, and he published two papers arising from this work the following year. He established a very good rapport with the Museum staff, and he used to manage to drop in almost every time he came down to New York from Boston in the succeeding years, even after *Lolita*. He also did some free-lance book-reviewing, and he was paid for this, not much, but it helped. This work came to him with the help of Edmund Wilson, whom he met in New York in 1940.

After the American edition of *Laughter in the Dark* in 1938 Nabokov had received many letters of inquiry from literary agents and agencies. All his Russian novels went the rounds of New York publishers, and all were rejected. Gradually the various agents lost interest and fell away, all except one, but even she did not last long. His first English novel was placed with New Directions with the help of Karpovich's friend Harry Levin, and on the recommendation of Delmore Schwartz. Edmund Wilson was at this time the literary editor of *The New Republic*, and James Laughlin of New Directions wrote to him to draw the novel to his attention. Nabokov received one hundred and fifty dollars for *The Real Life of Sebastian Knight* (which was less than he had got in Paris for the serialization of his last Russian novel, *The Gift*, which was later published with foundation support in the United States), and about twelve dollars apiece for a series of book reviews he was invited to do for Wilson and slightly more for those of another series he did, through an introduction provided by Wilson, for *The New York Sun*. As a result of these reviews he was asked to write a review for the *New York Times Book Review*, which did pay well, and an excellent magazine called *Decision*, edited by Klaus Mann, was going to use a humorous essay he wrote—in fact it was set in print, but then the magazine folded. Two of his Russian short stories which he translated were taken by *The Atlantic Monthly*. In his first year in America Nabokov was placed on the lecture circuit roster of the Institute of International Education, and one of his 1941 lectures was a March engagement at Wellesley College, and that eventually led to a loose association with Wellesley that lasted for seven years. At the time, it wasn't much of a livelihood, but it wasn't as bad as the Nabokovs' last months in Europe, and the pleasant prospect of Stanford and California was before them. The prospect was marred only by the fact that Véra Evseevna was seriously ill through much of that winter, and there was a question as to whether or not they could make the trip.

Nabokov worked harder during this first American year than he had ever before in his life. He did virtually no creative writing in this year, but the work he did was exceedingly pleasing to him. Besides his entomological work (in which he was able to classify several new butterflies), Nabokov threw himself into preparing lectures to deliver at Stanford in creative writing, drama, and Russian literature—actually, he had begun to do this preparation while he was still in Europe—and also, in anticipation of the full-time position as a teacher of Russian literature that he was hoping would materialize as a result of things that had been said at Wellesley. He prepared lectures for about one hundred teaching hours, and, working on a calculation of approximately twenty typed pages for a fifty-minute lecture, he wrote nearly two thousand pages. He would read his lectures at a slightly subdued pace, and he developed early on an extremely subtle way of glancing up and down, though he is sure that his more alert students were never in doubt of the fact that he was reading, not speaking from notes, including even the bits of local colour (these alone were changed from place to place over the years) and dramatic improvisations (Gogol pleading with his doctors to have the leeches removed from his nose) with which he conservatively spiced his hours. It was wise preparation for his two decades in America: —**The labour was tremendous, but I had no labour after that, thinking about them. I could think about something totally different while I was delivering my lecture.** He had given his lessons in Berlin in much the same spirit. He did it well, exceptionally well even, and yet he still contrived to save and hoard something, the essential something, of himself.

Nabokov enjoyed giving the lectures, but from the first he simply did not believe in the possibility of teaching, or teaching anything worth learning at any rate, in the traditionally honoured ways. He thought that the notion of a crowd of students attempting to take down in longhand a lecture which the instructor had himself written down was an idiotic medieval custom. He believed that his lectures should be recorded so that every student could listen to them whenever he or she felt like it and could stop the lecture to think, take notes, or replay a part of it. —**I used to tell my betters about it.** On odd occasions Nabokov had a little joke by which he gave himself empirical proof of the inadequacies of the classroom situation. After reaching some point in his lecture at which he thought it would be nice to stop, he would, and he would **237** begin to read again from the beginning of that same lecture. He found that for as long as two minutes absolutely no one would notice anything. All heads would be bowed and a roomful of pencils would continue to perform industrious exercises in place. Then, gradually, heads would rise. **—And not only that, some people would giggle, but you would hear other people say: "What's so funny?"**

On their first trip across America the Nabokovs were fortunate enough to have a driver. She was the last of Nabokov's private pupils, an American lady who had worked for years in the New York Public Library system. The Nabokovs had met her quite by chance, and she expressed a desire to learn some more Russian. Then, when they told her that they were going to California, she offered them her car, a brand-new Pontiac which she had just acquired, but at that point of time, of course, neither of the Nabokovs had had any more occasion to know how to drive an automobile than to understand, say, what banks were for—these were simple enough matters abstractly, but they had not yet obtruded upon their lives. Their friend and pupil, on learning that, simply told them: **—Oh, I'll drive you.** She not only drove them, she also planned their itinerary, which took a southerly course and had a particularly memorable stop in Arizona, for it was there, on the south rim of the Grand Canyon on a very cold day in June (they had departed on May 26) that Nabokov walking down a path into the gorge came upon and captured a new butterfly, which he gallantly named after their chauffeur, who had made the trip just to follow her whim and be kind to some newly arrived immigrants.

Nabokov acknowledges that the impressions of motel-America which began then contributed significantly to the genesis of his most famous novel. He recalls, too, that his six-year-old son, who had grown up to such a large extent in *pensions* in Europe, had the impression that they had somehow "come home" when they began to change from motel to motel (they must have stayed at a dozen as they drove westward) and, moreover, that this was the way all little boys lived: **—When somebody at a garage would say, "Sonny, where do you live?" he would say, "In little houses by the road." It was very exact.**

The place they rented in Palo Alto—the first house they had had since Russia—resembled a Riviera villa. It was a pleasant summer. Nabokov read his lectures, hunted butterflies, wrote his first poem in English for nearly twenty years, and almost every evening played chess.

When the summer session at Stanford was over the Nabokov family travelled back East. When they finally arrived in New York there was a telegram waiting for him: would he like to come and teach at Wellesley? He accepted at once. The position had a special title, Resident Lecturer in Comparative Literature, which had been created especially to accommodate him. The position, however, was only part-time (he was paid about what a teaching assistant in a large university receives, but the Nabokovs continued to live as they always had, and would, in modest rented quarters with few personal possessions, and so they found that when they left Wellesley they had saved roughly half of that income), and it did not even accord Nabokov the minimal status of a faculty member. All the same he liked it very much at Wellesley, and in spite of the fact that his situation at the college remained rather tenuous Nabokov chose not to pursue another tentative offer (—*I think I should point out that the Dartmouth students in general will be most interested in the social, economic, and political situation in modern Russia*) which came to him at the end of that year.

When Nabokov first visited Wellesley in 1941 he delivered a mixed bag of lectures, some of which had been written to serve double duty at both Stanford and as the Institute of International Education lectures. The eleven talks were: *Hard Facts about Readers; A Century of Exile; The Strange Fate of Russian Literature; The Artist and Commonsense; The Tragedy of Tragedy* (on modern drama); *The Art of Writing; The Novel; The Short Story;* and there were separate lectures on Pushkin, Lermontov, Gogol, and Tolstoy. The initial lectures, on the art of writing, were received so well that he was asked to stay an additional fortnight, during which time he gave his other general lectures on literature and the one on the strange fate of Russian literature. It is remembered at Wellesley that several influential faculty members such as Agnes Perkins and Amy Kelly (best known as the author of a scholarly book on Eleanor of Aquitaine, which to everyone's astonishment suddenly became a best-seller) were from the first strongly of the opinion that Nabokov should be made a faculty member. There were some minor problems: Nabokov had no higher degrees, Wellesley had no Russian department, but they did not prove insurmountable. Nabokov thinks that the thing which tipped the scales in favour of his special association with Wellesley was their discovery that he had done the Russian translation of *Alice in Wonderland,* a copy of which was in the college library's special collection of first editions and translations of Car- **239** roll's tale. —**Now we know you are the right person for the job,** he was assured. In translating *Alice* Nabokov had chosen the path of finding Russian equivalents to Carroll's parodies of well-known English verses. In later years he would say: —**It is not a very good translation, I'm afraid, except those bits of poetry. The prose is a little stilted.**

Fortuitous coincidence was repeated some months later when Nabokov dropped in to see Dr. Nathaniel Banks, Head of the Entomological Department at Harvard's Museum of Comparative Zoology. He wished to enter a complaint that one of the museum's collections was improperly preserved. It so happened that at that moment Banks had before him on his desk Volume 53 of *The Entomologist* opened to an article entitled *A Few Notes on Crimean Lepidoptera*. It was agreed that the collection should be rehoused, and Dr. Barbour, the genial Director of the Museum (who happened to be an admirer of Nabokov's short stories in *The Atlantic*) asked Nabokov to do the job. The task was gradually transformed into a regular part-time job. The salary wasn't grand, but of course he would have rapturously done the job for nothing. Nineteen forty-one to forty-two was a golden year. Nabokov had two ideal jobs (ideal first of all because he was doing things he liked doing in wholly congenial surroundings, and secondly because he was within reasonable limits beholden to no one else's authority in the execution of those jobs), his first English novel appeared in the fall of 1941, quietly but with some rather fine notices *(The New York Herald Tribune* called it —*a little masterpiece of cerebration and execution)*, there were the short stories in *The Atlantic Monthly,* and a much more extensive speaking tour had been arranged for that winter by the Institute of International Education. The following year was not to be quite so pleasant.

Nabokov gave a series of six general lectures on Russian writers when he began his Resident Lectureship at Wellesley. The first three, on Pushkin, Lermontov, and Gogol, were given in the first three weeks of October; the final three, on Turgenev and Tolstoy, Tiutchev, and Chekhov, began at the end of February and concluded in mid-March. They all took place in the afternoon, usually the late afternoon, in Pendleton Hall. All of the lectures concentrated upon the "Westernness" of each writer, as if to establish and underscore the intrinsic émigré quality of all of Russian literature. The titles were *Pushkin as a West European Writer, Lermontov as*
240   *a West European Writer, Gogol as a West European Writer,* etc.

The lecture on Pushkin explained how the great poet was an exile in his own country, unable to receive permission to go abroad, hated by officialdom, and always subject to the personal censorship of the tsar. The lecture's other main theme was *Pushkin in Relationship to the European Background of His Genius.*

In his lecture on Gogol, Nabokov spoke of that novelist as being one of the very first writers to apply techniques of art to literature, and he saw his influence upon Dostoevsky, Kafka, and Joyce. His remarks on Tolstoy seem to have been of some interest, because, after detailing the sad history of the relationship between Tolstoy and Turgenev, Nabokov spoke of Tolstoy as the writer who possessed the deepest and most human concept of time. In his talk on Chekhov he emphasized the effect which Chekhov creates by his subtle interweaving of seemingly random and insignificant details. The lectures were well attended and created a small but vital (as it turned out) Nabokov coterie on the campus. I dare say none of his listeners save Véra Evseevna realized how much of a personal statement about himself as an artist and about the historical tradition in which he saw himself—which to a certain extent he had created for himself, because he was a poet—those sparkling and intriguing lectures were.

In addition to these formal lectures Nabokov was frequently invited to talk on various books and subjects in the French and English departments, occasionally in other departments, too, such as Spanish. He had no students of his own at first or marking responsibility, but in the second semester it was arranged for him to teach Russian to a group of interested faculty members. There were difficulties on the horizon, however. A quite substantial and even insistent faction of the faculty wanted Nabokov to become a permanent member of the staff, but there was another faction (of only three or four)—which not only did not wish to see Nabokov given any kind of tenure, but wanted to prevent him from returning for a second year. The most important of these persons was the then President of Wellesley, Miss Mildred McAfee, who had heard of numerous less than respectful remarks about Stalinist Russia and acknowledged masters of modern Russian literature, such as Mikhail Sholokhov, which were being made by the eccentric Resident Lecturer. Miss McAfee was, in addition to being President of Wellesley, extremely active in the women's war effort, and shortly after Nabokov came to Wellesley she was appointed head of the women's naval reserve, or WAVES. Because of **241** the war, the declarations of friendship then current in Roosevelt's Washington for the Soviet Union, and perhaps the embarrassment she felt at such constant anti-Soviet remarks being made by a staff member at Wellesley in view of her official connection with the government, Miss McAfee, according to Nabokov, made the decision that she would not have him back for a second year. A large number of staff members and faculty wives—Nabokov remembers it as something on the order of twenty-five or thirty—arranged to study Russian under Nabokov's tutelage outside the auspices of the college. A kind of uneasy truce was reached after a few months. Nabokov returned to his official demi-position and stayed on in that capacity, but the administration would not establish a formal Russian department while Nabokov was there.

Nabokov had only one direct encounter with Miss McAfee over the question. She approached him one day and said: —**I want to ask you a great favour. Don't make these remarks about Soviet Russia. After all, we are allies.** To which, of course, Nabokov replied: —**I refuse. If you want me to lecture only on classical Russian literature, it's all right. But if I'm going to lecture on modern Russian literature, I'm *going* to make those remarks.** It was a victory—he was never interfered with—but a limited one, for the final word in such matters always is said by the administration. Wellesley lost Nabokov when the head of its publicity department, a Nabokov admirer, described him glowingly in one of the college's pamphlets, which chanced to be seen by Morris Bishop at Cornell. Bishop had been following Nabokov's American publications with admiration. —**Oho, so they've got Nabokov!** he thought, and he wrote to Nabokov inviting him to come and give a lecture at Ithaca. Nabokov came, lectured, was shown the library, the canyon. When he received an offer to come to Cornell—it was more than twice what he had been receiving—the Wellesley administration told him (the usual formula): —**After all, Mr. Nabokov, we don't want to stand in your way.**

Nabokov was then living in Cambridge and took part in a daily car pool to Wellesley (it will figure in the second volume of memoirs). He was the only participant to pay his ten cents by the day rather than the week, and he always sat in the front seat. Two moments are especially remembered by the other participants— Nabokov rubbing his forehead slightly with his fingers one morning and saying: —**My brother has perished in a concentration camp.** And Nabokov standing in front of the car with Isabel Ste-

242

phens, a Wellesley friend who was one of the other pool members and the person who had suggested the title *Bend Sinister* to him, and discussing his academic dilemma with obvious pain. **—All the same, shouldn't I stay at Wellesley?** he asked her after considering the sensible course of action. America was the place, Nabokov has declared, where he was happiest, and though he enjoyed his decade at Cornell enormously, Wellesley was the particular place in America where he was happiest of all.

When it came time to go on his lecture tour in the autumn of 1942, Nabokov was less than enthusiastic at the prospect, but it was too late. He had no particular obligations at Wellesley in October and November, and he arranged to have Véra Evseevna do one of his rather delicate chores involving the transfer of several series of specimens from one tray to another (*—perekolesh'* **—when you pin them from one box to another. Wonderful verb** *—perekolesh'* . . .) at the museum while he was away.

The tour went south to the border of Florida and then swung north to Illinois and Minnesota. Nabokov travelled by overnight train. At the beginning of the trip he had had to wait because he found someone already asleep in his berth, but they conversed amiably about their situation, and in a short while the first occupant was given another berth. But Nabokov did not sleep terribly well because of the groans and bumps of cars coupling and parting in New York. His first stop, on October 3, was Florence, South Carolina, where he was to be met and driven to Hartsville, the home of Coker College, a women's college. The heat and the sun of South Carolina in October reminded him of the sensation one experiences upon coming to the Riviera from Paris; in the next few days he would learn that the American South had the same (*—zverskie, riv'erskie*) mosquitoes as well.

The train to Florence was an hour late, but there was no one to meet him. He called Coker and was told that they would call him right back about a car for him. He waited an hour and a half for that call in a little station café (not of the Riviera variety) by the phone booth. He was irritable, for he had not had his bath or shaven, and he was tired from the night on the train. Finally a professor of theology from the college called and cheerfully informed him that he was in Florence on some personal business and would drive him to Hartsville in three hours. The lecturer indicated his discomfiture at this prospect but was told that he would be taken to a local hotel to rest until then. No one appeared, and, **243** after waiting a while longer, Nabokov learned from a cab driver that a fellow driver had had an accident on his way to pick someone up to take him to a hotel and the driver to whom Nabokov was speaking had asked him to do it for him. They knew nothing about it at the hotel. When all hope seemed to have been lost and fearful that the teacher from Coker would be left eternally searching for him, Nabokov chanced upon the theology professor by overhearing a conversation in the lobby: —**Oh no**, the man said. —**I am waiting for a Russian professor. —But I am the Russian professor. —Well, you don't look like one.** His photograph had not been sent ahead by the Institute for this particular lecture, as a result of which Coker College had been looking for and forward to someone —*with Dostoevsky's beard, Stalin's mustache, Chekhov's pince-nez, and [wearing] a Tolstoyan peasant blouse.* Since the good professor's business in town was still not completed, however, Nabokov had no prospects of reaching Hartsville until shortly before dinner at six-fifteen, after which the lecture was to follow, and so he went to the local barbershop to get a shave. That was not a wise thing to do; there was a howling five-year-old in the next chair, and Nabokov's barber was a nervous old man who attempted to aid his fellow barber by shushing the child, as a result of which Nabokov was left with a bristly tuft on his Adam's apple and was lucky to escape with only a slight slice under his nose.

The theology professor appeared punctually in his car, but as they were pulling away from the curb they were hailed by an emaciated woman who had thought they were a taxi—she needed to go to Hartsville and was terribly afraid she was going to be late for the Russian professor's lecture. The three had an animated conversation about Christianity and the war as they drove to the magnificent many-columned Confederate estate which belonged to the family of Major Coker, the college's founder. It was ten minutes before dinner was to be served. Nabokov dived through a bath in his haste to get groomed and dressed in time. Unfortunately his shirt was starched to the point where it was absolutely impossible to get his cuff links in, and anyway, one of them skipped away he knew not where. He made his appearance at twenty minutes to seven with his shirt slightly rolled up in his tuxedo sleeves. But his social sense prompted him to declare the disarray of his dress at once, and someone else's cuff links were promptly produced and fixed in place for him by one of the ladies, to the delight of the entire company. From that point onwards everything went beautifully: two days of lectures and a reading (*Mademoiselle O*), extensive butterfly-collecting in the perfumed and blue-green Crimean lushness of the southern countryside in the company of a Presbyterian minister who was also a passionate collector and who turned out to be the son of an authority in the field whose work Nabokov knew well, tennis with the local pro, and hospitality from the various and numerous Cokers who seemed to control half of Hartsville. He met with traditional Southern warmth and as much interest as had been shown in him at Wellesley, for his pieces in *The Atlantic* were known not only to the educators but also to all the Cokers who knew Edward Weeks, *The Atlantic*'s editor.

Nabokov's lecture stops were all different, but all were in this general continuing atmosphere of tiring and ultimately trivial but immensely educative (and remunerative) experience, the further Americanization of Vladimir Nabokov. After Coker College Nabokov was to have gone on to Richmond, but because of a wartime blackout there his lectures had to be cancelled, and his tour organizer sent him instead to Spelman College, the Negro women's college in Atlanta.

It was to be simply a stopover of a few days with lectures in exchange for food and board, but it turned out to be one of his most successful receptions, and he was surprised at the end when he was given his usual fee, a hundred dollars. His first talk at Spelman was on Pushkin, with particular emphasis on the poet's African (Abyssinian) blood, and it was met with wild enthusiasm. Nabokov became especially friendly with the President of Spelman, Miss Read, who went to great lengths to surround him with interesting people and even to see to it that he didn't run out of cigarettes and that his forward travelling arrangements were properly made. She visited the Nabokovs on several occasions in later years. Each morning Nabokov would breakfast with Miss Read and discuss the Negro problem and telepathy. Then at nine he would be dragged to chapel for hymns with the entire student body. At first he tried protesting that he was a heretic and hated all music, but Miss Read knew that he would like theirs. In his honour they read prayers thanking God for poets and those who delight in making things and make them well, and Nabokov responded by reading his own translations of classical Russian poems exalted enough to suit the occasion. Nabokov really liked Spelman, and all the more because he had been more depressed than amused by the Uncle Tomism he had observed at Hartsville. A magazine of the college, *The Spelman Messenger* (November 1942), ran a long article detailing his various talks and readings (including a still-unpublished "lightly Rabelaisian poem on Superman"—it described the explosion of Superman's honeymoon hotel on his nuptial night and was rejected by *The New Yorker*) and predicting that he might well someday be a great writer. The problem with the speaking tour was that people were so anxious to please and kept him so busy that he was scarcely ever left alone. Though this passion to please was certainly present at Spelman, Miss Read's wisdom evidently extended to understanding Nabokov's need to have some time to himself, and it was there that he finished writing his book on Gogol.

He managed to cut short the tour in mid-November instead of mid-December as had been planned. Nabokov was quite tired by the northern leg of the tour and exhausted when it was finally over. Once Nabokov went out for a walk and lost his hotel. Another time, to his extreme horror, he arrived for his speech without the text he thought he had in his jacket (but the impromptu version was wholly successful). It should be mentioned that, while he was on the whole in excellent health on this trip, he suffered several attacks of brief but very severe pains in his ribcage, intercostal neuralgia. Though *Pnin* had not yet begun to take shape in Nabokov's imagination, it seems clear to me that, just as the motels of the Nabokov's collecting expeditions made their contribution to *Lolita,* so various incidents and observations on this lecture tour of 1942 cast their shadow, albeit a much lighter one, on *Pnin.* The comic mural in Waindell, Nabokov's imaginary college, for example, with great figures passing on the torch of knowledge was, and for all I know may still be, at Macalester College in St. Paul, Minnesota, where he spoke to an audience of nine hundred (it was also broadcast on the radio) on November 10. A newspaper just prior to his arrival called him a —*celebrated Soviet writer and a personal friend of Joseph Stalin,* which may or may not have had something to do with the size of his audience.

Over the years Nabokov lectured at about thirty American colleges and universities, but he never undertook such an extensive tour again. One of his warmest memories is of his 1964 reading (perhaps because that was in the rosy dawn of literary awareness of him as more than the author of one book) at the Y.M.H.A.

in New York, though he was unnerved by the lighting in the auditorium, which prevented him from seeing the audience, because he likes to be able to watch faces as he reads. A less pleasant memory is the talk he gave in 1952 on the Columbia Broadcasting System in a symposium to mark the centenary of Gogol's death, because he was violently ill in the men's room just minutes before the symposium began, and, though he was able to carry on and give his little talk, he has only a dizzy recollection of the occasion. He was invited to speak at Yale once. They were "looking him over," but it turned out that the person who was at that time in charge of the Russian programme at Yale spoke Russian with an extremely strange regional accent, and Nabokov thinks he was not interested in the academic qualifications or capabilities of the new appointee so much as in finding someone who spoke Russian somewhat as he did. One of his most memorable speaking engagements, however, was at Dartmouth. He might have been warned by the letter of invitation, which was signed Vladimir Nabokov. The absent-minded professor who had arranged the lecture completely forgot to have it advertised or even announced, so that when the time came only eight people made up the audience. (Another, better publicized lecture was being given by a visiting celebrity at the same time.) The nervous professor pointed out to his speaker that, though there were not many people, they were **very well distributed** in the hall. Among the audience of eight were a lady with her son, and a noted popular scholar of Russian history. —**Under the circumstances I had either not to give it or to do the very best I could. It was a wonderful lecture.** Nevertheless, the scholar seemed to doze throughout.

Much less often, but from time to time, Nabokov gave lectures on butterflies. He lectured on mimicry at the Museum of Natural History, and once, during the Wellesley period when Dmitri was in grammar school, he spoke on butterflies at the Dexter School, with rather great success.

After his short but awkward period of non-appointment at Wellesley, Nabokov taught the Russian language there twice a week. Later, when there was a need for more advanced courses, this was increased to three days a week. It may have been another sign of the displeasure of the college's administration that the classroom hours assigned to him in the spring of 1943 were at night, which was neither a terribly common nor a popular practice at Wellesley. But the course did well, and eventually Nabokov **247** usually had enough students to require the use of one of the larger classrooms such as a chemistry hall for his elementary classes. Nabokov's pedagogic technique as a language teacher seems to have been founded on the belief that grammar could be driven in with a hammer of whimsy. In a letter to George Hessen in 1943 Nabokov explains how he will teach Russian by interlingual association. Thus the phrase *ya lyublyu vas (I love you)* is made to stand with *yellow-blue vase,* and *thank you (blagodaryu)* is paired with *blackguard you.* Whatever this creative method may have done for retention, it must have added something interesting to the pronunciation of his students.

A student of the Class of '45 has left us a sketch of the middle-aged Nabokov as a language teacher in the student magazine *We* (Volume 1, No. 2, December 1943). Nabokov is presented as a very shy and idiosyncratic teacher, timidly asking his students whether they have done their assignment and then later pouring guttural and fricative Russian upon them in a torrent. He would plead winsomely with his class to "like" a word and the next moment he would stride to a student's notebook and despair with mock ferocity ("Ai-yai-yai!") over poorly formed Slavic letters. The blackboard after several uses and improper erasures would assume a vaguely oriental aspect.

The teacher would handle his grammar with dead-panned gusto. **—And now we come to the saddest story ever told, 'She is here. He is there.'** Or: **—How am I supposed to know 'Where is the book?'** And, a preview of coming attractions, he would tell his students of exciting episodes in forthcoming chapters: **—'Those uncles are crossing these rivers.'** A difficult point of grammar was always introduced apologetically if not funereally, but then Nabokov would brighten and assure his students that, having crossed this hurdle **—You will know practically all there is to know about Russian!** It is doubtful whether any of the students could have fully appreciated the sarcasm behind the *Peterburzhets* Nabokov's praise of their recitations: **—So good to hear Russian spoken again! It's just like being back in Moscow!**

It is not too much to assume that at least a fair number of the students attended the course as much for the harsh pleasure of the lecturer as for knowledge of the obscure subject he taught. Nabokov's courses moved out into the light of day, and he became a well-known and popular figure on the campus, to the point indeed where he was "featured" in a little piece

248

headed "Men on Their Minds" in *Mademoiselle* magazine in September 1947. A determined co-ed was quoted as saying: — **He's quite a guy! I'm going to write a book about him!** They were such nice girls in his classes at Wellesley. Nabokov shakes his head in wonder at the thought that today a few of them may be grandmothers.

It was in this bloom of success as a teacher, rather than four years earlier when he had written *Sebastian Knight*, that Nabokov felt the worst pains of his decision to withdraw from Russian as his artistic medium. On Christmas 1942 he wrote George Hessen with a light skim of jocularity:

*—The Sirin in me is beginning to arise since the time you were here. Someday a sagacious professor [**doshlyi dotsent**] will write about my absolutely tragic situation. I am too old to change con-radically. It seems to me that not a single writer in the world has executed my **Kunstuck**. (It's as though I created the person who composed **The Real Life of Sebastian Knight** and the poems in **The New Yorker** and all the rest, but it's not I who am creating —my relation to it is in the category of the pleasure one experiences in sport.)*

The letter which he wrote to his wife near the end of his lecture tour, however, speaks of the same thing much more simply and movingly:

*—Yesterday after a tour of the area around the city, I was wildly bored, and so I went to the cinema and came back on foot. I walked more than an hour and went to bed at about eight. On my walk I was pleasantly pierced by a lightning bolt of inspiration, I had a passionate desire to write, and write in Russian, and I must not. I don't think that anyone who has not experienced this feeling can really understand its tortuousness, its tragic aspect. The English language in this light is illusion and **ersatz**. I am in my usual state of affairs, i.e., occupied with butterflies and translations or academic writing, and so I am not fully caught up in the sadness and bitterness of my situation.*

The uniqueness of Nabokov's change of language after having created an *oeuvre* in his first language may be challenged (two Russian writers who passed into other languages, Knut' and Yanovsky, have already been mentioned, and there are others). What is quite unique, of course, is the intensity of pain which Nabokov experienced at the loss of his native language. He told me that it equalled in many respects and was a logical continuation of the pain he had experienced at the loss of Russia. When *The Gift* at last appeared as a book in Russian in 1952 it was received with virtually unbroken silence in the Russian emigration—not even *The New Review* reviewed the novel—but when *Lolita* appeared in English a Russian poetess took an advertisement in *The New Russian Word* condemning those who betrayed their native tongue. The betrayal was by the emigration, though Nabokov did hold himself more and more aloof from the emigration and what he saw as its will to mediocrity. For Nabokov the extent of his unbroken tie (—**twined solely of love and despair**) to Russia and the Russian tradition which ended with himself and Khodasevich can be clearly seen in his Russian poems written in the forties and the fifties (among the very best of his poems in Russian, but much of their penetrating force derives from their quiet acceptance that this is the end), his monumental Pushkin scholarship in the fifties, his translation of *Lolita* into Russian in the sixties—it is a poetic rather than a prosaic translation, the best one he has ever done— and, of course, the pervasive presence of Russian allusions in his English poetry and prose.

At the same time that he was experiencing his torments of withdrawal from the Russian language, Nabokov, somewhat to his own surprise (—**that is what it was, one of my few idiotic moments**), found himself wishing to join the U.S. Army and fight against Nazi Germany. Nabokov told his wife that, if it were not for her, he would enlist and go to fight in Morocco (always true to himself even in his moments of greatest altruism, there was a particular kind of butterfly in North Africa which he longed to capture), though he added on consideration that, much more than that, he would like to write a book in Russian again. He successfully withstood the Russian temptation, but when he returned to Wellesley the other patriotism finally proved too great for him and he presented himself, a gentleman in his forties, for active service. Of course, just as he had been too young for World War I, he was now too old for World War II, even if he had been in perfect health, which he wasn't. He was told: —**Go home and think about it, fellow,** and finally was classified out of service.

Nabokov suffered from neuralgia from the time he was a young man, and he was hospitalized with severe neuralgia attacks in
Germany and in France. The pain from them could be quite

disabling. Apart from these rather rare attacks, throughout his life Nabokov has suffered from recurrent headaches, which no pills have helped enough, an occasional heart palpitation, and also a suspected shadow behind the heart—no firm medical conclusion was ever reached about it—which caused him difficulty when he had to undergo the usual medical examination prior to his term as Visiting Professor at Harvard in 1951. He was in reasonably good shape, in part because of soccer and (this applies to America) tennis and butterfly hikes, but it is Nabokov's judgment that, without even realizing it, he was always rather sickly until he stopped smoking in 1948.

At Wellesley, where one was not supposed to smoke in the classroom, Nabokov, always an extremely punctual person, would usually be seen smoking outside the door until the last minute. Working as he did for whole days at the Museum of Comparative Zoology—one of Harvard's uglier ivory towers, farther removed than many parts of that university from the hustle and bustle of academic commerce and reputation building, but a rather overcrowded-with-equipment, old-wood-and-brick ivory tower— Nabokov sometimes punctuated his day's investigations with more than a pack of cigarettes. His *real life* in these years—so he wrote George Hessen—was not so much in his writing or his teaching as in the enchanted stillness of the microscope and in drawing minute organs with the aid of the *camera lucida* (into which, he said, his *camera obscura* had been transformed). Virtually every day he would make some small discovery, and sometimes he had the intense pleasure of seeing some diminutive hook or thorn which no one had ever seen before. It was while working at the Museum on June 6, 1944, D-Day, that Nabokov had the first of two horrible attacks. This first attack was food poisoning.

Véra Evseevna was in New York with Dmitri, who was about to undergo an appendectomy, and so Vladimir Vladimirovich was temporarily on his own. Nabokov had been spending his days at the Museum and his nights working on *Bend Sinister*. But for two days prior to June 6 Nabokov had closeted himself with *Bend Sinister*, which was nearing completion, and, living on Rocquefort and pineapple, had written eleven pages, an extraordinary amount for him (Nabokov has calculated that on the average he produces only about two hundred and forty pages of prose a year). He hoped to have completed the novel before his wife and son returned from New York. That day, pleasant and breezy, Nabokov **251** took a break from his writing and set off to the Museum. He felt in perfect health. His plan was to spend the morning and early afternoon working, and then he had a late-afternoon tennis match arranged. At about one he strolled to Harvard Square and had Virginia ham and spinach with coffee for lunch. He was back at his microscope at about two, and at two-thirty the first wave of nausea hit him, and he barely managed to rush out of the building onto the street before he began to feel faint and to have spasms and retch. A colleague had seen Nabokov's distressed exit from the building and followed him to the street. He offered to accompany him home, but Nabokov thought that he had sufficiently recovered his composure to make it home by himself.

He had underestimated the extent of his illness. As he staggered home he became so weak that he had to stop and sit down on the sidewalk every few steps. People laughed at him good-naturedly because they thought, evidently, that he was celebrating the invasion. (It was, actually, a rather tense moment in history.) By the time he reached the apartment he was writhing on the floor and was quite unable to stand on his feet. He dragged down the telephone and, sitting on the floor, called the Karpoviches. One of the stops he had intended to make that day was to pay a visit on Karpovich, who had himself just been taken seriously ill. Madame Karpovich came at once—they did not live far from one another—and shrewdly called the police rather than an ambulance, calculating that that was by far the faster means to get Nabokov to a hospital. The police did in fact also arrive in just a few minutes, but it was to be still some time before Nabokov got any relief: first they had to work their way through a police farce (—**Who is this woman? What poison have you taken?**), following which he was taken into Boston to a *sinister hospital* (as he wrote his wife) from the inept clutches of which it took still more time to extricate him and transfer him to the Cambridge hospital.

At the hospital he was promptly washed out with saline solution, though he had to spend the night in a room with an old man noisily dying in Canadian French and so did not get much sleep. He was immensely cheered at dawn by a breakfast of bacon, which, it turned out, had been meant for another patient. By the next afternoon he felt much better and had a tremendous appetite and desire to smoke, but he was allowed nothing except water until that night. The day after that, feeling still better but not yet well, he was transferred to a general ward. They wheeled him out

252

to a very pleasant dining room, and after eating he had the first cigarette he had smoked for several days.

The ward was nice enough, but Nabokov soon found himself being driven to distraction by the hubbub all around him. A radio played ceaselessly, the sick moaned, the healthy laughed and talked loudly to one another from different ends of the huge ward, and a sixteen-year-old idiot followed the nursing staff about and played hospital jester, giving imitations of the groans of some of the older and more severely sick patients, to the general amusement of not quite everyone. Nabokov had drawn the curtain around his bed and was sullenly trying either to rest or to study in the semi-darkness a medical dictionary which he had filched from a bookcase while being wheeled down a hallway, but the staff vehemently objected to this, claiming that his drawn curtains were spoiling the appearance of the ward because they implied that a sudden death had occurred. The book was pronounced too technical and taken away. It was Wednesday, and the doctor had promised Nabokov that he could leave on Friday. When Madame Karpovich came to see him during visiting hours, he laid his escape plan. She left and waited in her car. Nabokov casually walked to an open side door, and, dressed only in his dressing gown, which was all he had, he made a sudden dash for freedom and the waiting car with two staff members in furious pursuit. He just made it, and they sped away to the Karpoviches' home, where he stayed for several days until he had completely regained his health. He eventually went back and staged a row at the restaurant where he had been served the fateful blue plateful.

The second attack came in 1948 near the time of his planned departure from Wellesley and Cambridge to Cornell. It was a few weeks after he had quit smoking because of heart palpitations, which doubtless bears no relation whatsoever to the bump and wobble of John Shade's old unstable heart in *Pale Fire* (lines 735–36). Late one night after Nabokov had taken his son, who was home from school, to a wrestling match, he suddenly began to cough up blood, tremendous amounts of blood. At the hospital, no one quite understood what was the matter with him. They began to perform an exploratory tracheotomy. **A vulcanized rubber tube** —Nabokov said these words very slowly, perhaps feeling that tube still, it seemed to me—was inserted into his windpipe. He was fully conscious under local anaesthetic during the whole operation, which lasted two and a half hours. **—The doctors kept cracking** 253 jokes at me to keep my morale up. I remember one asking me, "How do you feel?" I said, "Controlled panic." Though he wasn't told at the time, the doctors were looking for and expecting to find cancer, but they didn't. There was an unpleasant moment for him and a puzzling one for his doctor when the various tests were done and showed nothing, but on a second round one of them showed that Nabokov had tuberculosis. It turned out to have been a mix-up. No sure diagnosis was ever made, but Nabokov takes the view that it was his body's ridding itself of the damage done to his lungs by nearly thirty-five years of smoking. While he was sick his wife read his lectures for him at Wellesley. From this point onwards Nabokov enjoyed better health than ever before in his life, though for two full years after that at Cornell he could sometimes taste the medicinal oil that had been used in his lungs during the exploratory operation. To this day Nabokov prefers that people not smoke in his presence.

In 1944, shortly before his own illness, Nabokov happened to mention Dmitri's upcoming appendectomy to his friend Edmund Wilson, who immediately told him: —**You must take him to New York. I know all the best doctors there.** Nabokov accepted Wilson's offer of advice. (The humour of leaving Boston to find a doctor was evidently lost on both writers.) Nabokov came to New York, and he and Wilson were to meet Dmitri with his Aunt Sonya in the lobby of the building, just south of Central Park, which contained the doctor's offices. They waited and waited, but the boy and his aunt didn't appear. Nabokov had telephoned giving them the time and the address. Wilson grew triumphantly irritable: —**Well, that's just like Russians! They can never, never, never be anywhere on time!** Wilson went outside to telephone and returned somewhat sheepishly. He had by mistake taken Nabokov to the wrong building. —**He had taken** *me* **to the wrong house! We went next door, and there was Aunt Sonya. Isn't that a marvelous story?**

That trivial incident was quite probably the only time in the long friendship between Nabokov and Wilson, lasting more than twenty years in various forms and states, when a clear advantage of one man over the other was acknowledged by both men on *anything.* I have before me a huge pile of correspondence, the
254 most protracted and voluminous into which Nabokov (and per-

haps Wilson, too, for all I know) has ever entered. Its promised publication will show (and it will be interesting to see how fully, for the letters are often not cautious in their judgments about their contemporaries) an essential mask of each writer. They did like each other enormously, though there seems hardly a moment when the tension of being competitors (with too highly dissimilar minds, attitudes, and educations) is dropped, and they stubbornly maintain the will to friendship—invitations to visit one another, answering questions for each other, expressing concern and affection for each other's family—long after the possibility of real friendship had passed. There are always such warm references to their actual meetings that it may well be that the roughness of their exchanges of opinion on literary matters does not accurately reflect their full relationship. If the annoying business of the perception of "greatness" or "importance" had been attended to by historical chance for both of the writers before they met, the friendship might have been a much richer and smoother one. It wasn't, and as it happened both Nabokov and Wilson were for quite different reasons at somewhat awkward stages in their respective literary careers.

For Nabokov the recognition he had earned as an émigré writer, and the stature which he felt he had, as yet cast no shadow in America, where it was necessary to start all over again. Wilson, on the other hand, after many years of dogged literary journalism, had only then reached the point at which he was considered something more than just a critic. Through no fault of his own, Nabokov was wholly innocent of Wilson's unique position in American letters, which Wilson was in the process of consolidating when they met. (Wilson was to follow his literary editorship of *The New Republic*—to which he had returned after several years' absence—with a position as staff critic on *The New Yorker*, and *The Triple Thinkers* and *To the Finland Station*, his most important books since *Axel's Castle*, had appeared a few years before.) Wilson and Nabokov had one good friend in common, Roman Grynberg, Nabokov's former pupil. Nabokov met Wilson and Mary McCarthy, whom Wilson had married in 1938, several times in New York in 1940, once at the apartment of Avrahm Yarmolinsky, the director of the Slavonic Section of the New York Public Library and the husband of the poetess-translator Babette Deutsch, and once, at Wilson's request, they introduced Wilson to Aleksandr Kerensky.

Wilson encouraged Nabokov to write reviews and essays and praised them highly, cautioning him only, please, to avoid puns. The two had agreed to collaborate on a translation of Pushkin's *Mozart and Salieri,* though Wilson confessed that his Russian was still very weak and needed working up, which he proposed to do by reading Tolstoy. The primary translation was done by Nabokov, with Wilson making stylistic changes and suggestions. The piece appeared in *The New Republic.* Wilson was trying to arrange to have Nabokov do a regular article there on Russian literature, and Nabokov began to work on an article about Soviet drama, but nothing came of the proposed arrangement, which may have been dampened for both sides when a review Nabokov wrote, which touched on Russian politics and anarchism, was refused because, Wilson wrote his friend, the magazine had been scared of it politically. Although Wilson disagreed with the article's remarks about Lenin, he thought it too good not to be printed and graciously offered to assist in its publication elsewhere.

Wilson was tremendously active on Nabokov's behalf in those early years. Not only did Wilson ease Nabokov forward at *The New Republic* and *The Atlantic Monthly,* he aided his cause with the Guggenheim Foundation (Nabokov received his first of two grants in 1943); and at all the campuses which Wilson visited to give talks he made representations on Nabokov's behalf and tried to set up academic appointments for him at Bennington, Yale, and, some years later, Princeton.

Wilson was aware from the beginning—he knew not only Grynberg, but also Aldanov, Tchelitschew, Nicholas Nabokov, and many other Russians among whom were at least a few committed Sirin fans—that Nabokov had produced a large *oeuvre* in Russian. And it is clear that he was fascinated by Nabokov both personally and as an artist. He met Nabokov's friend from Cambridge Bobby de Calry and quizzed him at length about Nabokov's past. He also questioned his cousin Nicholas. He even met Nabokov's former Cambridge roommate, though he told Nabokov his roommate remembered almost nothing of him; and there was by chance living near Wilson on Cape Cod a woman with whom Nabokov used to go roller-skating in his English days. He happened upon and purchased a rare copy of *The Empyrean Path* in New York, and he also read *Mary* (which he liked enormously, though he protested that one couldn't copulate in the back of a taxi that way) and *Invitation to a Beheading* in Russian (he found the Russian of this novel too difficult and did not much like it) as well as the two Russian novels which were available in English. In letters written in 1945, 1947, 1951, and 1953 Wilson announces to his friend that he is on the verge, first for *The Atlantic,* later for *The New Yorker,* of doing a comprehensive study of him *(—I have been aiming to make you my next Russian subject after Turgenev),* and even as the intention fell into abeyance Wilson would from time to time declare that he was going to read Nabokov's complete works. Sadly, that comprehensive overview was one of the last things that Wilson wrote, as a note attached to his attack on Nabokov's translation of *Eugene Onegin* for the collection *A Window on Russia.* The note was hideously superficial. Seven novels are mentioned, several of them tossed away in a line or two, and only *Lolita* is praised. Wilson acknowledges at the beginning of his note that he has been moved to write it in order *—to correct any possible injustice that I might have seemed to have done to Mr. Nabokov's work in other departments of literature than the scholarly. . . .* He calls attention to and is obviously made awkward by Nabokov's latter-day fame, but his remarks only add up to an ill-tempered, somehow half-hearted, and yet frequently successful attempt to shoot a few arrows *ad hominem* as well: *—Like all persons who enjoy malicious teasing and embarrassing practical jokes, he is invariably aggrieved and indignant when anyone tries anything of the kind on himself.* The over-all tone of Wilson's remarks is somewhat kinder but harks back to the comments which used to be made about Nabokov by émigré critics such as Adamovich, Gippius, Ivanov, and Merezhkovsky.

In spite of his comments on the inadequacies of Wilson's Russian during their Pushkin controversy, Nabokov once thought well enough of it to propose, in April 1942, that he become his translator. It was certainly a mistake in judgment on Nabokov's part, for Wilson, having only stepped out onto the plateau from which he could single-handedly make or seriously hobble the reputation of any of his contemporaries, could not have wanted a literary relationship in which he would be subservient to a brilliant but impudent intruder into American literature. Wilson graciously declined, saying that he would gladly become his translator but did not have the time, and, moreover, that his still uncertain Russian would probably cause Nabokov more difficulty than if he were to do the translation himself.

About a year and a half later (November 10, 1943) Wilson **257** wrote to Nabokov with a proposal of his own: he wanted them to collaborate on a book about Russian literature in which he would contribute an essay on a particular poet and Nabokov would supply a series of translations from that poet. Nabokov was then under contract to give New Directions a book of his Russian translations, but Wilson suggested that Nabokov could perhaps withdraw from New Directions and that he could procure a substantial advance from Doubleday which they would divide evenly. He also said he hoped that Doubleday could be induced at the same time to contract for Nabokov's second English novel, parts of which Wilson had already read in its first draft and praised. (It will be of interest to note that it had been Nabokov's original intention to have his hero Krug **confront his maker,** that is, Nabokov, at the end of the novel.) And finally, Wilson reckoned that several of the paired pieces would certainly be used by Weeks in *The Atlantic.*

Nabokov accepted the proposal by return mail. He could not be released from his New Directions obligation (the book appeared in 1944), but there were, of course, other translations that he had done and could do for the Wilson-Nabokov book. But in the end only a single one of the pairs of what they called their "Siamese connection" appeared, in *The Atlantic* in 1944, and the project was put aside, first for the summer and then forever. Wilson made the arrangement with Doubleday, and they divided a fifteen-hundred-dollar advance evenly. The publishing house insisted, Wilson informed his friend somewhat awkwardly, that the book was to be *by* Edmund Wilson *with translations by Vladimir Nabokov,* but he volunteered the assurance that he would take care to see that Nabokov's name was set in the same size type.

Not long afterwards, Wilson's editor at Doubleday informed him that there had been a house decision to de-emphasise highbrow books and concentrate more on popular-appeal books. Wilson had been told that in view of this decision he had no future with Doubleday any more. So, in the summer of 1947, Wilson began conversations with the Oxford University Press to take over (or, he hoped, even raise) the advance paid by Doubleday, but now the connection had broken, and Wilson wrote Nabokov (July 18, 1947) that instead of the combined volume which Nabokov had wanted there would be a separate volume of Wilson essays, to include the Russian articles he had at hand, and a volume of Nabokov's translations. And then the New York editor of the Oxford University Press declined the poetic translations on economic grounds—the years immediately following the war were lean ones for publishing—and that was the end of it.

Nineteen forty-six was, in Nabokov's estimation, the year that marked the decline of the rather close relationship that had developed between Wilson and himself, though they remained friendly as late as the early fifties. To be sure, there were potentialities for awkwardness from the very beginning. In his eighth letter to Nabokov, Wilson, probably having learned his nickname from Nicholas Nabokov, Nabokov claimed, addressed him as Da-rogue-oy Val-odd-ya. Nabokov called Wilson "Bunny," which is not something everyone did to his face.

In their relationship Wilson seems often to have chosen to play the Russian; Nabokov, the American. When Nabokov visited Wilson at Stamford, Connecticut, in 1942 (it is Wilson's fridge which is the hero of Nabokov's poem *The Refrigerator Awakes*), they went for a long stroll during which Wilson initiated the conversation by asking whether or not Nabokov believed in God. —**Do you?** Nabokov replied. —**What a strange question!** muttered Wilson. Nabokov, for his part, could not always withstand the temptation to fool around in the American manner. Once, for example, he reached over from the back seat of a convertible being driven by Mary McCarthy and took off Wilson's brown hat, impersonating the wind. Wilson ignored him and turned to Véra Evseevna: —**Your husband has a rather strange sense of humour,** which, of course, was and is true.

When Wilson and Nabokov first met, Wilson was in the midst of one of his periods of intense interest in Russian literature and politics. *To the Finland Station* had just appeared. Wilson presented Nabokov with a copy inscribed: *To Vladimir Nabokov in the hope that this may make him think better of Lenin.* Nabokov sent Wilson a long letter praising the book but detailing what he felt were Wilson's misconceptions of Lenin the man and politician. In reply (December 19, 1940) Wilson acknowledged the weakness of his Russian background and gallantly allowed that there were weaknesses on the German side as well, but he held his ground about his judgment of Lenin. That is the way intellectual discussions between them usually went. Nabokov recalls that when he visited Wilson at Wellfleet they would have long arguments in which Nabokov had the impression that he had finally worn Wilson down and gained his acquiescence on whatever point was at question, but Wilson would always appear with fresh arguments **259** the next day as though their previous conversation had never been. Particularly in political matters in the early years (later on, more and more in literary matters as well) Nabokov and Wilson found themselves almost inevitably at friendly odds. After one such exchange Nabokov wrote Wilson (February 2, 1947): —*you are partisan of a certain interpretation which you regard as absolute. This means that we will have many a pleasant tussle and that neither will ever yield a thumb (inch) of terrain (ground).*

For all their arguments, Nabokov considered and still considers that they were alike in certain ways and not so very different in taste. Wilson was perhaps slightly more aggressive by nature than Nabokov, but the intrinsic need for an adversary can also clearly be seen in Nabokov's career. The slight difference may be observed in the way they walked: the younger Wilson was described (by Scott Fitzgerald) as walking briskly through New York crowds wrapped in his own thoughts and looking straight ahead, whereas the younger Nabokov was famous for his almost ethereal flying gait and seemed to some always to be looking at some far-off point. The point though is that both men to a large extent inhabited worlds of their own. The older, craggy Wilson whom I met was much softer in appearance and smaller than the photographs of his last years suggest, but descriptions of his contemporaries and photographs of the period when he was younger seem to concur that then he had the toughness of a handsome, unwrinkled bulldog. Wilson was born in Red Bank, New Jersey. His father was a very successful professional man. Something might be explained of the slight but essential difference between Nabokov and Wilson if we momentarily transpose the Nabokov family from Russia. Had the Nabokov family lived near the Wilson family in New Jersey, they surely would have lived not in professional Red Bank but in nearby Rumson, where that part of southern New Jersey's upper class (families such as the exploring Scotts and the mustard Guldens) lived. Nabokov had many skills which had been given to him in childhood by tutors and governesses, but Wilson compensated for that by the range of his interests, even in comparison with those of Nabokov. There can be not the slightest doubt that Nabokov looked upon his friend's efforts at catholicity not without a certain amount of condescension. I remember how he smiled when he told me how Wilson had specially asked him to include entomologists among the guests at a little party he was giving, and

how Wilson immediately went into a corner with them and attempted to "talk shop." But the entomologists had not turned up, and the guests from Wellesley were more than a little puzzled by Wilson's sudden interest in insects.

Nabokov particularly admired Wilson for his knowledge in those areas such as lower-level early American literature where it seemed to him that Wilson did have rare and deep knowledge, and Nabokov sometimes followed and accepted Wilson's recommendations. Also it was through Wilson that Nabokov's respect for Melville grew, and Nabokov was introduced to *Mansfield Park*, which eventually became a staple of one of his courses at Cornell, by Wilson. Most of all they shared an undimmed boyhood admiration for H. G. Wells. Russia and Russian literature were always a problem. —These were the two mirages of Wilson: that he knew Russian history better than I because of his Marxism, and that he knew at least as much about Russian literature as I. For many years, at least until 1948, Wilson simply classified his friend as a White Russian to explain his political views. (Afterwards, once Wilson had abandoned his former political sympathies, he was fond of saying that Nabokov was an ascetic, an austere worshipper of Pure Art, a monk, with no experience of women.) Mary McCarthy had somewhat the same politics as Wilson, but her opinions were held much more ferociously. Nabokov remembers Mary McCarthy once ripping into a book on Shakespeare because it didn't take the Industrial Revolution into account. They would have, according to Nabokov (he refers to this conversation in one of his forewords) conversations like this: —What exactly are you? You're not a Red, so you must be a White. —In a certain sense, I suppose so. —Then you're a fascist. —I come from a family of Russian liberals. —There were no Russian liberals. Gradually, over the years, politics became less of an issue, though Wilson continued to object to Nabokov's emphatic patriotism: —You new Americans with your enthusiasm. What a bore!

In addition to their exchange of letters, Wilson and Nabokov would usually see each other several times a year, in Cambridge, on Cape Cod, in New York, and later in Ithaca. Nabokov sometimes stayed in Wilson's cold-water flat in New York when he visited the city. It was there he met Allen Tate, with whom he grew quite friendly, and a young poet who would come to see Tate, Robert Lowell. He would also encounter Wilson in Cambridge at Harry Levin's and at the home of Billy James, the son of William James (and a tremendous admirer of Nabokov's writing; **261**

Billy James had promised Nabokov one of Henry James's desks but died before the desk was passed to Nabokov, who, anyway, thought less of Henry than William). He met Robert Lowell, again at Billy James's. They talked about Lowell's school, St. Marks, where Dmitri had been, and Nabokov flabbergasted Lowell with the extent of his knowledge about the school (he had been studying it; it is in *Pnin*). Once, Nabokov wrote to Wilson lecturing him for drinking with Billy, who was under doctor's orders not to. For his concern he received a telegramme from them in the old literary tradition: WE DRINK TO YOUR HEALTH   BUNNY AND BILL.

When Nabokov was sick in 1948, Wilson played an important helping role in his personal life. There was a very real question for some time as to whether or not Nabokov would have to cease all work and take a prolonged period of complete rest on doctors' orders. For nearly four weeks Wilson was extremely active on his friend's behalf, and he initiated a plan whereby *The New Yorker* would arrange to pay Nabokov, who by that time had become a reasonably regular contributor to the magazine, a modest "pension" during the time he was recovering. Indeed, Wilson was so energetic in Nabokov's interest that he even turned to friends with requests for loans, which rather embarrassed Nabokov because, as had been the case when he was leaving France, not all the requests were successful.

For anyone who has any awareness of the two men or their writing, the differences between them hardly need be stressed. What is no less obvious and yet perhaps needs be pointed out is the singularly similar position of Wilson and Nabokov in American culture. This similarity may be seen especially clearly in the attitudes towards and the experiences of both men in regard to universities and in their publishing careers.

The distance that Edmund Wilson kept from the American academy has perhaps been somewhat exaggerated. Wilson was willing enough to attach himself to a college or university. (In the Nabokov-Wilson correspondence there is reference to an appointment at Cornell on which Wilson was counting and which was lost at the last minute by the personal veto of Cornell's president.) Very much like Nabokov, Wilson was willing to associate with the academy and academics, both of which he thought provincial and restricting, but on his own terms. The university which each man perhaps felt was his due place if he were to have an academic position at all was Harvard. Their experiences with that university were quite similar. Both men had friends at Harvard, and yet the scholars of Harvard were not accustomed to and did not enjoy being regarded from a position of slight intellectual superiority as both Wilson and Nabokov were wont to do. Nabokov held the opinion that on the whole the scholarly calling was purer, less worldly at Wellesley than at Harvard. He taught at Harvard once (so, as a matter of fact, did Wilson), by invitation of Harry Levin, in the spring semester of 1952, but by then the possibility of a permanent appointment had been proven to be infeasible. Nabokov had had conflicts with a few of the people who would have become his colleagues. When he first began to teach at Wellesley, a dean had submitted his proposed syllabus to Samuel Hazard Cross at Harvard for approval. Cross, who was then Chairman of the Russian Department at Harvard, did not approve; Nabokov was infuriated at what he thought was interference which was both uncalled for and incompetent. Nabokov made him cross, too.

Equally serious opposition to the idea of inviting Nabokov to Harvard came later from the noted linguist Roman Jakobson. Nabokov and Jakobson had at first at least qualified respect for each other's abilities, but, after an initially friendly period when Nabokov accepted some of Jakobson's readings of the medieval *Song of Igor's Campaign*, differences in approach, belief (in many areas), and temperament made themselves felt. There is a tape recording that is perhaps symptomatic, on which Jakobson and Nabokov are reciting stanzas from *Eugene Onegin* in order to illustrate the difference between the St. Petersburg and Moscow accents. At one point in Jakobson's reading a subdued but quite clear *Uzhasno! (Horrible!)* escaped from Nabokov in the background. The two men became adversaries without quarrelling, though Nabokov did withdraw his contribution from the Festschrift which was being prepared in honour of Jakobson (Nabokov states that his reason was objection to what he viewed as Jakobson's pro-Sovietism), and the story is not apocryphal that one year Jakobson successfully led the opposition to Nabokov's appointment by rising in the committee room and sarcastically exclaiming in his richly Russian English: —Gentlemen, even if one allows that he is an important writer, are we next to invite an elephant to be Professor of Zoology?

The struggle between the pro- and anti-Nabokov factions was close though, and in 1946 it seemed that Nabokov was assured of appointment as Professor of Comparative and Slavic Literature. **263**

One evening Renato Poggioli, an Italian comparativist with a special interest in Russian, paid a courtesy call on him, and they spent a delightful evening discussing literature and all sorts of other things except the fact that Poggioli had, as Nabokov learned the next day, just been given the post that he was to have had. Two years later, when another scholar of more modest academic ability was given a temporary Harvard appointment, Nabokov wrote to Edmund Wilson (November 21, 1948): —*I sometimes wonder whether the curious disinclination on Harvard's part to avail itself of my services might not have been due to my taking a crack or two at some academic shibboleths (say, Goethe's* **Faust**) *in my book on Gogol.* The Gogol book was surely only one of innumerable signals to the academic community that he was not cut of their cloth, and the point was impressed upon his friends as well as the others. When Nabokov fiercely and at some length attacked Cervantes in his Humanities 4 lectures in 1952, Professor Levin was rather taken aback and told him primly: —**Harvard thinks otherwise.** However many hairs he may have raised on the backs of literary necks at Harvard, there was, Nabokov assured me, even greater hostility and opposition to him on the part of certain entomologists there. The unusual academic talents of both Edmund Wilson and Vladimir Nabokov may, it seems to me, be described in the same terms as the famous definition of democracy: they were undoubtedly the worst sort of academics except for all the others. And though he is, of course, much more of a pedant by nature than Wilson ever was, Nabokov fully shared his friend's views on PMLA-type people. —**I loathe them,** Nabokov told me, saying it practically as a single word.

Also as fellow contributors to *The New Yorker* over the years, Nabokov and Wilson had roughly parallel experiences. Both wrote for the magazine frequently. Nabokov was brought into *The New Yorker*'s stable on Wilson's recommendation by Katharine White, a senior editor who had followed and admired his work in *The Atlantic.* Each man found that he frequently strained the air of gentility which was its hallmark in those years. Wilson, much more than Nabokov, displeased the little old ladies from Dubuque with his provocative and often cranky essays after he replaced comfortable Clifton Fadiman as *The New Yorker*'s regular book reviewer. Nabokov always felt that it was a pleasure and a privilege to be a *New Yorker* author, both for the over-all level of the magazine and (which was especially important in the forties) for the fees, plus generous cost-of-living, or COLA, supplements, which were unequalled by any other serious magazine of the time; but, in spite of, or perhaps because of, *The New Yorker*'s concerned and discreet relationship with both its writers and its readers, Nabokov periodically found that pieces of his were turned back with what must surely be some of the most regretful and eloquent rejection notes in the history of literature. Two chapters of *Pnin* were rejected (although another portion of the novel appeared). The phrase "applesauce in your pants" in the short story "Lik" occasioned a pained explanation of *The New Yorker*'s traditional policy in regard to bodily functions. It is characteristic of the relationship between Nabokov and *The New Yorker* that he accepted occasional emendations, something he has never done for any other publisher or journal. Nabokov stresses an author's duty to stand firm in this regard in *Transparent Things.*

In 1947 Wilson supported Nabokov in connection with some editorial difficulties which had arisen over one of his short stories, "Signs and Symbols," and a chapter from Nabokov's autobiography. He wrote to *New Yorker* editor Katharine White on November 12, 1947, and complained at length about resistance which he felt certain aspects and portions of his own and Nabokov's work encountered at the magazine. (Both, of course, were publishing most of what they wrote in these years in *The New Yorker.*) "Signs and Symbols" had been treated as an overwritten parody, which had angered Nabokov. Wilson expressed surprise that he had not challenged someone to a duel. Wilson thought that the story was "everyday," and he suggested to Mrs. White that its editorial treatment bespoke a morbid fear on the part of a magazine which had come to the age when it was loathe to print anything which might jar its audience or seem to be unintentionally funny. Wilson recalls some short stories of his which were rejected by the magazine because, he thought, they were not silly and empty and pale enough. In regard to another piece of Nabokov's which had generated some doubts, "My English Education" (a chapter from the autobiography), Wilson thought it perfect for *The New Yorker,* a judgment which he specified with the opinion that the piece doesn't get anywhere and was just the sort of little reminiscence of which *The New Yorker* had already printed any number. The root of the difficulty, Wilson felt, was that *The New Yorker* always objected to any manifestation of an idiosyncratic style and sought to present only writing in which there was nothing vivid or startling.

It is certainly true that some of the work of both Nabokov and   **265**

Wilson through the forties and fifties was, for one reason or another, unsuitable for *The New Yorker* (such as Wilson's *Hecate County* or Nabokov's poem about the nuptial night of Superman and Lois Lane), but what is much more significant in Nabokov's case was the unqualified recognition of his talent, indeed unbounded enthusiasm for his writing on the part of certain *New Yorker* editors, a fact no less important to the first half of his career as an American writer than his association with *Contemporary Annals* had been to the second half of his Russian writing career.

Wilson did not abide by his own counsel in regard to Nabokov. Throughout their correspondence he counters Nabokov's pedagogy in points of Russian grammar and poetics with his own corrections of what he takes to be Nabokov's grammatical or stylistic errors in English. He noted some weak points in the language of *The Real Life of Sebastian Knight,* which was the Nabokov novel he praised most highly, and he spoke of other weaknesses in his slightly condescending *New Yorker* review of *Nikolai Gogol.* It was *Bend Sinister,* however, which initiated something very like artistic antagonism between the two writers, though, ironically, it was Wilson who found it a publisher, Henry Holt. Wilson did not like the novel and said so quite bluntly, appending to his opinion an extensive number of grammatical mistakes which he thought he had spotted. Nabokov patiently explained all the items Wilson raised, pointing out that *cries on havoc* is not only correct but taken from Shakespeare; that *lower and belowed* was intended to illustrate a common German mistake (the letter w used in place of v) in English; that the word *recurved* is a dictionary word and is used extensively in zoological studies; and so forth. Wilson found a few of these explanations to be worse than the supposed errors, and he reprimanded Nabokov for his silliness and bad taste. They clashed over the gender of arse in the French for "to wipe one's behind." Wilson was in error on this occasion and sent Nabokov a telegramme to correct his mistake when he discovered it. Nabokov is of the opinion—I for one doubt it—that it was this slip on his derrière that lay behind Wilson's later "linguistic rages."

For all the help which he extended to Nabokov on his own initiative in the early years, and though he clearly recognized Nabokov as a peer, Wilson simply was unable to do the main thing, recognize Nabokov in print as a major talent. This, in spite of the fact that several of Wilson's literary friends such as Allen Tate did
not hesitate at a very early date to use the word genius when

speaking of Nabokov. Wilson made every effort to contain his admiration of Nabokov within the bounds of a personal literary friendship. In March 1945 he wrote Nabokov saying that their conversations had been among the few consolations of his literary life in those years when old friends had been dying, petering out, and getting more and more neurotic. Wilson was not, Nabokov told him, a Nabokov fan. Wilson professed not to understand what he meant.

Perhaps the final rent in their friendship occurred in 1954 when Wilson read *Lolita* in manuscript. The novel had been given to Wilson's publishing house with strict instructions that the manuscript was not to be shown to anyone, but a copy found its way into Wilson's hands. Wilson wrote to Nabokov (November 30, 1954) and told him that he liked it less than anything else of his which he had read. The situation seemed to him to be too absurd to be tragic and too unpleasant to be funny, and he felt that the novel had too much background and description of places (the very things for which he praised *Lolita* in 1971). Wilson enclosed two notes with his letter. One was from Mary McCarthy—she was writing to Wilson, not Nabokov—and she took what she termed a midway position. There were various things in the book she liked, but she concluded by saying that she thought the writing was terribly sloppy throughout, worse perhaps in the second part. The other note was from Wilson's fourth wife, who wrote that she could not put it down and thought it a very important book. Nabokov later claimed that his contempt was excited not by Wilson's opinion but by the fact that Wilson had read only half the novel before delivering his verdict.

As was his custom, Wilson, notwithstanding his own opinion, offered to help find a publisher for the novel and enclosed a little list of grammatical errors which he had noted. Later, when *Lolita* became a best-seller, Wilson told Nabokov that he understood his purpose—to write a modern *Fanny Hill* which would enjoy runaway sales because of its sexual theme. (Wilson himself, some years before, had had very high hopes for his own *Memoirs of Hecate County*, but the book had been banned by court order in New York, and, when the ban was lifted years later, the literary climate had changed drastically and *Hecate* was no longer sensational. Wilson made only about thirty thousand dollars from the book, a considerable sum but, Nabokov thinks, less than he was hoping for.)

Their literary exchanges over the years usually began with an enthusiasm of Wilson's. After reading Malraux while staying in Nevada in 1946 (he was waiting for his divorce and preparing to remarry again), Wilson wrote Nabokov (November 17, 1946) that he had decided that Malraux was the greatest contemporary writer. Back came the reply (November 27), a four-page letter on the clichés, imprecisions, and pretensions in Malraux's writing. Nabokov concluded: —*The longer I live the more I become convinced that the only thing that matters in literature is the (more or less irrational) shamanstvo of a book, i.e. that the good writer is first of all an enchanter. But one must not let things tumble out of one's sleeves all the time as Malraux does.* Once, at an evening together with Wilson at the Levins', Nabokov told the story of how as a boy he had chanced to see a party conjuror packing his tricks away with all the mechanisms revealed, and Wilson held that that was precisely what Nabokov himself did as an artist. Wilson's reply to the anti-Malraux letter was that he had been counting on getting a rise out of Nabokov (an important part of their relationship), and that, moreover, inaccuracies, clichés, and clumsiness do not in themselves invalidate a writer. They had similar exchanges about Genet and Faulkner, and again they agreed to disagree, though Nabokov's heavy assault upon the syntactic tangles in Faulkner's prose may have had something to do with the reservations on that score which Wilson expressed when subsequently praising Faulkner in print. Their disagreement in 1960 on the merits of *Doctor Zhivago,* then, was only to be expected, though Wilson called Nabokov long distance in California (where he was at work on the screenplay of *Lolita*) to discover what he thought of the novel, on which Wilson was then writing for *The New Yorker,* perhaps the most enthusiastic essay of his critical career. Nabokov thought *Zhivago* was a third-rate sentimental novel inexplicably written by a rather good poet.

It is unnecessary, I hope, to tell again the story of the protracted and in the end rather bitter dispute between Wilson and Nabokov over Nabokov's translation of *Eugene Onegin,* which arose first in *The New York Review of Books* and was continued in *Encounter* in 1965–66. Suffice it to say that Wilson held that Nabokov betrayed Pushkin by the stilted language of his perfectly accurate pony while Nabokov held that Wilson was incapable of grasping either the basic sense or the nuances of what Pushkin

wrote. More than a few of the key issues in the dispute were ones they had argued for many years. It had all happened so long before it was committed to paper for the public! On the question of Pushkin's knowledge of English, for example, Nabokov had written Wilson eight years earlier (June 17, 1957):—*I have been studying the question of Pushkin's knowledge of foreign languages for about ten years now and really you should not send me to* **Rukoyu Pushkina.** *You will find a complete analysis of the matter in my commentary to* **E.O.** *Pushkin got what you call "Byron's rhythms" from Zhukovski's versions of English poems.* Wilson was extremely eager to get his hands on the *Onegin* commentaries (twenty-five-hundred pages in manuscript) and made efforts to get a copy from the publisher, this time, however, without success. When the translation and commentaries finally did appear, Wilson told Harry Levin that, whereas Nabokov concentrated upon the French sources of Pushkin's poetic language, he would focus in his review-essay upon the classical sources, an area in which he felt himself stronger than Nabokov. In the attack which he did write, however, he concentrated almost wholly upon the translation.

The last time that Edmund Wilson and Vladimir Nabokov saw each other was when Wilson while travelling through Europe in 1965 came to see his old friend in Switzerland. They had a delightful time together discussing all sorts of things, but Wilson neglected somehow to inform Nabokov of the essay he had completed only a short time before. After it was all over Wilson sent Nabokov two scribbled lines in pencil saying that he was sorry their controversy had come to an end, and that he had rarely enjoyed anything so much, to which Nabokov replied: —*Although I did not relish quite as much as you tell me you did our "controversy" I would like to thank you for your Christmas greetings. V.* Wilson's Christmas cards to Nabokov included on two occasions a paper butterfly powered by a rubber band. I happened to be present when the last Christmas butterfly from Wilson arrived in Montreux in 1968. It thrummed inelegantly straight to the floor, twitched a few times, and was still. It was black, and that was that.

After Nabokov came to America, the amount of time which he devoted to the collection and classification of butterflies and the intensity with which he gave himself to these pursuits was such that he eventually faced a choice as hard as the one he had to make between languages. It became obvious that he simply could not 269 carry forward his literary and his entomological careers at the same time. When Nabokov left Massachusetts the study of butterflies was relegated to a slightly lesser place in his hours if not his life.

Nabokov's major work in this field was done in the forties. There are two or three small groups of butterflies about which he knows more than anyone else in the world. A colleague who has worked with him in the field says:

—He cannot be called one of the ranking authorities, but his work had weight. If he had devoted more time to his work in this field he almost certainly would have been a major figure in the field. . . . There is general acceptance of his work and admiration for its thoroughness. It is not eccentric. Work in this field falls into a certain mold of reporting facts. If his treatment were not standard, he would have been thrown out, that is, his work would not have been taken seriously.

Or, from an entomologist who remembers Nabokov at the Agassiz (the more common name for the Museum of Comparative Zoology) when he was just a teen-ager:

—His work is painstaking, thorough. It has improved our knowledge of a particular group. He did not follow the beaten path in his writing by any means. His details and measurements are almost unique in their scale-by-scale meticulousness. It really has not been done that way before or since. Instead of saying "a broad stripe" or "a narrow stripe," he would count the scales, and this enabled him to come to conclusions he could not otherwise have reached.

In addition to his specialized knowledge of blues, Nabokov excelled in another, descriptive speciality: butterfly genitalia, which are extremely important because there can be great differences in the genital structure of butterflies which otherwise look quite alike. The organ in question is a tiny but sclerotic particle. After its removal, the organ is usually kept for a few hours in a certain solution (Nabokov made the discovery that a certain brand of dental cleanser does the job much quicker) until the fleshy portion dissolves away. The work preparing the genitalia for slides is very difficult and tedious. It is done with a fine needle. After proper preparation the piece is dipped first in alcohol, then in an organic solvent before mounting. But mounting prevents the genitalia from being freely turned while they are being examined under the microscope, and so Nabokov developed the technique of keeping each set in a weak solution of alcohol with a little glycerine in corked vials. For one of his major papers Nabokov might do nearly a thousand such examinations, representing months of patient work.

After he had returned to Europe in 1960 Nabokov eventually resumed the scientific study of butterflies in earnest. He devoted nearly three years of intensive work to the preparation of an inclusive study of European butterflies. He recalls these three years as very, very happy ones, but once again entomology surrendered to literature, and the butterfly book was abandoned. With four hundred species of butterflies and, on the average, about ten important subspecies to each species, there were nearly twelve thousand coloured photographs involved, with descriptions of locality and a bibliography for each subspecies. It might have equalled the Onegin commentaries in scope, but too much work would be required now, bringing the manuscript up to date.

In their first decade in the United States the Nabokovs spent the first summer in California, two summers in Vermont, one in Wellesley, one in New Hampshire (at a horrible lodge on a dismal lake), and the rest in the Rocky Mountains. They were virtually all excellent collecting summers; the one in Wellesley was a miraculous summer during which Nabokov caught many butterflies which hadn't been observed in the environs for years. It was only when they went to Cape Cod that they found collecting not so good. They had travelled by train or chauffeured car, but then Véra Evseevna learned to drive, rather fast as a matter of fact, and in the summer of 1949 they set out on the first of many cross-country meanderings which took them to nearly every state and several hundred motel rooms. Their destination was Utah where Nabokov had been invited to join a two-week writers' conference. Their first American car was a 1940 Plymouth four-door sedan. —We *never* went West in the Plymouth! —Wait a minute, darling, I have a note. A Plymouth four-door sedan, six cylinders, eight years old, which we acquired on August 19, 1948. There is a subdued but determined mumbling from his wife. —Wait a minute, I'm quite certain of all this. At Canandaigua we picked up my student Dick Buxbaum, who took turns driving the car to Salt 271

Lake City. But Nabokov's victory is a short-lived one: —**It was not the Plymouth. It was the Olds. We sold the Plymouth because it wouldn't go to Chicago.** It was in that Olds (1946, six-cylinder!) and a subsequent much grander green 1954 Buick, also a four-door sedan, with a dazzling white interior (his *buicka* he called it when someone referred to it as his winged troika—somehow many Russian intellectuals in America ended up owning one of those Buicks), in which Nabokov toured around America and across Canada too, and it was in the back seat of the Buick parked in shady roadside nooks that much of *Lolita* was written.

Their stay at Salt Lake City in 1949 was a very pleasant and comfortable one. In the Alpha Delta Phi house they had a good room with a private bath, a condition stipulated by Nabokov in agreeing to participate in the conference. Other staff members at the conference were Oscar Williams, John Crowe Ransom, Martha Foley, George Davis, Wallace Stegner, and Dr. Seuss (—**A charming man, one of the most gifted people on this list**). Nabokov spent a good deal of time with Ransom, and on several occasions they spoke together on live radio discussions which were broadcast locally. Then—the conference lasted only two weeks, though it seemed longer because the intellectual company had been so good —on July 16 the Nabokovs, still with their student, made a series of collecting stops, on one of which, they had some rather strange neighbors, playboys (—**gentle people, but in their cups they could be dangerous**) who had a World War II machine gun. One morning Nabokov came upon the awful stench of a machine-gunned horse by the roadside. He told them. —**They laughed. They chuckled and confessed that it was one of their neighbor's horses, and sometimes their 'aim wasn't too good.'** Nabokov remembers that returning from his collecting hikes he was far more concerned about the ra-ta-ta of that machine gun than about the rather ugly moose which lived in the surrounding willow bogs. In late August (the student had by now left) they started back to Ithaca, and a highpoint of that trip back was the capture of some specimens of a rare species on a pile of bear dung.

On several occasions in the Far West the Nabokovs visited the ranch (half house, half resort—the rent was very reasonable) owned by his current publisher, James Laughlin, of New Directions. It was in Alta, Utah, and Nabokov did some of his most important collecting in the Wasatch Mountains of the region.

Laughlin was tremendously impressed by Nabokov's energy, the pace at which he attended to both his writing and collecting. Nabokov was always, his publisher recalls, very secretive about what he was writing, but once Laughlin was invited to go on a collecting hike with his author. The two men hiked for four and a half hours. That was a fairly average day's go for rough terrain; on more level ground Nabokov covers about fifteen miles a day. At night he would collect the moths attracted in large numbers by the brilliantly illuminated plate-glass windows of the Alta Lodge lounge.

Colorado and Utah were two of the states in which Nabokov spent protracted periods of time. In 1951 the Nabokovs spent July in Colorado while waiting for Dmitri, then a high-school senior, who had won a New England debating championship and had gone to California to compete in the national finals. They met many people and saw many things. The portraits of the Windsors framed in toilet seats. The divorcée who sagged all over and who told Nabokov, as though she were discussing the weather: —**Men are interested in me.** Nabokov climbed and collected in the mountains of Wyoming, and they rented homes for weeks or months in Yellowstone, in Oregon, and in Arizona, where they stayed one summer until Véra Evseevna had had enough of the rattlesnakes. These collecting summers were among the most treasured times in the Nabokovs' American period. Nabokov has promised that he will set some of their magic in a composite portrait of a day's outing in *Speak On* (or *Laugh,* or *Smile*), *Memory,* a many-titled book, most recently *Speak, America.* The only real problem apart from rattlesnakes and occasional bears (not the mean sort which Nabokov recalls from the woods of Northern Russia) and once a mysterious creature which Nabokov discovered that local zoologists preferred not to discuss with him—the only real problem was that money tended always to run dangerously low in the course of the summer. A sale to *The New Yorker* made it possible not to curtail the summer on more than one occasion. The delightful story is told at Wellesley, and it is probably apocryphal, that one year Nabokov, impatient to be off on the hunt, went to the office of the Wellesley Registrar after the final day of classes and asked, in vain, whether he could submit his students' grades before they took their exams since he already knew precisely what each student would do on the exam.

After leaving Cambridge in 1948 the Nabokovs lived in New York on the West Side for the month of June, and they moved to **273**

Ithaca on July 1, 1948. Their first of many rented homes there was on East State Street, but after two months they transfered to another house on East Seneca Street. For whatever reason Nabokov was not as well known as a writer on the Cornell campus as he had been at Wellesley, even among his colleagues, but he very quickly acquired a reputation among the staff as a good keeper of houses, and staff members going on sabbatical used to vie with one another to have the Nabokovs as tenants in their absence. A professor of German told me that certain faculty members who were more or less friendly with the Nabokovs and used to be invited to their occasional little parties would play a game the object of which was to observe and catalogue, as the Nabokovs shifted from house to house, which items and objects actually belonged to the Nabokovs themselves. Many of the houses were excellent, one or two were horrid. This pattern of transitory dwelling was something of a reversion to their old émigré ways. In Cambridge, Massachusetts, they had actually remained in the same apartment (8 Craigie Circle, a living room, two bedrooms, and a kitchen—the author's view of a street at night in the final page of *Bend Sinister* is from a window of that apartment) from late 1942 until the beginning of summer 1948, whereas in Ithaca four months was about their usual duration in one place. Once only they stayed somewhere for a year and a half, at 880 Highland Road, their best Cornell house. They occasionally took in lodgers.

On May 14, 1950, in Ithaca, Nabokov finished writing his autobiography, then called *Conclusive Evidence,* which he had begun three years before in Cambridge. And on December 6, 1953, Nabokov finished *Lolita,* which he had started to write almost exactly five years before when he came to Cornell. The working title for the novel, until 1951, was *Kingdom by the Sea. Pnin* was written entirely at (and in part about) Cornell, and the greater portion of the staggering research for the *Eugene Onegin* was also done at Cornell. He started what was to have been a novel about Siamese twins at Cornell, but much to the relief of his friend Bishop, that project was put to the side and became a short story. He also did supplementary and very important critical work for his lectures.

Nabokov enjoyed Cornell. Nabokov, come to think of it, has enjoyed almost everywhere. He will say Yes to life in whatever form it presents itself to him. Nestled between the early abandoned title *Happiness* and the *Ah! Da!* of his late and longest novel, there is another abandoned title, *Yes (Da)*, which became *The Gift (Dar)*. It was time for Nabokov's fame by now, more than time. At least, he was not quite the sweet and puckishly shy teacher he had been at Wellesley any longer.

Morris Bishop, who had brought Nabokov to Cornell, remained the only person with whom he was at all close on the campus. Nabokov belonged to the Department of Nabokov. Morris Bishop smoothed the bureaucratic wheels for him and magically negotiated all the raises and promotions (from $5500 to $9580 and tenure). He never attended a faculty meeting. He had some fine students—Thomas Pynchon took his courses, and so did a noted science-fiction writer, and he once had a student who approached the celestial A+—but there were annoyances. He did not like the frequency of anti-Semitism among both students and staff. The students cheated a lot (Nabokov thinks that he was very good at catching them at it), and there were too many of them, a problem he also faced in his one term at Harvard, when he discovered he had a hall of over four hundred students not many of whom were actually interested in reading the books. At Cornell the survey course which he inherited had an enrolment of over two hundred, but that enrolment increased under Nabokov to four hundred. It is true that the course was called "dirty lit" on campus, but it is not true that this label derived from anything to do with Vladimir Nabokov; the course had been traditionally called that at Cornell because its readings included (ah, those were the days) such novels as *Anna Karenina* and *Madame Bovary*.

Nabokov seems to have become a sterner teacher than he had been at Wellesley. At the beginning of a term he told the students: **—The seats are numbered. I would like you to choose your seat and stick to it. This is because I would like to link up your faces with your names. All satisfied with their seats? O.K. No talking, no smoking, no knitting, no newspaper reading, no sleeping, and for God's sake take notes.** Before the examination Nabokov would say something like:—**You have almost a month to reread *Anna Karenina* twice before the midterm,** which always raised the expected roomful of groans. And at the exam: **—One clear head, one blue book, ink, think, abbreviate obvious names, for example, Madame Bovary. Do not pad ignorance with eloquence. Unless medical evidence is produced nobody will be permitted to retire to the W.C.** It worked, Nabokov remembers, like a charm.

When his students were studying Kafka, they had to know not

only precisely what sort of beetle Gregor turned into, but also the arrangement of the rooms and the position of doors in the Samsa flat. For *Ulysses* the students had to know the map of Dublin; for *Anna Karenina*, the map of Moscow. *Mansfield Park* and *Bleak House* were presented to the students with intricate blackboard diagrams. An examination question Nabokov once set was to describe the wallpaper in the Karenins' bedroom. Heaven knows Nabokov didn't pander to his students, but still they came and suffered and enjoyed it all reasonably well. Though Nabokov then professed scorn for the student who simply feeds back what he or she has been given (now he says that is all he ever demanded), campus wisdom had it that the high marks usually went to those few who could really do just that. He was not always fair. He nearly failed one student for dragging in categories from an academic study which he considered particularly idiotic. There can be no doubt that, the brilliance of his lectures notwithstanding, Nabokov would have had trouble trying to teach in this way on most American campuses in the decade that followed. He had only one taste of student radicalism, a student who stood up in class and suggested that Nabokov speak for twenty minutes, following which he would talk for the rest of the time so that the students could make up their own minds about the writer in question. Nabokov told him to sit down. After that the student did not attend the lectures in protest against Nabokov's treatment of committed writers. Needless to say, he failed the final exam. Sensationally.

There was, and still is, an unusual relationship between the teaching of literatures and that of foreign languages at Cornell University. Language instruction at Cornell is under the direction of a man who was one of the originators of the U.S. Army's language programme in World War II, and the system was transferred to Cornell, where all languages are taught from a single department on the basis of memorization of pattern sentences with great reliance on audio-visual techniques. There are languages for which the Cornell system is said to have worked well, but Russian was not one of them. The teaching of Russian was under the direction of a linguist who did not happen to know Russian, very much Russian at any rate, and the students were taught to make seal-like noises which were supposed to be Russian letters but were far from that. Nabokov was at first reasonably friendly with the director of the Division of Modern Languages
276 (they played tennis, until Nabokov mastered his trick shot), but it

was not long before they quarrelled over the wisdom of a Russian-language course taught by a battery of linguists who knew no Russian.

In his last year at Cornell Nabokov finally could stand it no more, and, when three students presented themselves for an advanced Russian course and proved unable to demonstrate even the most elementary knowledge of the language, Nabokov lodged a formal complaint in which he said in conclusion: —*The situation at the Russian Language Department has been steadily deteriorating over a number of years and now it has really reached a point at which continued silence on my part would be disloyal to the university.* The students, he said, were not taught to speak, read, or write Russian, but rather a method of teaching others to teach that method. For this reason, and because courses described in the prospectus as suited for students competent in the language did not take account of Nabokov's understanding of what constitutes competence in Russian (he never had a single advanced student), there was no Russian department in anything but name while Nabokov was at Cornell, and though in theory even graduate degrees in Russian were offered, this particular theory was never put to the test. So when Nabokov finally did leave his office at Goldwin Smith, there were many faculty members ready to note that Cornell had lost a celebrity but gained the possibility of having a Russian department. It was, after all, hard for them not to be jealous: Nabokov had so many talents, his Literature 311–312 was so popular, and then a best-seller . . . But there were those who were proud of his association with Cornell, too. When he gave a public lecture on "Readers, Writers, and Censors in Russia" on April 10, 1958, all of Ithaca came. It has been said that Nabokov's job was in peril when the Olympia Press edition of *Lolita* appeared. Nothing of the kind. The files of Cornell University contain only one anonymous letter of complaint, from Two Concerned Parents: —*Frankly, we have forbidden our youngster to enroll in any course taught by Nobkov, and we would be in fear for any young girl who consulted him at a private conference or ran into him after dark on the campus!*

Nabokov and his wife once told me that they considered *Lolita* a joke at first. Moreover, he told his cousin Peter de Peterson, who visited him in Ithaca, that he believed that love could exist in this form, and that it could last longer than most people assumed. There never was any question of concern about its theme—the   **277**

Russian story *The Magician* from which the novel grew would have been printed in *Russian Annals* except for the interruption of the war—but Nabokov found it very difficult to write and told Véra Evseevna: —**I think I could destroy this.** She said: —**Don't burn it. Wait till tomorrow.** And when it was clear that it was going to be difficult to find an American publisher, it was she who arranged to send it to Nabokov's French agent, who arranged publication with the Olympia Press, about which Nabokov knew nothing at all. Philip Rahv had agreed to use some of it in *Partisan Review* but declined upon lawyer's advice (so long ago this all seems now!). Jason Epstein, whom Nabokov met through Wilson and liked very much, arranged to use a portion of the novel in *The Anchor Review*, and that helped its fortune a good deal. Nabokov was on leave from Cornell for a short time and living in Cambridge, where he was using Widener Library to complete the final draft of his Pushkin commentaries, when he chanced to see an item in *The New York Times Book Review* stating that *Lolita* had been cited as one of the three best books of the year by Graham Greene. The transfer of the novel to America wasn't easy (Olympia was given one-third of the royalties, a considerable step-down on their part from what they originally asked), but there were no censorship difficulties. The book came much closer to being censored in England, where, I am told by Nigel Nicolson, discussion reached Cabinet level. When Nabokov came back to Ithaca from his summer collecting trip in September 1958, *Lolita* was selling very nicely in America. A colleague at Cornell remembers seeing Nabokov following the best-seller lists in the library as *Dr. Zhivago* slowly crept up on *Lo*.

It was time again. Nabokov arranged that Herbert Gold would replace him at Cornell, and he and Véra Evseevna set out on a leisurely last motor trip through the States—the Great Smokies, Tennessee, Big Bend, Texas, Arizona, and California—before sailing on the *Liberté*. As they were driving away from Ithaca that February 23, they had a horrible skid on a frozen road and were lucky to escape a serious accident. On one of their two return trips to the United States, they came back to Ithaca to visit with Morris and Alison Bishop. They came by train, a long dirty train with a single parlour car at the rear. Vladimir Vladimirovich and Véra Evseevna emerged from the car—the new European phase of their existence obviously suited them (*—Véra was a little more* *regal. I think she was somewhat reduced by falling into the bour-*

geois life and a difficult one at that. Now she looked very well and more beautiful than ever)—and Nabokov immediately raised his hands and clapped smartly for a porter. They were hundreds of miles from the nearest porter.